MW00474147

Module
5

Biblical Studies

Bible Interpretation

Biblical Inspiration:

THE ORIGINS AND AUTHORITY OF THE BIBLE

. . . .

Biblical Hermeneutics:

THE THREE-STEP MODEL

. . . .

Biblical Literature:

INTERPRETING THE GENRES OF THE BIBLE

. . . .

Biblical Studies:

USING STUDY TOOLS IN BIBLE STUDY

This curriculum is the result of thousands of hours of work by The Urban Ministry Institute (TUMI) and should not be reproduced without their express permission. TUMI supports all who wish to use these materials for the advance of God's Kingdom, and affordable licensing to reproduce them is available. Please confirm with your instructor that this book is properly licensed. For more information on TUMI and our licensing program, visit *www.tumi.org* and *www.tumi.org/license.*

Capstone Module 5: Bible Interpretation Student Workbook

ISBN: 978-1-62932-005-2

The Urban Ministry Institute is a ministry of World Impact, Inc.

Contents

About the Instructor

Rev. Dr. Don L. Davis is the Executive Director of The Urban Ministry Institute and a Senior Vice President of World Impact. He attended Wheaton College and Wheaton Graduate School, and graduated summa cum laude in both his B.A. (1988) and M.A. (1989) degrees, in Biblical Studies and Systematic Theology, respectively. He earned his Ph.D. in Religion (Theology and Ethics) from the University of Iowa School of Religion.

As the Institute's Executive Director and World Impact's Senior Vice President, he oversees the training of urban missionaries, church planters, and city pastors, and facilitates training opportunities for urban Christian workers in evangelism, church growth, and pioneer missions. He also leads the Institute's extensive distance learning programs and facilitates leadership development efforts for organizations and denominations like Prison Fellowship, the Evangelical Free Church of America, and the Church of God in Christ.

A recipient of numerous teaching and academic awards, Dr. Davis has served as professor and faculty at a number of fine academic institutions, having lectured and taught courses in religion, theology, philosophy, and biblical studies at schools such as Wheaton College, St. Ambrose University, the Houston Graduate School of Theology, the University of Iowa School of Religion, the Robert E. Webber Institute of Worship Studies. He has authored a number of books, curricula, and study materials to equip urban leaders, including *The Capstone Curriculum*, TUMI's premiere sixteen-module distance education seminary instruction, *Sacred Roots: A Primer on Retrieving the Great Tradition*, which focuses on how urban churches can be renewed through a rediscovery of the historic orthodox faith, and *Black and Human: Rediscovering King as a Resource for Black Theology and Ethics*. Dr. Davis has participated in academic lectureships such as the Staley Lecture series, renewal conferences like the Promise Keepers rallies, and theological consortiums like the University of Virginia Lived Theology Project Series. He received the Distinguished Alumni Fellow Award from the University of Iowa College of Liberal Arts and Sciences in 2009. Dr. Davis is also a member of the Society of Biblical Literature, and the American Academy of Religion.

Introduction to the Module

Greetings, in the strong name of Jesus Christ!

According to the clear testimony of the Scriptures themselves, God equips his representatives through the Spirit-breathed Word of God, the Scriptures. Everyone God calls into the ministry must determine to discipline themselves so as to master its contents, submit to its injunctions, and teach its truths. Like a workman (or work-woman!) they must strive to handle the Word of truth accurately, and so be approved of the Lord in their study (2 Tim. 2.15).

This module focuses on the facts, principles, and implications of interpreting the Bible. In our first lesson, *Biblical Inspiration: The Origins and Authority of the Bible*, we will outline the need for biblical interpretation, and what we need to do to prepare for this great task. We will explore both the divine and human dimensions of the Bible, clarify the goal of all interpretation, and lay out clearly our theological assumptions regarding the high place of the Scriptures in the Church. We will especially concentrate on the kind of life and heart preparation necessary to interpret God's Word accurately. We will also look at the Bible's claim to be inspired of God, and its authority and place in theological and spiritual judgments in the Church. In a day where biblical scholarship has exploded, we will also take a brief look at modern biblical criticism, and wrestle with its claims as it relates to our study of Scripture today.

In our second lesson, *Biblical Hermeneutics: The Three-Step Model*, we will introduce an effective method of biblical interpretation designed to help you approach your study of Scripture so as to bridge the gap between our ancient and contemporary worlds. We call it the Three-Step Model: understand the original audience, discover general principles, and make applications to life. In this lesson, too, we will actually examine a passage of Scripture employing this model, looking at a passage in Paul's letter to the Corinthians, in his first epistle, 9.1-14. Using the framework found in your *Keys to Bible Interpretation* appendix, we will canvass this great text of Scripture looking specifically at how a deliberate, careful, and prayerful approach can yield great knowledge and encouragement to us as we strive to understand God's will through his holy Word.

We focus upon the types of literature found in the Bible and how to interpret them in our third lesson entitled *Biblical Literature: Interpreting the Genres of the Bible*. We will define and outline the concept of genres (pronounced JOHN- ruhs) in biblical interpretation, laying out an overview of the idea, and giving a few basic assumptions of this kind of special hermeneutics. We will then discuss various forms of biblical genres, but will give special attention to two types of literature which represent the vast majority of the actual material in the Bible, narrative and prophetic. We will give brief but meaty discussions of both narrative study (i.e., story theology) as well as prophetic and apocalyptic literature, showing how attention to genres can help us better interpret Scripture.

Finally, we will close our module study with our fourth lesson, ***Biblical Studies: Using Study Tools in Bible Study***. Here we will explore the kind of solid scholarly reference tools available to us as we attempt to understand the meaning of a biblical text. The student of the Bible has access today to many remarkable tools, both written and software, all which can help him or her gain a mastery of the Word. We will concentrate first on the *basic* tools for solid biblical interpretation: a good translation of Scripture, Hebrew and Greek aids, a Bible dictionary, a concordance, and exegetical commentaries. We will also consider *additional* tools that may enrich our study of Scripture. These will include cross-reference aids, topical Bibles, cross-reference Bibles, and topical concordances. We will also discuss aids which focus on history and customs of the Bible: Bible dictionaries, Bible encyclopedias, atlases, and other related reference works. Finally, we will briefly look at Bible handbooks, study Bibles, and other helps, and conclude our discussion with the use of Bible commentaries, and the role of tools in general as you interpret your Bible for devotion, preaching, and teaching.

The Bible's own remarkable claim of its transforming power ought to be reason enough to challenge us to master the Word of God. "All Scripture is breathed out by God and profitable for teaching, for reproof, for correction, and for training in righteousness, that the man of God may be competent, equipped for every good work" 2 Tim. 3.16-17. The God-breathed Word of God in the words of humankind is sufficient to enrich us, delight us, and make us competent and equipped for every good work. Truly, the Word of God cannot be broken, will always accomplish its purpose, and will ensure the person of God enjoys good success in all they do to advance the Kingdom of God wherever they are (John 10.35; Isa. 55.8-11; Josh. 1.8).

My sincere prayer is that all of the these blessings and more become yours as the Holy Spirit enables you to explore the principles and practices of interpreting his holy and eternal Word!

With great anticipation of your edification,

- Rev. Dr. Don L. Davis

Course Requirements

Required Books and Materials

- Bible (for the purposes of this course, your Bible should be a translation [ex. NIV, NASB, RSV, KJV, NKJV, etc.], and not a paraphrase [ex. The Living Bible, The Message]).

- Each Capstone module has assigned textbooks which are read and discussed throughout the course. We encourage you to read, reflect upon, and respond to these with your professors, mentors, and fellow learners. Because of the fluid availability of the texts (e.g., books going out of print), we maintain our *official* Capstone Required Textbook list on our website. Please visit *www.tumi.org/books* to obtain the current listing of this module's texts.

- Paper and pen for taking notes and completing in-class assignments.

Suggested Reference Books for Purchase

Please note: These reference resources are highly recommended for purchase for your personal library. You will need to have access to these kinds of resources to complete assignments for this class.

- Douglas, J. D., N. Hillyer, and D. R. W. Wood, eds. *New Bible Dictionary*, 3rd ed. Downers Grove: InterVarsity Press (IVP), 2000.

- Strong, James. *Strong's Exhaustive Concordance of the Bible*. Iowa Falls: World Bible Publishers, 1986.

- Vine, W. E. *Vine's Complete Expository Dictionary of Old and New Testament Words*. Merrill F. Unger and William White, Jr., revision eds. Nashville: Thomas Nelson, 1996.

- Wenham, G. J., J. A. Motyer, D. A. Carson, and R. T. France, eds. *New Bible Commentary*. 21st Century ed. Downers Grove: IVP, 2000.

Suggested Readings

- Kuhatschek, Jack. *Applying the Bible*. Grand Rapids: Zondervan, 1990.

- Montgomery, J. W. ed. *God's Inerrant Word*. Minneapolis: Bethany, 1974.

- Packer, J. I. *"Fundamentalism" and the Word of God*. London: IVP, 1958.

- ------. *God Has Spoken: Revelation and the Bible*. Grand Rapids: Baker, 1979.

- Sproul, R. C. *Knowing Scripture*. Downers Grove: IVP, 1977.

Summary of Grade Categories and Weights

Attendance & Class Participation . . . . 30%   90 pts

Quizzes . . . . 10%   30 pts

Memory Verses . . . . 15%   45 pts

Exegetical Project . . . . 15%   45 pts

Ministry Project . . . . 10%   30 pts

Readings and Homework Assignments . . . . 10%   30 pts

Final Exam . . . . 10%   30 pts

Total: 100%   300 pts

Grade Requirements

Attendance at each class session is a course requirement. Absences will affect your grade. If an absence cannot be avoided, please let the Mentor know in advance. If you miss a class it is your responsibility to find out the assignments you missed, and to talk with the Mentor about turning in late work. Much of the learning associated with this course takes place through discussion. Therefore, your active involvement will be sought and expected in every class session.

Every class will begin with a short quiz over the basic ideas from the last lesson. The best way to prepare for the quiz is to review the Student Workbook material and class notes taken during the last lesson.

In a course on the Word of God, it should not be odd to expect an assignment on the task of Scripture memorization. Maybe above all the disciplines of ingesting the Word, the act of memorizing Scripture for meditation and review must become a central priority for your life and ministry, both as a believer and leader in the Church of Jesus Christ. There are relatively few verses in this module you will need to learn, but all of the passages are critical in both theological significance and biblical content. Each class session you will be expected to recite (orally or in writing) the assigned verses to your Mentor.

The Scriptures are God's potent instrument to equip the man or woman of God for every work of ministry he calls them to (2 Tim. 3.16-17). In order to complete the requirements for this course you must select a passage and do an inductive Bible study (i.e., an exegetical study) upon it. The study will have to be five pages in length (double-spaced, typed or neatly hand written) and deal with one of the four aspects of the nature and procedure of interpreting the Scriptures covered in the four lessons of this course. Our desire and hope is that your analysis of Scripture will encourage you spiritually, strengthen your skills in interpreting the Bible, and increase your knowledge and ability to use the Bible to both affect your life and the lives of those to whom you minister. As you go through the course, be open to finding an extended passage (roughly 4-9 verses) on a subject you would like to study more intensely. The details of the project are covered on pages 10-11, and will be discussed in the introductory session of this course.

Ministry Project

Our expectation is that all students will apply their learning practically in their lives and in their ministry responsibilities. The student will be responsible for developing a ministry project that combines principles learned with practical ministry. The details of this project are covered on page 12, and will be discussed in the introductory session of the course.

Class and Homework Assignments

Classwork and homework of various types may be given during class by your Mentor or be written in your Student Workbook. If you have any question about what is required by these or when they are due, please ask your Mentor.

Readings

It is important that the student read the assigned readings from the text and from the Scriptures in order to be prepared for class discussion. Please turn in the "Reading Completion Sheet" from your Student Workbook on a weekly basis. There will be an option to receive extra credit for extended readings.

Take-Home Final Exam

At the end of the course, your Mentor will give you a final exam (closed book) to be completed at home. You will be asked a question that helps you reflect on what you have learned in the course and how it affects the way you think about or practice ministry. Your Mentor will give you due dates and other information when the Final Exam is handed out.

Grading

The following grades will be given in this class at the end of the session, and placed on each student's record:

A - Superior work   D - Passing work

B - Excellent work   F - Unsatisfactory work

C - Satisfactory work   I - Incomplete

Letter grades with appropriate pluses and minuses will be given for each final grade, and grade points for your grade will be factored into your overall grade point average. Unexcused late work or failure to turn in assignments will affect your grade, so please plan ahead, and communicate conflicts with your instructor.

Exegetical Project

Purpose

As a part of your participation in the Capstone *Bible Interpretation* module of study, you will be required to do an exegesis (inductive study) on one of the following passages regarding the nature of the Scriptures and their application to our lives and ministries:

❏ Psalm 19.7-11 ❏ 2 Timothy 3.14-17 ❏ 1 Corinthians 2.9-16

❏ Psalm 1.1-3 ❏ Matthew 22.34-40 ❏ James 1.22-25

❏ Isaiah 55.8-11 ❏ 2 Peter 1.19-21 ❏ Proverbs 2.1-5

The purpose of this exegetical project is to give you an opportunity to do a detailed study of a major passage on the character of the Word of God and its role in our spiritual walk and ministry. Using one of the texts above as your ground and base, your assignment will be to think critically about the character and nature of the Word of God as well as how it transforms and builds up the Church to fulfill God's will in every area of life. As you study your text (either one of the passages above or a text that you and your Mentor agree upon), our hope is that your interpretation of the passage will help you better understand the role and function of the Word of God in your life, as well as those to whom you minister and teach. We are convinced that the Holy Spirit will give you insight into the power and meaning of the Word of God. The Scriptures indeed are food to our souls, weaponry in our spiritual warfare, and a mirror to our own personal walk of discipleship. As we master them, God can use them to equip you for the leadership role he has commissioned you for in both your local congregation and outreach to others.

Outline and Composition

This is a Bible study project, and, in order to do *exegesis*, you must be committed to understand the meaning of the passage in its own setting. Once you know what it meant, you can then draw out principles that apply to all of us, and then relate those principles to life. A simple three-step process can guide you in your personal study of the Bible passage:

1. What was *God saying to the people in the text's original situation*?

2. What principle(s) does *the text teach that is true for all people everywhere*, including today?

3. What is *the Holy Spirit asking me to do with this principle here, today*, in my life and ministry?

Once you have answered these questions in your personal study, you are then ready to write out your insights for your *paper assignment*.

Here is a *sample outline* for your paper:

1. List out what you believe is *the main theme or idea* of the text you selected.

2. *Summarize the meaning* of the passage (you may do this in two or three paragraphs, or, if you prefer, by writing a short verse-by-verse commentary on the passage).

3. *Outline one to three key principles or insights* this text provides on the nature, meaning, and/or function of the Word of God.

4. Tell how one, some, or all of the principles may relate to *one or more* of the following:

    a. Your personal spirituality and walk with Christ

    b. Your life and ministry in your local church

    c. Situations or challenges in your community and general society

As an aid or guide, please feel free to read the course texts and/or commentaries, and integrate insights from them into your work. Make sure that you give credit to whom credit is due if you borrow or build upon someone else's insights. Use in-the-text references, footnotes, or endnotes. Any way you choose to cite your references will be acceptable, as long as you 1) use only one way consistently throughout your paper, and 2) indicate where you are using someone else's ideas, and are giving them credit for it. (For more information, see *Documenting Your Work: A Guide to Help You Give Credit Where Credit Is Due* in the Appendix.)

Make certain that your exegetical project, when turned in meets the following standards:

*   It is legibly written or typed.

*   Is a study of one of the passages above.

*   It is turned in on time (not late).

*   It is 5 pages in length.

*   It follows the outline given above, clearly laid out for the reader to follow.

*   It shows how the passage relates to life and ministry today.

Do not let these instructions intimidate you; this is a Bible study project! All you need to show in this paper is that you *studied* the passage, *summarized* its meaning, *drew out* a few key principles from it, and *related* them to your own life and ministry.

Grading

The exegetical project is worth 45 points, and represents 15% of your overall grade, so make certain that you make your project an excellent and informative study of the Word.

Ministry Project

The Word of God is living and active, and penetrates to the very heart of our lives and innermost thoughts (Heb. 4.12). James the Apostle emphasizes the need to be doers of the Word of God, not hearers only, deceiving ourselves. We are exhorted to apply the Word, to obey it. Neglecting this discipline, he suggests, is analogous to a person viewing our natural face in a mirror and then forgetting who we are, and are meant to be. In every case, the doer of the Word of God will be blessed in what he or she does (James 1.22-25).

Our sincere desire is that you will apply your learning practically, correlating your learning with real experiences and needs in your personal life, and in your ministry in and through your church. Therefore, a key part of completing this module will be for you to design a ministry project to help you share some of the insights you have learned from this course with others.

There are many ways that you can fulfill this requirement of your study. You may choose to conduct a brief study of your insights with an individual, or a Sunday School class, youth or adult group or Bible study, or even at some ministry opportunity. What you must do is discuss some of the insights you have learned from class with your audience. (Of course, you may choose to share insights from your Exegetical Project in this module with them.)

Feel free to be flexible in your project. Make it creative and open-ended. At the beginning of the course, you should decide on a context in which you will share your insights, and share that with your instructor. Plan ahead and avoid the last minute rush in selecting and carrying out your project.

After you have carried out your plan, write and turn in to your Mentor a one-page summary or evaluation of your time of sharing. A sample outline of your Ministry Project summary is as follows:

1. Your name

2. The place where you shared, and the audience with whom you shared

3. A brief summary of how your time went, how you felt, and how they responded

4. What you learned from the time

The Ministry Project is worth 30 points and represents 10% of your overall grade, so make certain to share your insights with confidence and make your summary clear.

Biblical Inspiration
The Origins and Authority of the Bible

Lesson Objectives

Welcome in the strong name of Jesus Christ! After your reading, study, discussion, and application of the materials in this lesson, you will be able to:

- Define hermeneutics as the discipline and branch of knowledge which focuses on interpretation, especially the interpretation of texts.

- Give evidence that the Bible must be interpreted as a divine and human book, with both dimensions to appreciate and fully understand the nature of Scripture.

- Lay out the critical presuppositions that historically orthodox Christians have believed about the nature of Scripture including their divine origin, Scripture interpreting Scripture, the idea of progressive revelation, the Christ-centered nature of Scripture, and the necessity of the Holy Spirit to understand God's Word.

- Give an overview of the Three-Step Model of biblical interpretation which includes understanding the original situation, discovering biblical principles, and applying the meaning of Scripture to our lives.

- Recite the various elements involved in preparing the heart for biblical interpretation, including the need for humility and prayer, diligence and determination, and rigorous engagement of the Bible as a workman.

- Demonstrate a knowledge of the kinds of roles we ought to adopt as we prepare our mind for serious biblical interpretation including the role of an explorer, the role of a detective, and the role of a scientist—seeking the Word diligently, following up on clues, and weighing the evidence carefully before making judgments.

- Exhibit from Scripture its claim that the Bible is both inspired by God as well as written by human authors.

- Demonstrate and distinguish between the various theories of inspiration which seek to explain how and in what way the Scriptures can be inspired by the Holy Spirit and also be influenced by human authors.

- Present carefully the rationale and history of biblical criticism, and how this modern discipline seeks to trace the origins of the Scriptures from the original events spoken of in the Bible to the actual reports of those happenings recorded in the canonical books of Scripture.

- Give a brief explanation, including the benefits and problems associated with the major subsections of modern biblical criticism, including form, source, linguistic, textual, literary, canonical, redaction, and historical criticisms, as well as translation studies.

Our Ground of Confidence

Devotion

Isa. 55.6-11 - Seek the Lord while he may be found; call upon him while he is near; [7] let the wicked forsake his way, and the unrighteous man his thoughts; let him return to the Lord, that he may have compassion on him, and to our God, for he will abundantly pardon. [8] For my thoughts are not your thoughts, neither are your ways my ways, declares the Lord. [9] For as the heavens are higher than the earth, so are my ways higher than your ways and my thoughts than your thoughts. [10] "For as the rain and the snow come down from heaven and do not return there but water the earth, making it bring forth and sprout, giving seed to the sower and bread to the eater, [11] so shall my word be that goes out from my mouth; it shall not return to me empty, but it shall accomplish that which I purpose, and shall succeed in the thing for which I sent it."

God is unequivocal in his assertion of his absolute integrity and truth. The God and Father of our Lord Jesus Christ is a God of faithfulness and trustworthiness, one who has never and could never lie or mislead, whose word is completely veracious, and whose sovereignty and truth provides his people with profound confidence. Even a glance at some of the texts of the Bible about God's faithfulness underscores the remarkable certainty of God as the God of the faithful Word of covenant, and his bold proclamation of the operative power of his Scripture and promise. Here is a sampling of this confidence in the Word of God:

Ps. 19.7-10 - The law of the Lord is perfect, reviving the soul; the testimony of the Lord is sure, making wise the simple; [8] the precepts of the Lord are right, rejoicing the heart; the commandment of the Lord is pure, enlightening the eyes; [9] the fear of the Lord is clean, enduring forever; the rules of the Lord are true, and righteous altogether. [10] More to be desired are they than gold, even much fine gold; sweeter also than honey and drippings of the honeycomb.

Deut. 32.4 - The Rock, his work is perfect, for all his ways are justice. A God of faithfulness and without iniquity, just and upright is he.

Exod. 34.6 - The Lord passed before him and proclaimed, "The Lord, the Lord, a God merciful and gracious, slow to anger, and abounding in steadfast love and faithfulness."

Ps. 98.3 - He has remembered his steadfast love and faithfulness to the house of Israel. All the ends of the earth have seen the salvation of our God.

Ps. 100.5 - For the Lord is good; his steadfast love endures forever, and his faithfulness to all generations.

Isa. 25.1 - O Lord, you are my God; I will exalt you; I will praise your name, for you have done wonderful things, plans formed of old, faithful and sure.

John 6.63 - It is the Spirit who gives life; the flesh is of no avail. The words that I have spoken to you are spirit and life.

1 Pet. 1.23-25 - Since you have been born again, not of perishable seed but of imperishable, through the living and abiding word of God; [24] for "All flesh is like grass and all its glory like the flower of grass. The grass withers, and the flower falls, [25] but the word of the Lord remains forever." And this word is the good news that was preached to you.

Add to this modest list literally dozens of Scripture on the faithfulness of God and you essentially come full circle on the claim of Isaiah 55. God compares the certainty of his Word's fulfillment, both in terms of prediction and promise, to the organic power of the rain from heaven, that once mixed with the seed and the earth, brings forth abundance fruit. God essentially says that his Word is as productive, certain, successful, and potent as the rain mixing with the elements of the earth.

To what do we count this certainty of effect, this promise of fruitfulness and prosperity associated with the covenantal Word of God? It is rooted in his character, in his person, in his veracity as the faithful God, the God who cannot lie (Titus 1.2), whose Word is certain and sure, forever settled in the heavens. David sang of God's faithfulness and the reliability of his Word in Psalm 89: "I will sing of the steadfast love of the Lord, forever; with my mouth I will make known your faithfulness to all generations. [2] For I said, 'Steadfast love will be built up forever; in the heavens you will establish your faithfulness'" (Ps. 89.1-2). In this text God assures us that his Word is true. Because he is a faithful God, his Word will accomplish what God determines, and prosper in the thing, the affair, the task he appoints for it.

Let me ask you: what do you believe is the ground of our confidence that all that God has promised to us will in fact come about–on what grounds, what basis, do we believe that we will reap the life promised to us through faith in Jesus Christ? The answer is the veracious and truthful character of the living God who has spoken the truth to his people. Our God is a God of truth, and because of that we hold onto the promise of God, knowing full well that what he promised, he will do. This and this alone is our ground of confidence.

After reciting and/or singing the Nicene Creed (located in the Appendix), pray the following prayer:

Blessed Lord, who caused all holy Scriptures to be written for our learning: Grant us so to hear them, read, mark, learn, and inwardly digest them, that we may embrace and ever hold fast the blessed hope of everlasting life, which you have given us in our Savior Jesus Christ; who lives and reigns with you and the Holy Spirit, one God, for ever and ever. Amen.

~ Episcopal Church. **The Book of Common Prayer and Administrations of the Sacraments and Other Rites and Ceremonies of the Church, Together with the Psalter or Psalms of David.** New York: The Church Hymnal Corporation, 1979. p. 236

Nicene Creed and Prayer

No quiz this lesson

Quiz

No Scripture memorization this lesson

Scripture Memorization Review

No assignments due this lesson

Assignments Due

CONTACT

Why Should We Care?

 Many modern people today take for granted that science has once and for all debunked the truth value of the Bible, at least as it applies to history and the possibility of the supernatural. A small but vocal group of sincere Bible students believe it is their duty to prove to those who are skeptical about the nature of the Bible its historical accuracy and truth. They cite the fulfillment of prophecy, accuracy regarding predictions, internal coherence, and its preservation as evidence that our Scriptures must be divinely inspired. Another equally sincere yet less vocal group of Christians are convinced that you simply cannot with evidence persuade those who disbelieve the Scriptures of its historical and spiritual validity. Without the Holy Spirit, they argue, no person will ever be convinced of the claims and promises of God in Christ, let alone be convinced by arguing with skeptics about the believability of the Bible. As you consider these positions, why do you believe we ought to care or not care about the issue of the Bible's origin, authority, and inspiration by God?

Scripture and the Holy Spirit

Evangelical Christians have written thousands of books on the need to use excellent methods and principles in making sense of the Bible. One may go to any Christian bookstore or seminary library and find scores of texts all providing detailed instruction in the specific steps we should take to discover the "plain and literal sense" of the Bible's meaning. Despite all of these books, we still have many churches which demonstrate a deep lack of knowledge of the Bible, and, despite access to fine methods on how to do Bible studies, don't seem to love or read their Bibles any more than others. Some suggest that methods and approaches mean virtually nothing apart from the leadership and infilling of the Holy Spirit. These would downplay method entirely, and emphasize the *spiritual dimensions* of biblical interpretation, not the *intellectual dimensions*. As the Spirit is the one who inspired the Bible, he must also be the one to illumine it. *What is the relationship of methodology to the work of the Spirit in biblical interpretation?* Is it possible to understand the Bible in any substantive and life-changing way apart from the illumination of the Holy Spirit, even if we have good forms of hermeneutics to understand it?

1

A Literature or a Living Word of God, or Both?

For the last few decades a few scholars have emphasized the need to understand the **3**
Bible as literature in order to discover its meaning for our lives. Literature, they
argue, functions according to defined rules and forms, whether biblical or not.
Rather than reading the Bible as a human book with human forms and conventions,
these scholars claim that we have cut the Bible into little pieces, ignored the forms of
literature, and sought to use the Bible primarily as a proof text to make theological
claims about this, that, or the other subject. Others claim that although the Bible
was written by human authors, the text goes well beyond just forms of convention
and literary rules. It is the living Word of God, and we ought to discover within it
(and, for that matter, *everywhere* within it) the meaning regarding salvation and our
faith in Jesus Christ. What is your reaction to this kind of discussion: is the Bible a
book of literature, the living Word of God, or both?

Biblical Inspiration: The Origins and Authority of the Bible

CONTENT

Segment 1: Preparing for Solid Biblical Interpretation

Rev. Dr. Don L. Davis

Hermeneutics is that discipline and branch of knowledge which focuses on **Summary of**
interpretation, especially the interpretation of texts. As a methodology, **Segment 1**
hermeneutics seeks to understand the way in which the Bible must be interpreted as
both a divine and human book, with both dimensions needed to appreciate and
fully understand the nature of Scripture. Historically orthodox Christians have,
from the beginning, believed in the inspiration of Scripture, the need for Scripture
to interpret Scripture, and the idea of progressive revelation that culminates in the
revelation of Christ. Only through the Holy Spirit can the Scriptures be
understood. The *Three-Step Model* of biblical interpretation includes understanding
the original situation, discovering biblical principles, and applying the meaning of
Scripture to our lives. In order to rightly interpret the Word of God, we must
prepare our hearts, minds, and our wills to humbly and rigorously study it,
carefully analyze it, and heartily obey it, all to God's glory.

Our objective for this segment, *Preparing for Solid Biblical Interpretation*, is to enable you to see that:

- Hermeneutics is that discipline and branch of knowledge which focuses on interpretation, especially the interpretation of texts. Biblical hermeneutics focuses specifically on the methods and science of interpreting the Bible.

- By all accounts the Bible must be interpreted as both a *divine* and *human* book, and both dimensions of the divine and human must be appreciated to fully understand the nature of Scripture.

- Since the beginning, orthodox Christian faith has held to certain fundamental presuppositions regarding the nature of Scripture, including its divine origin, the necessity of Scripture to interpret Scripture, the idea of progressive revelation which culminates in the revelation of God in the person of Christ, and the necessity of the working of the Holy Spirit in order to understand God's Word.

- The Three-Step Model of biblical interpretation, which seeks to take seriously the historical and linguistic difference between the world of the text and our modern world, includes efforts to understand the message in light of its original situation, discovering biblical principles from the text, and finally applying the meaning of Scripture to our lives.

- In order to rightly interpret the Word of God, we must prepare our hearts, minds, and our wills to humbly and rigorously study it, carefully analyze it, and heartily obey it, all to God's glory.

- We prepare our hearts through humility and prayer, diligence and determination, and rigorous engagement of the Bible as a workman. We prepare our minds as we embrace the roles of explorer, detective, and scientist, seeking the Word diligently, following up on clues, and weighing the evidence carefully before making judgments. We prepare our wills by obeying the Word, not merely hearing it, and embracing the truth that wisdom comes from responding to God's Word, not merely reflecting upon it.

I. The Need for Biblical Interpretation

A. Introductory terms

1. "Hermeneutics" - the discipline and branch of knowledge which focuses on interpretation, especially the interpretation of texts

2. "Interpretation" - the act or process of interpreting or explaining; providing the sense and the meaning of a message, text, or object

B. Why the Bible must be interpreted

1. The Bible is a *divine* book: no one knows the thoughts of God save God himself, 1 Cor. 2.10-11.

   a. God has spoken clearly, Deut. 30.11-14.

   b. God has spoken so that the seeker may understand his mind, Isa. 45.19.

   c. God has spoken comprehensively (i.e., giving us the things that we need to know to believe and obey him), Deut. 29.29.

2. The Bible is a *human* book, 2 Pet. 3.15-16.

   a. Differences exist in language, culture, and experience.

b. The Scriptures were written over 1,600 years by 40 different authors, whose experience and understanding was radically different from our own.

3. God asks us to handle the Scriptures accurately, that is, to read it in such a way as to get the meaning he intends for us to receive.

   a. 2 Tim. 2.15

   b. 1 Cor. 2.6

   c. 2 Cor. 4.2

C. The goal of biblical interpretation: *to make the meaning clear and plain*

   1. To "rightly handle" the Word of truth, 2 Tim. 2.15

   2. To give the meaning and make it clear, Neh. 8.1-3, 7-8

   3. To know the truth and experience God's liberty, John 8.31-32

   4. To benefit spiritually from our commitment to the Word of God, Ps. 19.7-11

D. Critical presuppositions (*things we will accept as the truth before we begin to interpret the Scriptures*)

1. The Scriptures have both *divine* and *human* authorship.

2. Biblical interpretation is about *exegesis*, not *eisegesis*.

   a. Exegesis - to explain, make clear, and interpret the meaning from *within* a text (*to draw out of*)

   b. Eisegesis - to explain and interpret a text, especially a biblical text, using one's own ideas (i.e., *to read into*)

3. Scripture must interpret Scripture.

   a. 1 Cor. 2.13

   b. Matt. 22.29

   c. Luke 24.44-47

4. *Progressive revelation*: The revelation unfolds until it culminates in Jesus Christ (i.e., Jesus is the standard by which all interpretations of Scripture must be judged).

   a. Heb. 1.1-2

b. Matt. 17.5

c. John 1.17-18

d. 2 Cor. 4.3-6

5. Scripture must be read illumined by the Spirit.

a. 2 Pet. 1.20-21

b. Mark 12.36

c. Acts 1.16

d. Acts 3.18

E. Overview of the "Three-Step Model" of biblical interpretation

1. Understand the original context and situation: *a passage cannot mean what it never meant.*

2. Find general principles: *the Spirit reveals universal truths in the Word of God binding on the mind, the conscience, and the will.*

3. Make connection and application: *the Word of God is to be believed and obeyed, not merely analyzed and studied.*

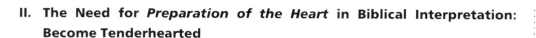

II. The Need for *Preparation of the Heart* in Biblical Interpretation: Become Tenderhearted

2 Chron. 16.9a - For the eyes of the Lord run to and fro throughout the whole earth, to give strong support to those whose heart is blameless toward him.

A. We approach the Word of God humbly in prayer: the importance of prayer, Ps. 119.18.

   1. Pray for the leading of God's Spirit, 1 John 2.20-21.

   2. Pray for an openness to God's instruction, Ps. 32.8-9.

   3. Pray for God's power to trust and obey.

      a. Heb. 11.6

      b. James 1.22-25

   4. Pray for God's leading to share it with others, Ezra 7.10.

B. Be-attitudes of Scripture study

   1. Be a workman, being diligent and determined, Prov. 2.1-9; cf. Prov. 2.2-5; 2 Tim. 2.15.

   2. Be humble and contrite, Isa. 57.15.

3. Be teachable and open, Ps. 25.4-5.

C. "Break up that fallow ground": *become familiar with the Word of God through constant and rigorous reading and meditation*, Hos. 10.12.

1. Read the Bible, Neh. 8.8.

2. Memorize the Bible, Ps. 119.11.

3. Meditate on the Bible, Ps. 1.1-3.

4. Hear the Bible preached and taught, Acts 17.11.

III. The Need for *Preparation of the Mind* in Biblical Interpretation: Become Tough-minded

1 Cor. 14.20 - Brothers, do not be children in your thinking. Be infants in evil, but in your thinking be mature.

A. Approach the Word of God as an *Explorer* (a seeker determined to discover its treasure), Matt. 13.52.

1. Recognize that the world of the Bible is quite different yet very similar to ours.

2. The first movement of all Bible study is becoming familiar with "their world."

3. All Bible study involves some "time travel."

4. Open my eyes that I may see: observing, participating, and discovering.

B. Approach the Word of God as a *Detective* (searching for clues to understand its larger meanings and connections).

1. The power of truth is in the jots and the tittles; the need to train yourself to look for clues, Matt. 5.17-18.

2. Seek with such thoroughness as to not miss a single detail: Agassiz and what do you see?, Luke 16.16-17.

3. Follow every possible lead; interview every witness of Scripture.

4. Check out every possible story and alibi.

5. The Word of God cannot pass away, Luke 21.33.

C. Approach the Word of God as a *Scientist* (one dedicated to check all ideas out and verify everything according to the facts), Acts 17.11.

1. Test every theory and hypothesis against the Word, holding all ideas accountable to the Word of God.

    a. 1 John 4.1

b. Isa. 34.16

c. 1 Thess. 5.21

d. Isa. 8.20

e. Rom. 12.2

f. Eph. 5.10

g. Phil. 1.10

2. Accept no explanation that is not backed up with the Word of God.

a. 1 John 4.5-6

b. 1 Pet. 1.10-12

3. Strive to connect all meaning of Scripture to the person of Messiah.

a. 2 Tim. 3.15-16

b. John 5.39

4. In your thinking be fully mature.

    a. Get your facts straight; do not make snap judgments or over generalize on points, John 7.24.

    b. Make valid arguments: *logic and the laws of thought*.

       (1) The law of identity ("A is A")

       (2) The law of non-contradiction ("A is not B")

       (3) The law of the excluded middle ("X is either A or B")

    c. Learn to think *dialogically*: both A and B are true (AB).

       (1) God's truth is A: *Jesus is fully God*

       (2) God's truth is B: *Jesus is fully man*

       (3) God's truth is *both A and B* (equal, different, unified)

D. "Do not lean on your own understanding," Prov. 3.5-6.

    1. Learn to suspend your judgment until you get all the facts.

    2. Discipline yourself not to jump to conclusions.

    3. Double check everything you think you have found.

    4. Let others judge the fruit of your study.

IV. The Need for *Preparation of the Will* in Biblical Interpretation: Make Yourself Available to Practice the Word of God.

A. Be a doer of the Word, James 1.22-25, cf. Ezra 7.10.

    1. Listen to the *voice* of the Lord as you study the Word of God, Heb. 3.7-13.

    2. Carry out God's promptings immediately.

    3. Don't get into the habit of *reading for others* and not *reading to hear God speak to you*.

    4. Expect the Word of God to affect your life, not just your study habits.

B. Wisdom comes from *obeying* God's Word, not merely *interpreting* it, Ps. 111.10.

    1. Solid biblical scholars do not *live to study*, rather, they *study to live*.

        a. Deut. 4.6

        b. Joshua 1.7-8

    2. Understanding occurs as *God's Word* is our meditation, not just notes and outlines, Ps. 119.98-101.

1

3. We grow from infancy to childhood to maturity through a steady obedience to the Word of God.

    a.   1 Pet. 2.2

    b.   Heb. 5.12-6.1

Conclusion

» In order to properly interpret the Scriptures, we must prepare our hearts, minds, and wills to engage the eternal Word of the Living God.

» As a divine and human book, we must depend on the resources of the Holy Spirit to understand the Word of God, and be ready to allow that Word to transform our lives *before* we engage it.

Segue 1

Student Questions and Response

Please take as much time as you have available to answer these and other questions that the video brought out. We must never view the subject of biblical hermeneutics as merely a bunch of rules and methods to be woodenly applied that will yield the treasured insights of Scripture. Rather, the entire subject is a *spiritual issue*, and authentic biblical interpretation will always demand a spiritual preparation, a godly foundation that seeks not only to *understand* the Scriptures, but to *fulfill* it in every dimension of our lives. Review the following questions which summarize the key insights of the first segment with these truths in mind, and always support your answers with Scripture!

1. What is the science of hermeneutics, and what does it concern? What is the specific challenge and goal of biblical hermeneutics?

2. What does it mean to suggest that the Bible in a fundamental way must be perceived as a *divine* as well as a *human* book? Does calling the Bible a human book detract or dismiss its claims to be of divine origin? Explain.

3. What is the goal of all biblical interpretation, in other words, what ought we to strive for as we study the Bible? What does it mean to "rightly handle the Word of truth" (2 Tim. 2.15)?

4. What is a presupposition, and what are the "critical presuppositions" that Christians have always held true about the Bible as they have sought to interpret it rightly? Why are these presuppositions important to know as *faithful followers of Christ BEFORE* we engage in various methods to understand the nature of Scripture?

5. Why is it important to see the Bible as a progressive revelation that culminates in the revelation of Jesus Christ? What do you think the relationship is between the *written* Word of God and the *personal* Word of God, our Lord Jesus? How do they relate to one another?

6. Explain the role of the Holy Spirit in the inspiration of Scripture and the illumination of Scripture in biblical interpretation?

7. What is the *Three-Step Model* of biblical interpretation, and how does this approach seek to take seriously the historical and linguistic difference between the world of the text and our modern world?

8. Why is it simply impossible to interpret the Word of God without the preparation of the heart, mind, and will to engage it as God determines? Does this mean that we should ignore the necessity of a solid biblical hermeneutic strategy as we read the Word of God?

9. What are some of the roles we ought to take as we seek to use our minds wholeheartedly in our study of Scripture? Why is obedience so central to fully grasping the meaning of Scripture, and not merely study and reflection alone?

Biblical Inspiration: The Origins and Authority of the Bible

Segment 2: Biblical Inspiration and Modern Biblical Criticism

Rev. Dr. Don L. Davis

1

According to the Bible's own claim, it is inspired of God, recognizing both the divine and human dimensions ingredient in its origin and authority as the very Word of the living God. Christians have confessed that because God's Word is inspired by God, it contained no errors in its original autographs, and thus represents the absolute authority in the Church of God for what we are to believe and to do. Modern biblical criticism attempts to trace the origins of the Scriptures from the original events spoken of in the Bible to the actual reports of those happenings recorded in the canonical books of Scripture. These major subsections include form, source, linguistic, textual, literary, canonical, redaction, and historical criticism, as well as translation studies. Regardless of the claims made by many scholars today, we may be confident that the Scriptures are in truth the Word of God which lives and abides forever.

Our objective for this segment, *Biblical Inspiration and Modern Biblical Criticism*, is to enable you to see that:

- The Scriptures clearly and boldly state that the Word of God is inspired of God, "God-breathed," through the power and working of the Holy Spirit. The Bible is a book of human authorship and divine inspiration, yet no Scripture is of any private interpretation, but the authors were "carried along" by the Holy Spirit.

- Five major theories of inspiration have surrounded the explanation of how precisely the Holy Spirit carried along the human authors of the Scriptures. These include the Mechanical or Dictation Theory, the Intuition or Natural Theory, the Illumination Theory, the Degrees of Inspiration Theory, and the Verbal/Plenary Theory. The Verbal/Plenary Theory argues that the entire text of the Scriptures, including the selection of words the author chose, are the product of God's leading and choice.

- Modern biblical criticism seeks to trace the origins of the Scriptures from the original events spoken of in the Bible to the actual reports of those happenings recorded in the canonical books of Scripture. Beginning with the regulatory event, it seeks to track God's message from the event to the translation of Scripture we have today.

Summary of Segment 2

- The major subsections of modern biblical criticism include form criticism (tracing oral tradition), source criticism (finding initial written sources), linguistic criticism (language, words, and grammar), textual criticism (copies of texts), literary criticism (rules of literature), canonical criticism (how books were selected), redaction criticism (the purposes of the authors), historical criticism (history and culture), as well as translation studies.

- Regardless of the claims made by many scholars today, we may be confident that the Scriptures are in truth the Word of God which lives and abides forever.

Video Segment 2 Outline

I. **Although Written by Human Authors, the Bible Is by God.**

A. Names and titles

1. "Bible" comes from the Greek word *biblos* (Matt. 1.1) and *biblion* (Luke 4.17) meaning "book."

2. Ancient books written upon the *biblus* or papyrus reed, from this came *biblos* and finally associated with the sacred books of Scripture (cf. Mark 12.26; Luke 3.4; 20.42; Acts 1.20; 7.42)

3. "Scripture" or "the Scriptures" (i.e., *the Holy Writings*) (Mark 12.10; 15.28; John 2.22; 10.35; Luke 24.27; Acts 17.11; 2 Tim. 3.15; 2 Pet. 3.16)

4. The Word of God (Mark 7.13; Rom. 10.17; 2 Cor. 2.17; Heb. 12; 1 Thess. 2.13)

B. The Bible is written by *human authors.*

    1. Isaiah, Isa. 1.1-2

    2. Paul, Gal. 1.1-5

    3. Moses, Ps. 90.1-2

    4. David, Ps. 19.1

C. The Scriptures are also *inspired by God.*

    1. They are *"breathed out"* by God himself, 2 Tim. 3.16-17.

    2. Their authorship are of no private interpretation, 2 Pet. 1.19-20.

    3. The authors were carried along by the Holy Spirit, 2 Pet. 1.21.

D. Implications of the divine inspiration of the Scriptures

    1. Because the Scriptures are inspired by God, we assert that they contain no errors in regard to their teachings or affirmations of truth (the doctrine of *inerrancy*).

2. Because the Scriptures are inspired by God, we further assert that the Scriptures alone are the final and absolute authority for all things to the Church, in what we believe and what we practice (the doctrine of *infallibility*).

II. Theories of Inspiration: How Exactly Did the Holy Spirit Lead the Human Authors?

These theories seek to answer the question as to just how the Lord, the Spirit, actually inspired the authors so that the product they came up with could be called "inspired by God."

The structure of argument in this section is adapted from H. Wayne House, "Theories of Inspiration." **Charts of Christian Theology**. Grand Rapids: Zondervan, 1992.

A. *Mechanical or Dictation Theory: passive human authorship*

1. The human author was a *passive instrument* in God's hands.

2. The author *wrote down each word* as God spoke it (verbatim reporting, like a secretary).

3. This dictation *protects the Scriptures* from error.

4. Reactions to the *Mechanical or Dictation Theory*

    a. Books of the Bible reveal too much diversity in styles of writing, language, and expression for this to be true.

    b. Why didn't God merely give us the book whole, then?

1

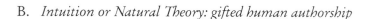

B. *Intuition or Natural Theory: gifted human authorship*

1. The Holy Spirit selected gifted people of deep spiritual wisdom to write the Bible.

2. The authors *wrote* the Bible informed by their own experience and insight.

3. Reaction to the *Intuition or Natural Theory*: the Scriptures claim that God, the Spirit, is the author of the Scriptures, not humans, however chosen or gifted, 2 Pet. 1.20-21.

C. *Illumination Theory: heightened human authorship*

1. The Holy Spirit heightened the normal capacities of human authors.

2. This heightened ability enabled the authors to have and express special insight into spiritual truth.

3. Reactions to the *Illumination Theory*: the Scriptures reveal not just human authors who wrote with added giftings, but those who spoke the very words of God ("Thus saith the Lord," and Rom. 3.2).

D. *Degrees of Inspiration Theory: more-and-less inspired human authorship*

1. Certain parts of the Scriptures are more inspired than others.

2. Portions dealing with key doctrine or ethical truths are more inspired than those dealing with history, economics, culture, etc.

3. Some parts of the Bible may be uninspired altogether.

4. Reactions to the *Degrees of Inspiration Theory*

   a. All Scripture is inspired by God, 2 Tim. 3.16-17.

   b. Asserting degrees of inspiration flies in the face of all that Jesus taught concerning the Word of God, Matt. 5.17-18; John 3.34-35; John 10.35.

   c. Who determines which parts are more or less inspired for us?

E. *Verbal-Plenary Theory: passive human authorship*

1. The Scriptures display both divine and human elements in its writing.

2. The entire text of the Scriptures, including the selection of words that the author chose, are a product of God.

   a. They are expressed in *human terms and conditions*.

   b. They are expressed in *human language and idiom*.

3. The authors were foreknown and chosen by God, and guided in their writing of the text (e.g., Jeremiah, Jer. 1.5).

4. Reactions to the *Verbal-Plenary Theory*

   a. Answers credibly the issue of human and divine authorship

   b. Concentrates on the entirety of the text, *including the words*

   c. How could finite, culture-bound human elements be described as the *unchanging and eternal Word of God?*

F. Final issues

1. The Holy Spirit carried the authors along, 2 Pet. 1.20-21.

2. The Scriptures (the result of the carrying along) are all, therefore, "breathed out" by God, 2 Tim. 3.16-17.

III. Biblical Criticism and the Origins of the Bible: From Event to Story to Text

A. The issue: the *evolution of the text*

1. How did the Bible come to us? What were the steps that led us to have our present translations of the Bible?

2. Can we trace the origins of the Bible from the actual events as they happened to our present Scriptures in our own mother tongue?

3. Modern historical criticism is concerned with *tracing the origins of the Scriptures from the original events to the actual stories and reports about them to the texts of Scripture, and finally to the translations we have today.*

   a. Original events: *revelatory events* (e.g., the Christ event)

   b. Actual stories and reports about them (*the oral traditions which circulated before the accounts were written down*)

   c. To the texts of Scripture (*the actual construction of the books themselves*)

   d. To the translations (our present translations)

B. A biblical example of criticism: Luke

   1. The testimony of Luke, Luke 1.1-4

      a. Compiling a narrative of historical facts

      b. Based on eyewitness accounts of those who believed

      c. Orderly account for Theophilus

d. For the purpose of certainty regarding *the things you have been taught*

2. Opening to the book of Acts, Acts 1.1-2

   a. Acts as "Volume II" of Luke's account regarding the person and work of Jesus

   b. Historical nuance and accuracy

3. Basic premise of Luke's criticism: *to provide an accurate account of the historical facts surrounding Jesus's life and work*

4. Modern biblical criticism: *to trace the text back to its original event, moving from the event itself, to its oral traditions, to textual copies, to standardized translations*

C. The Revelatory Event: God at work in the world and in the man and/or woman of God

   1. Decisive (*in terms of revelation*)

   2. Authoritative (*in terms of apostolic tradition, e.g., the resurrection, 1 Corinthians 15*)

   3. Unrepeatable (*tied to God's actions in history*), e.g., 2 Cor. 5.19

Note: Biblical studies is the attempt to recapture the meaning of the text in the context of the community as the community understood, transmitted, recorded, and theologized about the revelatory event.

4. Divinely revealed (*its meaning can only be interpreted by God himself to us, not from our own thinking or analysis*)

D. Form Criticism: *tracing the oral traditions (stories, reports, testimonies) associated with the events and the texts*

1. Studies the oral traditions of the people of God and the early Church

2. Views the Bible as the product of human tradition

3. Has a very low proof level

4. Strength: emphasizes that the Scriptures probably had *oral* beginnings before *written* products

5. Weakness: *speculates and guesses too much about how the community shared its story*

E. Source Criticism: *discovering the written sources used in the creation of the books*

1. Compares texts in various books to *see similarities and contrasts*

2. Views the Bible as the product of *human tradition*

3. Has a very low proof level

4. Strength: emphasizes the Scriptures' ability to identify *key sources*

5. Weakness: *proving its claims is not possible*

F. Linguistic Criticism: *studying the ancient languages, words, and grammar*

   1. Studies ancient Hebrew, koine Greek, and Aramaic

   2. Views the Bible as the *product of human culture*

   3. Has a middle range proof level

   4. Strength: in-depth meaning of *ancient languages*

   5. Weakness: *too far removed from the language*

G. Textual Criticism: *comparing the variant manuscripts to find the best reading*

   1. Focuses on *different manuscripts and their families* of texts

   2. Views the Bible as the product of *textual research*

   3. Has a very high proof level

   4. Strength: has a *multitude of reliable manuscripts* available

5. Weakness: *far too extensive number*

H. Literary Criticism: *determining the author, style, recipient, and genre*

1. Studies different types of literature, background study on the books

2. Views the Bible as the product of *literary genius*

3. Has a very high proof level

4. Strength: discovers what types (*genres*) of biblical literature mean and how they should be handled to interpret them properly

5. Weakness: *tendency to read too much into the text without allowing them to speak for themselves*

I. Canonical Criticism: *analyzes the Church's acceptance, view and use of the text*

1. Focuses on the history of the Bible in ancient Israel and the early Church (councils, conventions)

2. Views the Bible as the *product of the religious community*

3. Has a very high proof level

4. Strength: takes *the community's view* of the Bible seriously

5. Weakness: *tends to reduce the entire meaning of Scripture to what it meant within the believing community, and not what the Bible claims*

J. Redaction Criticism: *focuses on the theology of the person who wrote it*

1. Intense study of individual books to understand the meaning of the *author's theme and views*

2. Views the Bible as the product of *creative personality*

3. Has a mid proof level

4. Strength: deep analysis of an *author's entire collection* of writings and their interests

5. Weakness: *does not correlate the Bible with other books*

K. Historical Criticism: *investigating the historical setting, culture, and background*

1. Researches the *ancient cultures, their customs, and their history*

2. Views the Bible as the *product of historical forces*

3. Has a middle range proof level

4. Strength: has a firmer grasp of *the historical issues* of the text

5. Weakness: *too far removed from the history*

L. Translation Studies: *provides a clear, readable translation based on the best manuscripts*

1. Focuses on gaining an understanding of the receiving culture's language along with the meaning of the text for *the best translation*

2. Views the Bible as the product of *dynamic interpretation*

3. Has a middle range proof level

4. Strength: pursuing a *version of the Bible in one's own tongue* and thought world

5. Weakness: *reflects our own opinions about what the text means*

IV. Summary of Modern Biblical Criticism

A. Useful for understanding the surrounding situation of the Bible's history and customs

B. Beneficial in providing in-depth knowledge of biblical languages

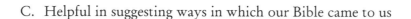

C. Helpful in suggesting ways in which our Bible came to us

D. Deep problems

1. Pursues truth from a *scientific study of religion*, not the word of Jesus and the apostles

2. Seeks to interpret the Bible *according to the limits of what they consider meaningful and possible*

3. It tends to undermine the Bible as *revelation*, and rather sees it primarily as record of religious community.

Let His Word Be True, and every man a liar!

Isa. 40.8 - The grass withers, the flower fades, but the word of our God will stand forever.

Conclusion

» The Word of God is inspired by God, for the authors were carried along by the Holy Spirit and the Scriptures they wrote, therefore, are the very inspired words of the living God.

» And while modern biblical criticism offers many helps to aid our understanding of the Bible, its general skepticism about the Bible's inspiration suggests that we must be careful at the things produced by them.

Segue 2

Student Questions and Response

The following questions were designed to help you review the material in the second video segment. The question of the origins, authority, and inspiration of the Bible lies at the heart of all biblical interpretation. We cannot proceed in defining our hermeneutic until we settle the question of the Bible's divine origin as well as its human authorship. Modern biblical criticism seeks to articulate the precise relationship between the claims of the divine and the human. As you discuss together the questions below, seek to make plain your own views as you review the key ideas of the segment. Read the following questions carefully, and seek to answer them in light of the teaching of the Scriptures.

1. List at least three Bible verses which claim that the Scriptures are inspired of God, "God-breathed," through the power and working of the Holy Spirit. What does it mean that the Bible is a divine book as well as a book of human authorship? How do you understand the text in 2 Peter that says that no Scripture is of any private interpretation, but the authors were "carried along" by the Holy Spirit (cf. 2 Pet. 1.19-21)?

2. What is the Mechanical or Dictation Theory, what does it hold, and what do you think about its believability?

3. Explain the Intuition or Natural Theory of biblical inspiration, and how ought we to interpret it in light of the Bible's own claim about itself?

4. What are the key elements of the Illumination Theory of biblical inspiration, and how do the Scriptures answer the question of the gifting of the authors and the Bible's divine authorship?

5. How does the Degrees of Inspiration Theory line up with the biblical teaching about the nature of the Word of God?

6. List the major concepts associated with the Verbal/Plenary Theory of biblical inspiration. Why does this theory, more than the others, provide us with a clear answer of the relationship of the divine and the human in the Bible's origins and authority?

7. What is the goal of modern biblical criticism? Is this a realistic goal? Explain your answer.

8. Summarize the various subsections of biblical criticism that traces the process from the divine event to our own copies of the Scriptures? What is the difference between "higher" criticism and "lower" criticism? What are the problems and benefits associated with these disciplines?

9. Of all the different approaches to biblical criticism, which do you believe offers orthodox students of Scripture the best and most useful support in their efforts to interpret the Word accurately?

10. Why can we be confident that our translation of the Scriptures is reliable and authoritative, even in light of the deep skepticism shown by many scholars today regarding the authority and inspiration of the Word of God?

Read the Appendix "Christ's View of the Bible" by Paul Enns to gain a critical perspective on the way in which Jesus of Nazareth both perceived and used the OT Scriptures, and how he foresaw through the apostles the coming NT.

CONNECTION

Summary of
Key Concepts

The Nature of Modern Biblical Scholarship

The multiplicity of methods currently available for biblical exegesis is confusing and can tempt the interpreter to focus on method(s) rather than on the dynamics of the process of understanding. When the full scope of the problem (including its "ontological" dimensions) is taken as the point of departure, it becomes possible to classify methods in terms of the specific aspect they address and to select the most suitable method in each case.

The historical aspect of the problem has mainly to do with the relationship between sender and message. From this important area of research a number of specialized techniques evolved. Background studies (Zeitgeschichte) focus on the historical environment from which the text emerged. Form criticism assumes an oral tradition behind the written text and is interested in its transition from the pre-literary form to the literary form. Source criticism studies the relationship between individual texts in a wider literary context and their dependence on sources. Redaction criticism proceeds from the assumption that the individual authors of biblical books had a strong influence on their eventual form and analyzes the composition of these texts from the perspective of the final redactor. Textual criticism is a specialized and technical discipline aimed at restoring the presumed original form of the text as accurately as possible. Questions of authorship, the history of individual books, and the formation of the canon all have to do with the historical aspect of the relationship between sender and message.

~ Bernard C. Lategan. "Hermeneutics." **The Anchor Bible Dictionary**.
D. N. Freedman, ed. Vol. 3. Doubleday: New York: Doubleday, 1997. pp. 152-153.

The following concepts summarize the critical truths we have discussed and reflected upon in this lesson on the origins, authority, and inspiration of the Scriptures. Before we can critically and reasonably lay out our own hermeneutic for understanding the Bible, we must be completely confident that the Scriptures are the Word of God, and that they merit the kind of attention, seriousness, and rigorous study that his inspired text deserves and demands. The truths listed below offer you a great opportunity to review the insights covered in your lesson.

- Hermeneutics is that discipline and branch of knowledge which focuses on interpretation, especially the interpretation of texts. Biblical hermeneutics focuses specifically on the methods and science of interpreting the Bible.

- By all accounts the Bible must be interpreted as both a *divine* and *human* book, and both dimensions of the divine and human must be appreciated to fully understand the nature of Scripture.

- Since the beginning orthodox Christian faith has held to certain fundamental presuppositions regarding the nature of Scripture, including its divine origin, the necessity of Scripture to interpret Scripture, the idea of progressive revelation which culminates in the revelation of God in the person of Christ, and the necessity of the working of the Holy Spirit in order to understand God's Word.

- The Three-Step Model of biblical interpretation, which seeks to take seriously the historical and linguistic difference between the world of the text and our modern world, includes efforts to understand the message in light of its original situation, discovering biblical principles from the text, and finally applying the meaning of Scripture to our lives.

- In order to rightly interpret the Word of God, we must prepare our hearts, minds, and our wills to humbly and rigorously study it, carefully analyze it, and heartily obey it, all to God's glory.

- We prepare our hearts through humility and prayer, diligence and determination, and rigorous engagement of the Bible as a workman. We prepare our minds as we embrace the roles of explorer, detective, and scientist, seeking the Word diligently, following up on clues, and weighing the evidence carefully before making judgments. We prepare our wills by obeying the Word, not merely hearing it, and embracing the truth that wisdom comes from responding to God's Word, not merely reflecting upon it.

1

1

☞ The Scriptures clearly and boldly state that the Word of God is inspired of God, "God-breathed," through the power and working of the Holy Spirit. The Bible is a book of human authorship and divine inspiration, yet no Scripture is of any private interpretation, but the authors were "carried along" by the Holy Spirit.

☞ Five major theories of inspiration have surrounded the explanation of how precisely the Holy Spirit carried along the human authors of the Scriptures. These include the Mechanical or Dictation Theory, the Intuition or Natural Theory, the Illumination Theory, the Degrees of Inspiration Theory, and the Verbal/Plenary Theory. The Verbal/Plenary Theory argues that the entire text of the Scriptures, including the selection of words the author chose, are the product of God's leading and choice.

☞ Modern biblical criticism seeks to trace the origins of the Scriptures from the original events spoken of in the Bible to the actual reports of those happenings recorded in the canonical books of Scripture. Beginning with the regulatory event, it seeks to track God's message from the event to the translation of Scripture we have today.

☞ The major subsections of modern biblical criticism includes form criticism (tracing oral tradition), source criticism (finding initial written sources), linguistic criticism (language, words, and grammar), textual criticism (copies of texts), literary criticism (rules of literature), canonical criticism (how books were selected), redaction criticism (the purposes of the authors), historical criticism (history and culture), as well as translation studies.

☞ Regardless of the claims made by many scholars today, we may be confident that the Scriptures are in truth the Word of God which lives and abides forever.

Student Application and Implications

Your ability to carefully and slowly reflect and apply insights is key to your own ongoing enrichment and development as a Christian leader. This section of your lesson is your time to discuss with your fellow students the specific questions that have arisen in your minds about the origins and authority of the Scriptures. The concept of the inspiration of Scripture lies at the heart of both your own ability to grow in Christ as well as proclaim its promises and claims confidently in your ministry. Think now of those particular questions that have come to mind in light of the material you have just studied, and discuss them together. The questions below may spur your own questions, concerns, and issues.

* Is it necessary for every Christian to have some kind of "hermeneutic" as they seek to understand the meaning of the Bible? Why are these issues important for laymen as well as clergy, for ordinary Christians as well as scholars?

* Is there any final way to really know the precise relationship between the *divine* and *human* dimensions of how the Bible was created? What happens if we can't perfectly explain it; ought we to be overly alarmed at it? Explain your answer.

* Why is it so important to *begin* our study of the origins of the Bible with the truths that Christians through the ages have always held to and believed?

* Explain the reason why all hermeneutic strategies are essentially attempts to bridge the gap between the world of the text and our modern world? Is this really possible or necessary, given that there are so many centuries separating us and the authors of the Bible?

* What steps do I take to prepare my own heart, mind, and will to understand and apply the Word of God? What is the greatest challenge I have in this area?

* Do you have to believe that the original autographs of the Bible were "inerrant" and "infallible" in order to believe that they are inspired of God and "God-breathed?" Explain your answer.

* Of all the theories you read about in this lesson, which is most convincing to you about the nature of the divine and the human in the Bible? Which is least convincing, and why?

* To what extent do you think that urban Christian leaders need to know the general theories associated with modern biblical criticism? Do these fields enhance or interfere with our ability to really master the Word of God for personal discipleship and ministry? Explain.

* Of all the major subsections of modern biblical criticism, which do you think may provide urban Christian leaders with the best resources to both understand and apply the Word of God to life and ministry?

Tradition and/or Scripture

For the vast majority of Christians alive today, the role of church authority takes precedence over personal interpretation of the Bible. The authority of the pope for Catholics provides the outline and impulse whereby Catholic Christians come to interpret the Bible; although the Bible has personal application, they would hold, it should not be interpreted exclusively as a *personal book*. To be a Christian, they argue, is to be a part of the "communion of saints," the faithful of Christ who throughout the ages have clung to the hope of eternal life with all those who hold the truth in Christ as dear. For many Protestants, on the other hand, they understand the Bible as the "inerrant" and "infallible" authority in the lives of all Christians. The only problem with this view of the Bible is that it has spawned thousands of independent movements and sects, all of which claim connection to the "authority of the Bible." What do you make of these arguments about tradition and Scripture, and how ought we to view the role of tradition in the interpretation of the Bible?

No Way to Know for Sure

In a rather heated conversation among seminarians on the authority of the Bible, one student demanded answers on the *usefulness* of discussions about inspiration and authority issues. She argued that "Since we cannot know any of these theories as the *true* theory, it seems that we are wasting a lot of time talking about ideas that cannot be proven. What difference does it make if we can't even prove that *any* of these theories is actually the *right* one. Why not simply take the Bible at its word and confess that the Bible is the Word of God, that God inspired it, and that it is reliable for our faith and our ministry?" Others argued that this was a naive position. As seminarians and Christian leaders, they were obligated to ask the "tough questions" and go as far they could to make sense of these and related questions on the Bible. Who do you think is correct in their view about these arguments?

Only Christians Really Care

A pastor was asked by the elders of the church why he had been in the church for five years but had never done a series on the reliability of the Bible, and its inspiration. He replied, "It is not that I do not believe that the Bible is reliable. I do. The problem is that the only ones who are interested in hearing messages about the Bible's inspiration are those who already believe it. I have found in my years in the ministry that very few unbelievers have been converted on the basis of long-winded arguments about the possibility of miracles and the theories of inspiration. They are more convinced by the living epistles of our lives, the kind of generosity, hospitality, and genuine servanthood that disciples of Jesus show, not the length of their essays and the weight of their intellectual arguments. Really, only Christians care about issues of inspiration." What do you think about the pastor's evaluation of these kinds of preaching and teaching on the inspiration? Why is he right–or wrong–in his judgment?

First Things First

4 One Christian leadership training center offers a full array of biblical, theological, and pastoral training to its students through a solid and dedicated faculty. In all of the programs they offer, they only demand of their students a single course: biblical hermeneutics. Their reasoning is clear and simple: the center deeply believes that the central and most important skill for Christian leadership development is gaining a mastery of the Scriptures. No other field of learning, no other skills or experience, can begin to compare with the necessity of being grounded in Scripture, of gaining the ability to preach, teach, and apply the message of the Scriptures to the various issues of family, church, work, and service. What do you make of this claim: in terms of all the things that urban leaders must learn to do and be, what place should the Word of God play in their development? Why is it simply impossible to be the kind of leader God desires for you to be if you remain ignorant and ill-equipped to "rightly divide" the Word of truth?

Restatement of the Lesson's Thesis

Hermeneutics is that discipline and branch of knowledge which focuses on interpretation, especially the interpretation of texts. Biblical hermeneutics focuses specifically on the methods and science of interpreting the Bible. Since the beginning, orthodox Christian faith has held to certain fundamental presuppositions regarding the nature of Scripture, such as the inspiration of the Bible, the necessity of Scripture to interpret Scripture, and the idea that Scripture progressively reveals God's will, ending with the person of Jesus. The *Three-Step Model* of biblical interpretation seeks to bridge the gap between the world of the text and our modern world, understanding the original situation, discovering biblical principles, applying Scripture to life. In order to rightly interpret the Word of God, we must prepare our hearts, minds, and our wills to humbly and rigorously study it, carefully analyze it, and heartily obey it, all to God's glory.

1

The Scriptures are "God-breathed" through the power and working of the Holy Spirit. The question of human authorship and divine inspiration has been explained through five major theories of inspiration, including the Mechanical or Dictation Theory, the Intuition or Natural Theory, the Illumination Theory, the Degrees of Inspiration Theory, and the Verbal/Plenary Theory. The Verbal/Plenary Theory argues that the entire text of the Scriptures, including the selection of words the author chose, are the product of God's leading and choice.

Modern biblical criticism seeks to trace the origins of the Scriptures from the original events spoken of in the Bible to the actual reports of those happenings recorded in the canonical books of Scripture. The major subsections of modern biblical criticism includes form criticism (tracing oral tradition), source criticism (finding initial written sources), linguistic criticism (language, words, and grammar), textual criticism (copies of texts), literary criticism (rules of literature), canonical criticism (how books were selected), redaction criticism (the purposes of the authors), historical criticism (history and culture), as well as translation studies. Regardless of the claims made by many scholars today, we may be confident that the Scriptures are in truth the Word of God which lives and abides forever.

If you are interested in pursuing some of the ideas of *Biblical Inspiration: The Origins and Authority of the Bible*, you might want to give these books a try:

> Bacote, Vincent, Laura C. Miguelez, and Dennis L. Okholm. *Evangelicals & Scripture: Tradition, Authority and Hermeneutics*. Downers Grove, IL: InterVarsity Press, 2004.

> Barton, John. *People of the Book: The Authority of the Bible in Christianity*. Louisville, KY: Westminster John Knox Press, 1989.

> Bruce, F. F. *The Canon of Scripture*. Downers Grove, IL: InterVarsity Press, 1988.

> ------. *The New Testament Documents: Are They Reliable?* Grand Rapids: Eerdmans Publishing Company, 2003.

Resources and Bibliographies

The doctrine of the origins and inspiration of the Scriptures does have immediate application to our ministry to others. The inability to have confidence in the power of the Word of God will in every way affect how you preach, to whom you preach, and what you expect from your ministry of the Word. Take time now to explore

Ministry Connections

the ramifications of these important truths about the God-breathed Scriptures, and seek to make a tangible and practical ministry connection to an area where you serve and teach. As you have discussed and meditated upon these truths throughout this lesson, perhaps some concepts have "jumped out" at you as deeply significant for your own walk and ministry, and deserving of further prayer, meditation, and study this next week. Explore the particular direction that the Holy Spirit suggests to you regarding the authority and inspiration of the Scriptures, and the confidence it provides as we claim its promises, obey its commands, and cherish its claims about God, his Son, and the Kingdom.

Counseling and Prayer

A significant element in your learning experience ought to be open, focused intercession and supplication for your fellow students during the class session. In light of the various truths, challenges, and needs shared throughout the time, spend time praying specifically for the needs and concerns of your colleagues. Never underestimate the power of faithful prayer to make the truth of God come alive in our lives. Only as the Holy Spirit provides us with insight and grace can we truly be transformed, and make the truth our very own (1 Cor. 2.9-16).

ASSIGNMENTS

Scripture Memory

2 Peter 1.19-21

Reading Assignment

To prepare for class, please visit *www.tumi.org/books* to find next week's reading assignment, or ask your mentor.

Other Assignments

You will be quizzed on the content (the video content) of this lesson next week. Make sure that you spend time covering your notes, especially focusing on the main ideas of the lesson. Read the assigned reading, and summarize each reading with no more than a paragraph or two for each. In this summary please give your best understanding of what you think was the main point in each of the readings. Do not be overly concerned about giving detail; simply write out what you consider to be the main point discussed in that section of the book. Please bring these summaries to class next week. (Please see the "Reading Completion Sheet" at the end of this lesson.)

. . . .

In today's lesson we explored the need for biblical interpretation, and for our own preparation of our hearts, our minds, and our wills to engage the eternal Word of the Living God. As a divine and human book, we must depend on the resources of the Holy Spirit to understand the Word of God, and be ready to allow that Word to transform our lives *before* we engage it. In our next segment we examined the inspiration and authority of the Bible, and discuss the role of modern biblical criticism in the understanding of the Word of God today.

In our next lesson we will go into greater detail into our *Three-Step Model* of biblical interpretation, a simple yet effective way designed to help us understand the truth of Scripture and bridge the gap between our ancient and contemporary worlds. The model includes a prayerful yet disciplined use of Bible study tools to enable us to grasp God's message to the original audience, discover general principles for today, and make applications of them to our lives.

Looking Forward to the Next Lesson

Name _____

Date _____

For each assigned reading, write a brief summary (one or two paragraphs) of the author's main point. (For additional readings, use the back of this sheet.)

Reading 1

Title and Author: _____ Pages _____

Reading 2

Title and Author: _____ Pages _____

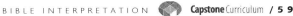

Biblical Hermeneutics
The Three-Step Model

Lesson Objectives

Welcome in the strong name of Jesus Christ! After your reading, study, discussion, and application of the materials in this lesson, you will be able to:

- Give evidence to show how the *Three-Step Model* is an effective method of biblical interpretation designed to help us understand the truth of Scripture and bridge the gap between our ancient and contemporary worlds.

- Provide a definition of the *Three-Step Model* of biblical interpretation, and recite it without aids: "to so understand the meaning of the original situation that we may discover general principles of truth which may be applied in our personal lives in the Spirit's freedom."

- Highlight the ways in which all study of the Word of God must unfold the meaning and message of God's final revelation to us in the person and work of Jesus Christ.

- Demonstrate your knowledge of how the *Three-Step Model* corresponds to the grammatical-historical method of Scripture interpretation, which affirms the plain sense of its meaning, God's progressive revelation in Christ, the unity of the Bible, and the integrity of the text.

- Reproduce the critical reasons for each step in the *Three-Step Model*, including why each is necessary, the difficulties associated with each, the key attitude required in each step, the activities associated with each one, as well as an example of each step in Scripture.

- Distinguish between the kinds of attitudes necessary for each phase of study in the *Three-Step Model*: humility, thoroughness, and liberty for each of the phases respectively.

- Reproduce an example of the *Three-Step Model* using 1 Corinthians 9.1-4 as a case study of its application, employing each step of the method practically as you go through the text.

- See how the study of a particular passage must be done in light of the message of the entire chapter, section, book of the Bible, and ultimately, in light of the Bible's message to us in Christ.

- Show through personal use of *Three-Step Method* how each of the key stages focuses *on the text* in such a way as to credibly discern its purpose of illumination of the text's meaning, and the transformation of our lives through the joy of discovering biblical principles for life.

- Discern the key elements, cautions, and procedures in investigating the original situation of the text, discovering biblical principles, and making correct applications of the Scripture's teaching to your life.

A Heart Prepared to Study, Do, and Teach the Word of God

Devotion

Ezra 7.10 - For Ezra had set his heart to study the Law of the LORD, and to do it and to teach his statutes and rules in Israel.

Is your heart prepared before God?

A glance at the major saints of the Scriptures reveals that our God uses men and women whose hearts have been prepared before him to study his Word, to practice it diligently within their lives, and then be used as his vessel to communicate his truth to others. Perhaps one of the clearest examples of this is recorded in the OT historical book of Ezra which details the return of the Israelites during the post-exilic era back to Judah from Babylon in order to spiritually revive the faithful and reestablish the worship of the Lord in the temple. The worship of the Lord in a way that is appropriate and right is a key theme in all the books of the OT written during the time after Israel and Judah were sent into captivity because of their sin against God. Included in these books are 1 and 2 Chronicles, Ezra, Nehemiah, Haggai, Zechariah, and Malachi (with perhaps the book of Esther being the only exception). Those who returned were ready and willing to acknowledge their guilt before the Lord, their confidence that he would reestablish them in the land he had given them, and that he and he alone was worthy to be worshiped and able to usher in his kingdom reign through the coming Messiah.

Actually, there were three returns to the land of Israel from Babylon, which occurred approximately in the years 538, 458, and 444 B.C.E. This corresponds to the fact that there had been three times that the population was deported to Babylon from Israel in the years 605, 597, and 586 B.C.E. respectively. The returns were led by godly servants of God, the first in 538 B.C.E. by Zerubbabel (Ezra 1-6; Haggai; Zechariah), whose efforts resulted in the rebuilding of the temple. The second return occurred in 458 B.C.E. under the leadership and supervision of Ezra (Ezra 7-10), which focused on the reform and instruction of the people, their *spiritual revival*, and the need for them to come back to the Lord through the fulfillment of the covenant. Finally, Nehemiah led the third return to the land in 444 B.C.E., whose major concerns dealt with rebuilding devastated Jerusalem's broken down walls, and with Ezra, to bring God's people back to the Lord with spiritual renewal and covenant obedience. Many scholars believe that Malachi was probably written in Nehemiah's time, and that Esther was written during the events recorded in Ezra 6 and 7. This eventful time in Israel's history provides key insights in the need for prepared men and women for the task of God.

Our single text for the devotion records the kind of inner life and motive of the person that God uses to bring revival, renewal, and refreshment to his people. "For Ezra had set his heart to study the Law of the LORD, and to do it and to teach his statutes and rules in Israel." According to our text, Ezra had "set his heart," literally "fixed his soul" to do three things on behalf of the Lord.

First, Ezra had set his heart to study the Law of the Lord. There would be no half-hearted, sleepy-eyed scanning of God's Word, but a disciplined, passionate, focused *study* of God's law. The Bible simply can be mastered in no other way; without seeking the knowledge of the Lord as treasure hunters seek gold, the hidden depth and meaning of the text simply cannot be found nor understood (Prov. 2.1-9). The lazy, undisciplined heart will never come to know the riches of God's wisdom regarding his plan of salvation in Christ.

Second, he had set his heart to *do it*. Simply put, Ezra was not *living to study*, rather, he was *studying to live*. The intent of the Word of God is not merely to hear the will of God regarding faith, obedience, love, and service. The purpose is to do it, and the blessing of the text is associated not merely with those who reflect upon it but to those who respond to it with humility and diligence as it is the very Word of God (James 1.22-25). The wisdom of the Lord comes to those who actually carry out his will as they discover it in his holy Word (cf. Psalm 111.10 The fear of the Lord is the beginning of wisdom; all those who practice it have a good understanding. His praise endures forever!).

Finally, Ezra has set his heart to "*teach his statutes and rules in Israel.*" Once the Word of God is mastered through study and fulfilled through obedience, then the servant of God is ready to fulfill his or her ministry through the teaching ministry. Ezra's priorities regarding his approach and ministry of the Word were in the proper order: he prepared himself to study God's perfect Law, to do it, and *then* to teach it. This kind of careful consideration and heart preparation is the veritable *stuff* of which saints, Christian workers, prophets, and apostles are made of. The focus is not upon the mission, or the work, or the blessing, or the gifts. The focus is upon the Word of God-on studying it, mastering it, putting it into practice, and then, once known and obeyed, sharing it with passion and clarity. This is precisely what occurred in the ministry of Ezra to the people; because of his heart priorities, God used him mightily to bring revival and renewal to God's people, and lay a foundation for a movement that would eventually prepare the nation for the coming of Messiah. And all this, because a single person in love with God prepared his heart for the Word.

Is your heart set before God to study, do, and teach his Word to his people, for his glory? Do you focus on *yourself–your* gifts, *your* blessing, *your* opportunities, or are you clear in your desire simply to master the Word of God so *you* can put it into practice in your life, and be released of the Holy Spirit then to teach his Word to the people of God? Let's learn from the example of this humble and brave preacher of the Word of God whose ministry began not with grand plans of influence, but the humility of a heart set to know and do God's will as he learned it from the Word of God. Truly, *this* is the pattern for all fruitful ministry in the name of the Lord.

After reciting and/or singing the Nicene Creed (located in the Appendix), pray the following prayer:

Nicene Creed and Prayer

> *O God Almighty, Father of our Lord Jesus Christ: Grant us, we pray, to be grounded and settled in your truth by the coming down of the Holy Spirit into our hearts. That which we know not, reveal; that which is wanting in us, fill up; that which we know, confirm; and keep us blameless in your service; through the same Jesus Christ our Lord. Amen.*

> ~ Presbyterian Church (U.S.A.) and Cumberland Presbyterian Church. The Theology and Worship Ministry Unit. **Book of Common Worship**. Louisville: Westminister/John Knox Press, 1993. p 26.

Quiz

Put away your notes, gather up your thoughts and reflections, and take the quiz for Lesson 1, *Biblical Inspiration: The Origins and Authority of the Bible.*

- -

Scripture Memorization Review

Review with a partner, write out and/or recite the text for last class session's assigned memory verse: 2 Peter 1.19-21.

- -

Assignments Due

Turn in your summary of the reading assignment for last week, that is, your brief response and explanation of the main points that the authors were seeking to make in the assigned reading (Reading Completion Sheet).

- -

CONTACT

2

Only Formal Training Will Do

1 Many churches and denominations today are convinced that those who desire to go into ministry must have some formal training in a Bible Institute, Christian liberal arts college, or graduate school/seminary. Those who hold such a view are simply convinced that the rigors, problems, and situations of ministry cannot be left to one's own personal preparation. Rather, the likelihood that one will be successful in urban ministry increases greatly, they argue, if a student is given the opportunity to receive formal training. Unfortunately, for those able neither to afford nor to qualify for such training, they are de facto eliminated from the candidate pool of ministry. What is your opinion about the role of formal training in biblical, theological, and pastoral training and the prospect of urban ministry? Is it possible to have a fruitful urban ministry without having been trained formally? If it is, then what is the role and function of formal academic preparation for urban ministry?

Discerning the Mind of the Holy Spirit Is My Method

2 While many believe that having a clear, rational method for approaching Bible study is essential to discern the meaning of Scripture, a great many today remain skeptical of the role of *method* for spiritual discernment. Having seen the doubt and confusion produced by modern historical criticism of the Bible, many hold that any allegiance to a form of method is dangerous in study. Rather than using scientific methods of approach, these often argue for a more spiritual, intuitive approach to

Bible study. They approach study as a *spiritual* discipline not an intellectual one, and want to be taught by the Holy Spirit. This is perceived not as the wooden following of some method, but a heart and soul preparation that allows the Holy Spirit himself to be their teacher. If, in fact, the Holy Spirit alone is the true teacher of the Word of God, what is the usefulness of seeking a method to read, study, and apply the Scriptures? In what ways might a commitment to method in biblical interpretation either help or hinder our understanding of the Word of God?

Attitude vs. Method: Which One Is Most Critical in Biblical Interpretation?

While most acknowledge that some form of disciplined approach to the Scriptures is helpful to understand God's purpose and meaning in the Bible, it is often not clear how to weigh the importance between *attitude* and *method* in study. On the one hand, many believe that without the proper attitude, no understanding of Scripture is possible. Whatever method we employ to discern the meaning of the Bible, it requires the humble, broken, and contrite spirit that God says throughout Scripture is his true sacrifice and the requirement for his leading and teaching. On the other hand, we can point to many examples where humility and kindness, zeal and passion severed from knowledge produced horrible spiritual results. Attitude without knowledge did not produce spiritual discernment but resulted in tyranny, confusion, even heresy. What is the relationship between proper heart preparation and attitude, and following a disciplined method and approach to the Bible? How should we order and place them in our study of Scripture?

CONTENT ► **Biblical Hermeneutics: The Three-Step Model**

Segment 1: Bridging the Gap between the Ancient and Contemporary Worlds

Rev. Dr. Don L. Davis

Summary of Segment 1

The *Three-Step Model* is an effective method of biblical interpretation designed to help us understand the truth of Scripture and bridge the gap between our ancient and contemporary worlds. It focuses upon our efforts to understand the original audience, discover general principles, and make applications to life.

Our objective for this segment, *Bridging the Gap between the Ancient and Contemporary Worlds*, is to enable you to see that:

- The *Three-Step Model* is an effective method of biblical interpretation designed to help us understand the truth of Scripture and bridge the gap between our ancient and contemporary worlds.

- A clear and concise definition of the *Three-Step Model* is "to so understand the meaning of the original situation that we may discover general principles of truth which may be applied in our personal lives in the Spirit's freedom."

- While studying individual words, phrases, paragraphs, chapters, sections, and books of the Scriptures is both edifying and necessary, all of our insights into the Scriptures ought to be in sync with the message of the whole Bible, i.e., the meaning and message of God's final revelation to us in the person and work of Jesus Christ.

- The *Three-Step Model* resonates and corresponds to the grammatical-historical method of Scripture interpretation, which affirms the plain sense of the Bible's meaning, God's progressive revelation in Christ, the unity of the Bible, and the integrity of the text as it communicates to us in different genres and forms.

- Each step associated with the *Three-Step Model* has its own particular aim and logic, reasons and basis, and key attitudes, and are fulfilled with a particular sequence and list of activities. To master the model we must become familiar with and skilled at these steps and activities.

- The critical preparation for the use of any form of biblical study is the attitude of the student of the Scriptures, as the phases of study in the

Three-Step Model demands humility, thoroughness, and liberty for each phase respectively.

• As slaves to righteousness under Christ's lordship, we are called to obey his Word in every facet of our lives and ministries, and therefore, all legitimate biblical interpretation seeks to discern God's Word for the purpose of *life transformation*, not *mind information*.

Everyone Has a System for Bible Interpretation

Believe it or not, everyone has a method of interpreting the Bible. But not all methods are equally profitable. Some use the magic finger approach. It consists of acting upon some supposed divine directive, locating a particular verse—usually with the eyes closed—and taking that portion of Scripture as an answer or truth provided by God. We may laugh at that, but often come quite close to that when we ignore contexts. Then there are those who read the Bible a lot, but never seem to get very far in putting it altogether. They can quote at great length, but have difficulty seeing what the passage means. Others follow an extreme devotional approach. They read only what "warms" them at the moment, as if the Bible were intended to make them feel good continually. All of these people have systems of interpreting the Bible, and it is not difficult to see why such methods do not lead to spiritual soundness. As a result of these approaches—which are really partly Bible study methods and partly interpreting methods—many are spiritually weak and discouraged about their prospects of getting anything solid from the Bible. Such practices never lead to a mature ability to handle the Bible with power and fruitfulness. Methods of interpretation can be haphazard or systematic, and even systematic interpretation can be either profitable, or unprofitable, so that it does violence to the meaning of the Bible. God's desire is that believers come to the place where they are able to read the Bible with understanding, balance, and facility in relating various portions of the Scriptures to each other.

~ Paul Karleen. **The Handbook to Bible Study**. (electronic ed.). New York: Oxford University Press, 1987.

**Video Segment 1
Outline**

I. Definition, Purpose, Elements, Benefits of the Three-Step Model of Biblical Interpretation

A. Definition: "To so understand the meaning of the original situation that we may discover general principles of truth which may be applied in our personal lives in the Spirit's freedom"

1. *To so understand the meaning of the original situation*: the first step focuses on understanding what the text meant in its original setting.

2. *That we may discover general principles of truth*: the second step focuses on drawing out of the text biblical principles which are binding and applicable to believers today.

3. *That may be applied in our personal lives in the Spirit's freedom*: the third step is applying the principle of truth in our personal lives in the power of the Spirit.

B. Purpose

1. To learn what the author meant in the context of its original writing

2. To discover biblical principles which summarize the teaching of Scripture and offer God's wisdom and insight which are binding upon all and can be applied to all

3. To change our belief and practices and conform our lives to the truths contained in the Word of God

C. Elements

1. It corresponds to the *grammatical-historical method*: determine the meaning of the text in its *original setting* before applying its meaning to another time and place.

2. This model looks for the *plain sense* of the text.

3. This model affirms *progressive revelation*.

   a. The Bible shows that God unfolds the meaning and method of his purpose, culminating (i.e., "summing up") in Jesus Christ, Heb. 1.1-3.

   b. Jesus *surpasses* and *fulfills* the meaning of all that God communicated before (i.e., John 1.14-18; Matt. 5.17-18; John 5.39-40; Luke 24.27, 44-48).

4. It affirms *the unity of the Scriptures*.

   a. The Bible is a single canon (collection, library) of texts, written by a single author, 2 Tim. 3.16-17; 2 Pet. 1.20-21.

   b. The explicit subject of the Scriptures is *Jesus Christ and his Kingdom*, Acts 28.23,31; Col. 1.25-27; Eph. 3.3-11; Rom. 16.25-27.

5. This model assumes the *integrity of the text*: the authors carried along by the Holy Spirit communicated the perspective and truth God intended for the original hearers, which we can discover and appropriate, 1 Cor. 10.1-6.

D. Benefits

1. An *exegetical* approach to the Scriptures

2. A method emphasizing understanding *before* application

3. Searching for the *timeless principle* arising from the *temporal particulars*

Discovering the Word and Works of God in the Lives of the People of Scripture

Physical Environment

Worldviews

Religions

Beliefs

Cultures

Their Ancient World

What it meant to them then

Peoples

Languages

History

Politics

Kuhatschek's Categories:

Understanding the Original Situation

The Eternal Truth of the Living God

Finding General Principles

What it means to us now

World

Job

Our Contemporary Situation

Applying General Principles Today

Family

Character

Neighborhood

Relationships

Church

Applying Principles of God's Word to our Lives in the Church and in the World

2

II. Step One: Understanding the Original Situation (*Engaging the Text on its Own Terms*)

A. Critical reasons exist for seeking to understand a text *first* in its original situation.

1. *Major cultural barriers* exist between the original culture and our time.

2. The *languages* are different from our own (Hebrew, Aramaic, and koine Greek).

3. We are *ethnocentric* (completely immersed in our own culture, and believe naturally that ours is *preferable*).

4. We read the Bible *anachronistically* (i.e., we tend to read our own situation in the present day *back into* the biblical time).

5. We are prone to make *geographical, historical, and social blunders*.

B. Why is it so difficult to understand the original situation?

1. We weren't there!: *no one alive today was present* during the events when the reports of the Scriptures were given.

2. We do not know *the usages or nuances of the biblical languages* (Greek, Aramaic, and Hebrew).

3. Our *personal opinion filters* constantly interfere with our understanding of the original situation.

4. We are conditioned to *read it the way we've always read it* (i.e., we allow past readings to bias our present readings).

5. We *jump to conclusions* without considering what it meant to the people.

C. Key attitude needed: ***humility***, James 1.5

1. Acceptance of the distance between ourselves and the actual situation of the text

2. Willingness to admit the differences and the barriers that exist between our own time and that of the authors and audiences of the text

3. Openness to suspend judgment until we learn more of the situation *before we pass judgment on what the text meant*

4. Cultivating a deep respect for the original meanings and situations

D. Steps in understanding the original situation

1. Take the time to do your homework on the original situation, Prov. 2.1-6.

2. Respect the process of critical analysis, Ezra 7.10.

3. Recognize and take seriously the reality of distance: *Sitz im Leben* (situation in life).

4. Acquire and learn to use the proper Bible study tools that will help recreate for you the original situation.

E. Example: the Passover, 1 Corinthians 5.7, 8

III. Step Two: Discover and Draw Out General Principles

A. Why do we need to discover general principles?

1. "Facts are dumb things": biblical facts require *interpretation*, and interpretation leads to *understanding*.

2. Without principles we are left with pieces and no mosaics: we confront thousands of unconnected facts in the Bible.

3. General principles allow us to draw out wisdom from the experience of others: the power of biblical case studies, Prov. 24.30-34.

   a. *Careful personal observation* of a particular situation

   b. Reflection and *consideration of the meaning* of those facts

   c. The *formation of a principle* (*proverb*) that can be applied to a number of different but related situations

4. General principles allow us to predict with accuracy *what will occur if certain conditions are met*, drawing clear conclusions from universal truth.

5. Principles provide us with *the big picture underlying particular events*, giving us insight into the whole of human experience and God's spirituality.

B. Why is it hard to draw out general principles from Scripture?

1. *Too many facts, stories, and details* to process

2. Irony: there are not enough facts to process!

3. *Personal reading and devotional habits* interfere with our ability to generalize rightly.

4. *Most principles*: many principles are not explicitly written.

5. *Requires labor and time* to check our findings against the Word of God for their validity

    a. Prov. 8.17

    b. Matt. 7.7-8

    c. Prov. 9.9

d. Eccles. 7.25

C. Key attitude: *thoroughness*, Acts 17.11

   1. Develop a willingness to search out the Word to find universal truths.

   2. Refuse to jump to conclusions without checking them against the Scriptures.

   3. Orient yourself to patiently pray and discuss, in your search, for principles in the Word of God.

D. Steps to discover principles

   1. Expect to find God's practical wisdom in your study of the Word of God, 2 Tim. 3.16.

   2. When analyzing individual texts, always be on the lookout for larger patterns, structures, principles, and connections in the text to other Scripture.

   3. Do not be hasty in declaring one of your proverbs a universal principle: test your findings against Scripture.

      a. 1 Thess. 5.21

      b. Prov. 23.23

     c.   Phil. 4.8

     d.   2 Thess. 2.15

  4. *Acid test of principle formation*: if your proverb is true, you ought to be able to find cases in life where the truth of your proverb is easily observed to be true.

E. Examples: "The Love Commandment" and "Sowing and Reaping"

  1. Loving God and loving neighbor is the summation of all God's moral demands in the OT.

     a.   The entire ethical demand of God hinges on loving him with all the heart, and one's neighbor as oneself, Matt. 22.36-40.

     b.   Love is the fulfilling of the law of God, Rom. 13.8-10.

  2. You will certainly reap what you sow, Gal. 6.7-8.

IV. Step Three: Apply the Principle to Life in the Power of the Spirit

A. What are the reasons for applying God's Word to our lives?

  1. We are to be doers of the Word and not merely hearers (i.e., students) of the Word, James 1.22-25.

2. Disciplined practice of the Word produces godliness, 1 Tim. 4.7-9.

3. By consistent application of the Word we mature and become able to teach others, Heb. 5.11-6.2.

4. Faith without works is useless, James 2.14-17.

5. Applying the Word establishes our lives on a firm foundation, Matt. 7.24-27.

B. Why is it so difficult to apply the Word?

1. Our sin nature: we are naturally inclined to disbelieve and disobey, Gal. 5.16-21.

2. We avoid the challenge and stimulation of other believers.

    a. 2 Cor. 9.2

    b. Heb. 10.24-25

    c. Heb. 3.13-14

3. We seek to apply the truth of the text in fleshly power and effort, Phil. 3.2-3.

4. We are easily distracted by things that do not matter.

    a. 2 Tim. 4.10

    b. Luke 9.62

    c. Luke 14.33

    d. Luke 16.13

    e. Luke 17.32

    f. Phil. 2.21

    g. 1 Tim. 6.10

    h. 1 John 2.15-16

5. We embrace a common fallacy: "knowing about something is the same as doing."

C. Key attitude: *liberty in Christ*

Gal. 5.1 - For freedom Christ has set us free; stand firm therefore, and do not submit again to a yoke of slavery.

Rom. 7.6 - But now we are released from the law, having died to that which held us captive, so that we serve not under the old written code but in the new life of the Spirit.

2 Cor. 3.17 - Now the Lord is the Spirit, and where the Spirit of the Lord is, there is freedom.

1. Freedom is the dominant theme of Jesus' liberation.

    a. John 8.34-36

    b. Rom. 6.18

    c. Rom. 8.2

    d. 2 Cor. 3.17

    e. Gal. 4.26

    f. Gal. 4.31

    g. Gal. 5.13

    h. 1 Pet. 2.16

2. As slaves of righteousness under Christ's lordship, we are free to express obedience to the Word in every facet of our lives.

3. We must cultivate a willingness to experiment in our obedience under the Spirit's direction, 2 Cor. 3.17-18.

4. Openness to the *voice of the Lord* as he calls us to do certain things day by day, Heb. 3.7-8

D. Steps to applying the Word of God

1. Be prayerful and open to *the Holy Spirit*.

2. *Listen to your heart* and let God speak, Heb. 3.15.

3. Set practical, feasible goals, Ps. 119.164.

4. Ask your mentors and body members to hold you accountable.

E. Example: Zacchaeus, Luke 19.1-10

Conclusion

» The *Three-Step Model* of biblical interpretation takes seriously the need to understand the meaning of the Bible in its own context, to draw out biblical principles, and to apply them in our lives today through the Spirit's direction and leading.

» This method is a sure and certain way to approach the Word with reverence and clarity as we seek to become disciplined students of the Word of God.

Please take as much time as you have available to answer these and other questions that the video brought out. In this session we saw how the *Three-Step Model* is an effective method of biblical interpretation designed to help us understand the truth of Scripture and bridge the gap between our ancient and contemporary worlds. As students of Scripture, we need a method that respects the nature of the Scriptures as ancient literature, as well as the living Holy Spirit in the Church who is our teacher and guide as we seek the mind and will of God (1 Cor. 2.9-16). Review the materials of the video segment through the following questions, and use the Scriptures themselves to support your claims.

1. What is the definition of the *Three-Step Model* of biblical interpretation? How is this method particularly designed to help us bridge the gap between our ancient and contemporary worlds? Why is this activity of overcoming the distance between us and the world of the Bible so important for an *accurate interpretation* of the Bible?

2. Where in the Bible does it mention that an attention to method is important for understanding its meaning (cf. Acts 17.11; Isaiah 8.20; Ezra 7.10; etc.)?

3. What are the benefits and cautions associated with using *any method* in biblical interpretation? What safeguards do we have against becoming overly dependent on methods and our own understanding as we seek to discover the truths of God in Scripture and apply them to our lives?

4. Why is it always important to keep the "big picture" and "whole message" of the Bible in mind when engaging in studies of particular "parts" of the Scriptures? In what way should any study of the Word of God somehow directly connect with and explain the meaning and message of God's final revelation to us in the person and wok of Jesus Christ? Give examples of your answer.

5. What is the "grammatical-historical" method of Bible study, and how does the *Three-Step Model* relate to it? In the same way, how does the *Three-Step Model* help us understand the plain sense meaning of the text, and the overall unity of the Bible?

6. Why is it key to respect the *integrity of the text* as it has come to us in its various forms (e.g., poetry, songs, epistles, history, etc.), and how does the *Three-Step Model* do so?

7. Outline briefly the critical reasons involved in each step of the *Three-Step Model*. How does each of the three steps help us overcome some of the

2

Segue 1

Student Questions and Response

Not Just Knowing What It Is, but Also How to Handle It

When Paul tells Timothy to strive to be someone who "correctly handles the word of truth" (2 Tim. 2.15), the assumption is that it is dangerously possible to be someone who does not correctly handle the word of truth. And that raises important questions about how to interpret the Bible. To approach the Bible wisely it is necessary not only to know what it is, but how to handle it.
~ Donald A. Carson. *New Bible Commentary: 21st Century Edition.* (electronic ed. of the 4th ed.). Downers Grove, IL: InterVarsity Press, 1997.

difficulties associated with understanding what the Bible teaches as an *ancient text* written in *languages which are no longer spoken or used as they were at the time of the Bible's writing*? Explain your answer thoroughly.

8. How do humility, thoroughness, and a love of liberty in Christ affect our ability to know and apply God's Word? What is the relationship between attitude and method in seeking to discern the Bible's meaning? Which is most important? Give an example that illustrates your opinion.

9. Explain and defend the statement: "all legitimate biblical interpretation seeks to discern God's Word for the purpose of *life transformation*, not *mind information*." How does the *Three-Step Model* help keep our focus on life transformation and not just analysis of texts and words?

Biblical Hermeneutics: The Three-Step Model

Segment 2: Using the Model: A Pauline Case Study

Rev. Dr. Don L. Davis

Summary of Segment 2

The *Three-Step Model* of biblical interpretation is an effective method to discern the meaning of Scripture, and can be practically demonstrated through a case study of Paul's letter to the Corinthians, in his first epistle, 9.1-14. By using the method in analyzing this passage, we see just how fruitful a disciplined approach to the study of Scripture can be.

Our objective for this segment, *Using the Model: A Pauline Case Study*, is to enable you to see that:

- The *Three-Step Model* is an effective method of biblical interpretation that may be fruitfully employed with a number of units of Bible materials (words, paragraphs, chapters, books, sections). Paul's instruction to the Corinthians in 1 Corinthians 9.1-4 offers us a clear case study of the application of our method that illustrates its usefulness.

- All study of the Word of God begins with our submission to the Holy Spirit, who alone is the Author of the Scriptures and the only one sufficient to instruct us in its meaning and significance for our lives today.

- The first step in employing the *Three-Step Model* is observing the details of the text, establishing the background of the book, its author and audience, its purpose for being written, as well as its rendering in different translations.

- Finding general principles of the text or passage is the second step of the *Three-Step Model*, and involves finding the central messages, truths, commands, or teachings contained in the text. This step involves going from what the text *meant in its original setting*, to what the text now *means to us in our lives today*. These principles must be stated clearly, compared with teachings throughout the Scriptures, and made plain for further study and application.

- After we have observed the details and drawn out principles, we go to the third step of the *Three-Step Model* which is our goal to apply the spiritual principles in the power of the Holy Spirit. An application is an *expression of the heart to the truth of God as the Spirit leads*. It demands discernment and a readiness to obey God's will for our lives.

- All biblical interpretation is given in order to strengthen our discipleship in Christ, and is essentially a *variation on the common themes* emphasized throughout the Scriptures. Love for God and neighbor and using our freedom to build up others and glorify God, constitute the heart of the Bible's ethic in both the Old and New Testaments.

Humility the Key to Interpreting Scripture

Because the Bible is God's word, it is vitally important to cultivate humility as we read, to foster a meditative prayerfulness as we reflect and study, to seek the help of the Holy Spirit as we try to understand and obey, to confess sin and pursue purity of heart and motive and relationships as we grow in understanding. Failure in these areas may produce scholars, but not mature Christians.

Above all, we must remember that we will one day give an account to the one who says, "This is the one I esteem: he who is humble and contrite in spirit, and trembles at my word" (Isa. 66.2).

~ Carson, Donald A. **New Bible Commentary: 21st Century Edition.**
(electronic ed. of the 4th ed.). Downers Grove, IL: InterVarsity Press, 1997.

**Video Segment 2
Outline**

I. **A Study of 1 Corinthians 9.1-14: Observe the Details (Follow these observations in the same order found in "Keys to Interpretation" in the appendix)**

1 Cor. 9.1-14 - Am I not free? Am I not an apostle? Have I not seen Jesus our Lord? Are not you my workmanship in the Lord? [2] If to others I am not an apostle, at least I am to you, for you are the seal of my apostleship in the Lord. [3] This is my defense to those who would examine me. [4] Do we not have the right to eat and drink? [5] Do we not have the right to take along a believing wife, as do the other apostles and the brothers of the Lord and Cephas? [6] Or is it only Barnabas and I who have no right to refrain from working for a living? [7] Who serves as a soldier at his own expense? Who plants a vineyard without eating any of its fruit? Or who tends a flock without getting some of the milk? [8] Do I say these things on human authority? Does not the Law say the same? [9] For it is written in the Law of Moses, "You shall not muzzle an ox when it treads out the grain." Is it for oxen that God is concerned? [10] Does he not speak entirely for our sake? It was written for our sake, because the plowman should plow in hope and the thresher thresh in hope of sharing in the crop. [11] If we have sown spiritual things among you, is it too much if we reap material things from you? [12] If others share this rightful claim on you, do not we even more? Nevertheless, we have not made use of this right, but we endure anything rather than put an obstacle in the way of the gospel of Christ. [13] Do you not know that those who are employed in the temple service get their food from the temple, and those who serve at the altar share in the sacrificial offerings? [14] In the same way, the Lord commanded that those who proclaim the gospel should get their living by the gospel.

A. *Ask God to open your eyes to the truth.*

1. The Holy Spirit is the author of Scripture, 2 Pet. 1.20-21.

2. As the author of Scripture he can instruct us in its meaning, 1 John 2.20.

3. As the original author speaking in the original context, the Holy Spirit can provide us with insight into the Scriptures.

   a. John 15.26-27

   b. John 16.13-14

B. *Establish the background of the book: Corinthians* (an "epistle," *letter*).

   1. Tools to use in *understanding the original situation*

      a. Several different English translations of the Bible

      b. Bible dictionaries

      c. Exegetical commentaries

      d. Bible atlas

      e. Bible handbook

   2. What this step wants you to do:

      a. Generate who, what, when, and where questions about the book, its author, and the audience.

b. Make an outline of the text.

c. Observe the details of the text (see the Oletta Wald "Overview of the Three-Step Model" in segment one of this lesson).

3. These tools should be consulted for *background information on the original situation first*, not for their interpretation of the text.

C. Who was the author of the book and what do we know about him: *the Apostle Paul*

1. Wrote it with Sosthenes, a brother in Corinth, 1 Cor. 1.1-2

2. There were factions around his personality in the congregation, 1 Cor. 1.12-13.

3. Deemed himself a servant assigned by the Lord to preach the Gospel, 1 Cor. 3.4-5

4. Felt himself to be a gift to the Corinthian church, 1 Cor. 3.22

5. His personal greeting is included at the book's conclusion, 1 Cor. 16.21.

D. *Who was the audience, where did they live, and what were their concerns?* (cultural and historical elements)

1. Called the "sin center" of the Roman Empire in Paul's time

2. Located about 40 miles west of Athens, Greece

3. A great commercial center of the Roman Empire, with 3 harbors

4. The temple of *Aphrodite*, built on the elevated ground, *Acrocorinthus*, was attended by 1,000 priestesses of vice (actually prostitutes).

5. There were various issues that needed to be addressed in the church.

    a. Divisions, 1 Cor. 1.10-4.21

    b. Scandals, 1 Cor. 5.1-6.20

    c. Marriage, 1 Cor. 7

    d. Christian liberty, 1 Cor. 8.1-11.1

    e. Women's dress, 1 Cor. 11.2-16

    f. The Lord's Table, 1 Cor. 11.17-34

    g. Spiritual gifts, 1 Cor. 12-14

    h. The Gospel and the resurrection, 1 Cor. 15

    i. Collections for the saints, 1 Cor. 16

E. *What is Paul's purpose in writing the book?*

1. 1 Corinthians is Paul's answer to a previous letter which he had written to them, 1 Cor. 5.9 - I wrote to you in my letter not to associate with sexually immoral people.

2. Paul is replying concerning questions they had, and conditions within the church that needed to be addressed.

F. *How does this passage contribute to the author's purpose?*

1. He discusses the idea of Christian liberty in chapter 8, affirming that he would not eat meat if it caused his Christian brother to stumble, 1 Cor. 8.1-13 (*note where the passage begins and ends, what section it is in*).

2. Paul here defends his apostleship before the Corinthians, *discussing the rights that he has as an apostle*, 1 Cor. 9.1-7.

    a. He defends his right as an apostle to eat and drink, v. 3.

    b. He defends his right to *take a believing wife along with him on his apostolic journeys as the other apostles*, v. 5.

    c. He defends his right to refrain from living and be supported on the Gospel itself, v. 6.

3. He gives ordinary analogies to prove that the one who serves in a context can be supported from that context.

2

a. A soldier, v. 7

b. A farmer, v. 7

c. A shepherd, v. 7

4. He closes by quoting a text from Deuteronomy, Deut. 25.4 - You shall not muzzle an ox when it is treading out the grain. (Cf. 1 Tim. 5.18 - For the Scriptures say, "You shall not muzzle an ox when it treads out the grain," and, "The laborer deserves his wages.")

a. A chapter speaking about practicing just relations among God's people

b. The principles

(1) Forty lashes are the limit on flogging (more than forty is considered unjust).

(2) Do not muzzle an ox while he is treading out the grain.

(3) Brother-in-law marrying a brother's widow (the family name is not to be lost)

(4) The hand of a woman seizing the private parts of another engaged in a fight with her husband shall have her hand removed (dirty fighting is absolutely not to be tolerated, especially since this kind might prevent a person from having descendants).

G. *Read the passage in other translations to get a sense of its flavor.*

Discovering Principles and Themes in the Bible

Especially where biblical themes are complex and intertwined, it is important to observe the Bible's use of such themes, to determine their specific functions, and to resolve to follow such biblical patterns in our own theological reflection.
~ Donald A. Carson. *New Bible Commentary: 21st Century Edition.* (electronic ed. of the 4th ed.). Downers Grove, IL: InterVarsity Press, 1997.

II. Step Two: Finding General Principles

A. Focus of the step: *finding the central message, truth, command, or principle that teaches God's truth and purpose for all people*

1. Summarize what you believe the author is trying to say.

2. Generalizing is a biblical practice:

   The legitimacy of such generalizing practices is affirmed repeatedly in the biblical text itself. Not only did God summarize His whole law in ten commandments (Exod. 20.1-17; Deut. 5.6-21), but He also gave seven other summaries of the law as well. Psalm 15 preserves God's law in eleven principles, Isa. 33.15 sets it forth in six commands; Mic. 6.8 encapsulates it in three commands, Isa. 56.1 further reduces it to two commands; and Amos 5.4; Hab. 2.4, and Lev. 19.2 each summarize the whole law in one general statement. Jesus Himself continued this same tradition by summarizing the whole law in two principles: "Love the Lord your God with all your heart and with all your soul and with your mind. . . .And the second is like it: Love your neighbor as yourself."

   ~ Walter C. Kaiser. **An Introduction to Biblical Hermeneutics**. p. 276.

B. Definition of a biblical principle

1. Simple declarative sentence statement (or proverbial saying) (*The moral of the story in a fable is the principle.*)

2. That expresses *a clear truth found within a Bible passage*

3. Supported *throughout the entire Bible*

4. That is *binding on everyone in every place* (expresses God's will or God's mind on a subject or theme)

5. Can be expressed in a *clear and understandable manner* to others

C. How to draw out a biblical principle

1. Study your passage thoroughly, observing the details and getting in touch with the meaning in "their world."

2. Look for the central teachings or ideas expressed in the text.

3. State your principle(s) in simple declarative form: those called to the ministry are permitted to make their livelihood through the ministry.

4. State it in *a few words*.

5. Put it in *a statement or proverb form*.

6. Use the *clearest, simplest language* you can.

7. Make sure that your statement:

   a. *Summarizes your study findings*: don't do a thorough and careful job in Step One and then ignore your results when drawing a principle.

   b. Expresses *the meaning* of the passage: gets at the core of the text's message

D. *Test your principle (i.e., your proverb or statement)* against what the rest of the Bible says (1 Thess. 5.21).

1. Check *BACK* to the passage itself. (*"Does this passage really teach what I am suggesting it does?"*) Ask yourself honestly, "If someone else were to read through this passage would they be likely to discover this principle?"

2. Check *THROUGH* other Bible passages. (*"Are there other passages in the Bible that clearly state and support my proposed principle?"*)

3. Check *OUT* Bible examples, stories, and illustrations. (*"Do the lives and experiences of the people in the Bible line up with my proposed principle?"*) If you can find no other statements or stories in the Bible that support your principle then you probably have not found a biblical principle.

4. Check *INTO* Bible commentaries and Church teachings to see if your findings are supported by other scholars. (*"Have others found the same insights I claim to have found here?"*)

   a. If no one else you read has ever found the principle you discovered, it does not automatically mean you are wrong, but it should make you extremely cautious.

   b. Without support from others you must make a very careful biblical case and at least attempt to explain why others may not have seen this principle.

5. Adjust your statement to fit the results of your test.

2

E. Paul the Rabbi: drawing out principles for the Corinthians

1. Paul's first illustration: 1 Cor. 9.10 - Does he not speak entirely for our sake? It was written for our sake, because *the plowman should plow in hope and the thresher thresh in hope of sharing in the crop.*

2. Paul's second illustration: 1 Cor. 9.13 - Do you not know that *those who are employed in the temple service get their food from the temple, and those who serve at the altar share in the sacrificial offerings?*

3. Paul's principle: 1 Cor. 9.14 - In the same way, the Lord commanded that *those who proclaim the Gospel should get their living by the Gospel.*

F. Paul's discerning of a principle from Scripture

1. He begins with an overwhelming concern: the defense of his apostleship.

2. He compares Scripture with Scripture: 1 Corinthians 9.10 with Exodus 29.32-33; Numbers 18.21.

3. He illustrates the principle in real life: soldier, shepherd, farmer, temple worker.

4. He applies it to his own situation: 1 Cor. 9.11-12 - If we have sown spiritual things among you, is it too much if we reap material things from you? [12] If others share this rightful claim on you, do not we even more? Nevertheless, we have not made use of this right, but we endure anything rather than put an obstacle in the way of the gospel of Christ.

III. Apply the General Principles to Life in the Power of the Spirit

A. Definition: *an application is an expression of the heart to the truth of God as the Spirit leads.*

1. An expression of the heart: application has to do with the convicted conscience and ready will to the truth of God in the Word.

2. As the Spirit leads: the Holy Spirit, the same one who inspires the Word, illumines the heart, will also ignite the will to respond to God's truth.

B. Application demands discernment.

1. The Holy Spirit is involved in all movements of truth in the Christian's life, John 15.26-27.

2. Insight is the gift of the Lord.

    a. Ps. 119.33

    b. John 14.26

    c. James 1.5

    d. 1 John 2.27

2

3. Insight comes from rigorous pursuit of the truth and a readiness to obey it.

    a. Ezra 7.10

    b. Ps. 119.99-100

    c. 2 Tim. 3.14-17

    d. Heb. 5.14

4. Application is about *listening to the Lord to reveal what should be known in order to do what must be done*, Ps. 139.23-24.

C. Recognize that the goal of all application is Christlikeness and the advancement of the Kingdom of God.

    1. Jesus and his Kingdom are the core of the apostolic tradition and message, Acts 28.23, cf. Acts 28.31.

    2. We are to seek the rule of God and his righteousness above all else, Matt. 6.33.

    3. Obedience to the commands of Christ is central to Christian discipleship, Matt. 7.24-27.

D. Celebrate that all obedience to God's truth and commands is done in an environment of freedom and liberty.

1. The principle of freedom lies at the core of all Christian discipleship.

    a. Rom. 7.6

    b. 2 Cor. 3.17-18

    c. Gal. 5.1

    d. Gal. 5.13

    e. 1 Pet. 2.16

    f. James 1.25

2. Avoid stern legalistic tendencies in your application, Col. 2.20-23.

    a. Beware of wolf applications in sheep clothing: *nothing is a good application that eclipses the freedom we have in Christ to obey him freely.*

    b. Man-made, legalistic applications are completely ineffective in dealing with the issues of the flesh.

2

3. Allow for differences in applications and appropriation of the text: *Jesus is alive!*

    a. One size does not fit all: we cannot know precisely how the Lord may want another to apply his Word, John 21.20-22.

    b. We are to use freedom in our expressions, but in sync with Christian charity and edification.

       (1) 1 Cor. 6.12

       (2) 1 Cor. 10.23

       (3) 1 Cor. 8.13

    c. Distinguish between *suggestions* and *mandates* in regard to your application of biblical principles (e.g., God tells me to love my wife as Christ does the Church, but there is no application that can mandate flowers and a movie every week!)

E. Remember that all applications are *variations on a theme*: the essentials.

    1. Love for God and neighbor are the first and second commandments, Matt. 22.36-40.

    2. We are to use our freedom not as a license for sin, but as an opportunity to love others, Gal. 5.13.

    3. All that we do is to be done for the good of our neighbors, for the building up of the body, 1 Cor. 10.24.

4. No matter what the application, we ought to be able to do it openly and for the glory of God.

   a. Col. 3.17

   b. 1 Pet. 4.11

   c. 1 Cor. 10.31

Conclusion

» The *Three-Step Model* is an effective tool to employ in seeking to discern the meaning in the units of biblical investigation: words, sentences, paragraphs, chapters, and books.

» A careful and prayerful approach to the Word of God can unlock to us the untold treasure of truth and knowledge contained in God's holy Word.

Segue 2

Student Questions and Response

The following questions were designed to help you review the material in the second video segment. As in our last segment, in this section we say how the *Three-Step Model* of biblical interpretation can be a very effective method to discern the meaning of Scripture, and we illustrated its uses through the study of Paul's letter to the Corinthians, in his first epistle, 9.1-14. Like any skill, the method of biblical interpretation can be mastered with much effort, long practice, and careful instruction from those who know it well. The first step in gaining skill at this method is understanding the various steps involved in effective and methodical Bible study. Review your understanding so far with the questions below, and concentrate on the actual way the method was illustrated in your video segment.

1. To what extent can the *Three-Step Model* prove to be an effective method of biblical interpretation with *any or all* of the units of Bible materials (words, paragraphs, chapters, books, sections)? In your illustration above, what kind of unit is Paul's instruction to the Corinthians in 1 Corinthians 9.1-14?

2. Why is it always important to start our study of the Word of God with prayer to God for wisdom, guidance, and instruction? How can we so pray as to avoid making this become an empty habit, and not a real request for the wisdom that only God can provide us as we study his Word?

3. Why is it simply impossible to discern the meaning of the text of Scripture without the aid of the Holy Spirit (cf. 1 Cor. 2.9-16)? Nevertheless, why can prayer to the Holy Spirit for guidance never be, in and of itself, a substitute for rigorous, disciplined study of the Word of God as *literature*? Explain your answer.

4. What tools did we use in our first step of the *Three-Step Model* in our exegesis of 1 Corinthians 9.1-14? How do these tools help us understand the original situation better, i.e., what Paul was intending to communicate to the Corinthians in their own context?

5. What are the kinds of questions that we ought to ask as we seek to discern the original situation in which the text was written? How might we go about answering those questions?

6. Define the meaning of a "general principle of the Scriptures." How do such summary statements like proverbs, sayings, and other general principles help to give us a more *holistic understanding* of God's will?

7. Give examples of three summarizing statements or general principles in the Bible. How can you tell that your summarizing statement *in your own personal study* is actually a *principle of Scripture*? What must you do to verify whether or not your discovery is actually a principle of the Word?

8. Why must we seek the mind of God as we apply the meaning of the Bible to our lives? What is the role of freedom and liberty in expressing our heart obedience to God in response to his teaching in the Scriptures?

9. Why is it always important to keep the *larger message of the Scriptures* concerning Christ and his Kingdom in mind when we seek to apply the Word of God to our lives? What kind of errors may occur if we fail to keep Christ central to every phase of our reading and application of the Scriptures? (Read together John 5.30-47 and discuss Jesus' own rebuke of the Pharisees concerning this kind of practice, of reading the Bible but failing to find Christ as the heart of its meaning and message.)

CONNECTION

Summary of Key Concepts

The Importance of the First Reader: The Key to the Three-Step Model

When interpreters and translators ask themselves how the first readers would have understood a passage, they are not asking a merely hypothetical question impossible to answer (since we have no access to their minds). Rather, this is simply a way of getting at a host of subsidiary questions: How would these words have been understood at the time? What issues and themes were of resounding importance? What kind of conceptual framework would the biblical text confront? To raise such questions is not to affirm that we can always find perfect answers. Sometimes we can infer responsible answers by "mirror-reading" the text itself.
~ Donald A. Carson. *New Bible Commentary: 21st Century Edition.* (electronic ed. of the 4th ed.). Downers Grove, IL: InterVarsity Press, 1997.

To master the Word of God is the central and definitive skill for the man or woman of God, for it is the God-breathed Scripture that is able to make us competent workers and faithful servants of the Church, to enable us to equip others for ministry, and minister to the real needs of those both within and outside the Church (2 Tim. 3.16-17). There is no way that we can overemphasize the importance of your ability to handle the Word accurately (2 Tim. 2.15), to meditate upon it day and night in order to ensure success in the endeavors of God (Josh. 1.8), and guarantee the kind of fruitfulness and power you desire in every phase of your work for the Lord (Ps. 1.1-3). Listed below are the central concepts covered in this lesson on the *Three-Step Model*, so please review them diligently and carefully. Understanding this model can enable you to gain the knowledge and skills to become a workman of the Scriptures, approved of God and without shame as you handle his Word accurately and rightly.

- The *Three-Step Model* is an effective method of biblical interpretation designed to help us understand the truth of Scripture and bridge the gap between our ancient and contemporary worlds. The *Three-Step Model* defined is "to so understand the meaning of the original situation that we may discover general principles of truth which may be applied in our personal lives in the Spirit's freedom."

- While studying individual words, phrases, paragraphs, chapters, sections, and books of the Scriptures is both edifying and necessary, all of our insights into the Scriptures ought to be in sync with the message of the whole Bible, i.e., the meaning and message of God's final revelation to us in the person and work of Jesus Christ.

- The *Three-Step Model*, as a logical and methodical way of understanding Scripture, resonates and corresponds to the grammatical-historical method of Scripture interpretation, which affirms the plain sense of the Bible's meaning. It also takes into account God's progressive revelation in Christ, the unity of the Bible, and the integrity of the text as it communicates to us in different genres and forms.

- The critical preparation for the use of any form of biblical study is the attitude of the student of the Scriptures, and the phases of study in the *Three-Step Model* demand humility, thoroughness, and liberty for each phase respectively.

- As slaves to righteousness under Christ's lordship, we are called to obey his Word in every facet of our lives and ministries, and therefore, all legitimate

2

biblical interpretation seeks to discern God's Word for the purpose of *life transformation*, not *mind information*.

➻ The *Three-Step Model* may be fruitfully employed with a number of units of Bible materials (words, paragraphs, chapters, books, sections).

➻ All study of the Word of God begins with our submission to the Holy Spirit, who alone is the author of the Scriptures and the only one sufficient to instruct us in its meaning and significance for our lives today. Our dependence on the Holy Spirit *enhances our diligent study of the Word* and is not meant to be a *substitute for it*.

➻ The first step in employing the *Three-Step Model* is observing the details of the text, establishing the background of the book, its author and audience, its purpose for being written, as well as its rendering in different translations.

➻ Finding general principles of the text or passage is the second step of the *Three-Step Model*, and involves finding the central messages, truths, commands, or teachings contained in the text. This step involves going from what the text *meant in its original setting*, to what the text now *means to us in our lives today*. These principles must be stated clearly, compared with teachings throughout the Scriptures, and made plain for further study and application.

➻ After we have observed the details and drawn out principles, we go to the third step of the *Three-Step Model* which is our goal to apply the spiritual principles in the power of the Holy Spirit. An application is an *expression of the heart to the truth of God as the Spirit leads*. It demands discernment and a readiness to obey God's will for our lives.

➻ All biblical interpretation is given in order to strengthen our discipleship in Christ, and is essentially a *variation on the common themes* emphasized throughout the Scriptures. Love for God and neighbor, using our freedom to build up others and glorify God constitute the heart of the Bible's ethic in both the Old and New Testaments.

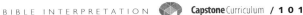

Student Application and Implications

Now is the time for you to discuss with your fellow students your questions about your understanding of the *Three-Step Model*, and methodical Bible study in particular. The kinds of relationships between our own attitude, our chosen method of study, the Spirit, resource tools, other Christians, and our leaders demand clarity and wisdom. Scholars, church workers, pastors and preachers, and lay-persons alike have struggled with the questions of biblical interpretation for centuries, and now is your chance to join the conversation! Use the questions below to start you on your journey of exploration about the nature of your own biblical study.

* With all the confusion and doubt caused by modern biblical criticism, should we be skeptical at using any method, including the *Three-Step Model* as our way of studying Scripture? How do we know that even the *Three-Step Model* won't be twisted and lead to a denial of the orthodox doctrines of the Christian faith?

* How can we say that employing a method like the *Three-Step Model* is not merely an enlightened form of "don't lean on your own understanding" (Prov. 3.5-6)?

* With the abundance of studies being done on every imaginable subject under the sun, how do we ensure that all of our insights line up with the message of the whole Bible? How do we avoid "majoring on the minors" in our study of the Bible? Give practical examples.

* What role do our leaders (i.e., bishops, pastors, mentors, well-known Christian leaders, etc.) play in taking our own personal interpretations as *authoritative*? Should we hold to an interpretation of Scripture that we have found in our study if it is contradicted by what Christianity has taught in the creeds and throughout Church history? Explain.

* Why should we be open to having others criticize our findings and ideas *before* we begin to suggest that we have discovered general principles that are binding on all members of the Church? What kind of attitudes should we demonstrate when we speak about new things we have learned from the Lord in our studies?

* How should we take a person, however scholarly or well-studied, who is unwilling to have their own ideas weighed and checked against the teaching of the Scriptures themselves? How does the Berean example and reaction to

2

the teaching of Paul inform our own need to be open to checking the findings of others against the Scriptures themselves (cf. Acts 17.11)?

* Since we are not all Bible teachers and scholars, what ought to be our goal as we engage in our own work of biblical interpretation? Should it concern us that some members of the body will discover more in their study than we did? How do spiritual gifts figure into this equation?

* Why is it important not merely to depend on others for the insights and wisdom that the Bible provides for us? What kind of errors may occur when we become overly dependent on others for our instruction and growth in Christ?

* Why is it impossible to suggest that our dependence on the Holy Spirit in our personal study is a substitute for the hard work of biblical interpretation? How can you know if you are not depending on the Holy Spirit for insight in your personal study? Likewise, how can you tell when you are being lazy in the way you are handling the Word of truth?

* Why is it always important to study the Bible in the light of the *great themes* emphasized by our Lord, along with the apostles and prophets? How do their teachings on love for God and neighbor help us understand that both the Old and New Testaments have a *common subject and purpose*? Explain.

CASE STUDIES

Only What the Pastor Says Counts

In many traditions, whatever the method of personal study employed to understand the meaning of the Bible, the heart of what the Scriptures teaches is dependent upon the church tradition and/or official leaders of the church. This is plainly seen, for example, in the Catholic approach to biblical interpretation. While individual study is encouraged and applauded as good and edifying, the discoveries of the individual can never take precedence over the teaching of the Church as we have understood it down through the centuries, and as it is represented presently in the teaching of the bishops and the Pope. Protestants do not hold to this view, but in many Protestant churches, individual interpretation is not considered credible unless it corresponds to what the pastor or spiritual leaders believe and teach. What is the place of pastoral and spiritual leadership authority in our personal interpretation of the Bible? Should all that we discover be confirmed by our leaders, or are they, like us, subject to the same responsibility to align their views with the Scriptures in order for them to be considered credible and acceptable?

How Then Do We Prove Anything from Scripture?

▶ **2** (Based on a true story). While in a graduate school situation, a budding pastor encountered an idea that challenged and somewhat confused him. During a class on the methods of the *scientific study* of religion, he was told by the professor that simply using the Bible to prove the points of the Bible is "tautological," or arguing in a circle, proving nothing. The professor went on: "If you want to prove that something in the Bible is true, you cannot use the Bible to prove it. In the scientific method you prove things on the basis of *independent verification*, not on the basis of those who have something to gain from the outcome of the study." The professor went on to suggest that because the prophets and the apostles were believers in Christ, they had too much at stake to say anything about Jesus except *what they wanted other people to believe.* As a result, he held, we cannot take their word as true regarding Jesus of Nazareth and his claims. Confused and bewildered, the pastor in the class felt handicapped. How can he prove the teaching of the Scriptures *without using the Scriptures themselves as proof?* What do you think about the professor's comments, and what would you advise the pastor to do in order to complete his study in that course?

Your Native Tongue Bible Isn't Enough

▶ **3** (Based on a true story). While turning in an exegetical project for credit during a class on Romans, a student was advised by his professor (who had skimmed his first attempt at the study) that he had broke fundamental rules in using tools of language. The professor explained: "You simply cannot go to a theological dictionary or lexicon and assume that all the usages written down of a word are the *meanings in this particular place.* You wouldn't use an English or Spanish dictionary that way; you would look up the word, find the definition that fit, and then apply *that single meaning* to the text. You applied all the meanings of the term to your study, and therefore made a fundamental error in your study." The professor went on to say that only when you know how an individual author used a word (e.g., Peter's, Paul's, or John's use of a word in all of his writings) could you then be sure that you were using your language sources right. Since the Bible was written in Hebrew, Aramaic, and Greek, and since many of us do not know these languages, how then are we to know that we are reading the text right? How are we to use language tools if we don't know an author's *entire use of a word or phrase?*

Confusing the Twigs for the Trees and the Forest

One of the immediate problems with those who discover the *Three-Step Model* is that they begin to use their new-found methods to analyze the specific details of numerous passages as a single part. With no guidance as to how to *connect and integrate* their insights into the overall meaning of the Scriptures, they multiply themes, topics, and studies without ever bringing them all together under a single, understandable banner. In your opinion, do the Scriptures have a single, coherent theme that would allow all of our study to be placed underneath it, allowing us to interpret our insights in light of it? How do we as students of the Bible avoid becoming focused on the details of single passages so much so that we miss the "big picture," the larger message and meaning of the Bible itself? How do we avoid the distinctive problem of the Pharisees, who mastered the details of the Scriptures but had great difficulty in seeing and applying the weightier matters of Scripture to their lives (i.e., they saw trees fine, but missed the forest). How can we see the Bible as a *whole* and still find nourishment as we study its *parts*?

The *Three-Step Model* is an effective method of biblical interpretation designed to help us understand the truth of Scripture and bridge the gap between our ancient and contemporary worlds. The *Three-Step Model* defined is "to so understand the meaning of the original situation that we may discover general principles of truth which may be applied in our personal lives in the Spirit's freedom." This method corresponds to the grammatical-historical method of Scripture interpretation, affirms the plain sense of the Bible's meaning, and respects the integrity of the text as it communicates to us in different genres and forms. The Bible's central message of salvation in Jesus Christ must take precedence over all study of individual words, phrases, paragraphs, chapters, sections, and books of the Scriptures. All study demands a spirit of humility, diligent thoroughness, and a love for Christ's liberty as we seek to be transformed by the life-giving message of Scripture.

All study of the Word of God begins with our submission to the Holy Spirit, who alone is the author of the Scriptures and the only one sufficient to instruct us in its meaning and significance for our lives today. Our dependence on the Holy Spirit *enhances our diligent study of the Word* and is not meant to be a *substitute for it*. The steps of the *Three-Step Model* are simple and clear. First, we observe the details of the text, establishing the background of the book, its author and audience, its purpose for being written, as well as its rendering in different translations. Next, we discover general principles which summarize our findings about what the text *meant in its*

Restatement of the Lesson's Thesis

2

original setting, and what the text now *means to us in our lives today.* Finally, we apply the spiritual principles in the power of the Holy Spirit. As we express our heart obedience to God, we ought to remain mindful of *the common themes* emphasized throughout the Scriptures which underlie his will for all believers in both Old and New Testaments–loving God and love neighbor through faith in Christ, all for the glory of God.

Resources and Bibliographies

If you are interested in pursuing some of the ideas of *Biblical Hermeneutics: The Three-Step Model,* you might want to give these books a try:

Fee, Gordon D. *New Testament Exegesis: A Handbook for Students and Pastors.* 3rd ed. Louisville, KY: Westminster John Knox Press, 2002.

Grenz, Stanley J., and Roger E. Olson. *Who Needs Theology?: An Invitation to the Study of God.* Downers Grove, IL: InterVarsity, 1996.

Grenz, Stanley J., and John R. Franke. *Beyond Foundationalism: Shaping Theology in a Postmodern Context.* Louisville, KY: Westminster John Knox Press, 2000.

Stuart, Douglas K. *Old Testament Exegesis: A Handbook for Students and Pastors.* 3rd ed. Louisville, KY: Westminster John Knox Press, 2001.

Traina, Robert A. *Methodical Bible Study.* Grand Rapids: Zondervan Publishing Company, 1985.

Ministry Connections

The use of the God-breathed Scripture in many ways is the very center of valid kingdom ministry. Like Ezra in our devotion, your ability to study the Law of the Lord and to do it is the key to your teaching the truth of God in the midst of his people, the Church, and to those who do not believe. Every facet and strand of ministry relates directly to your mastery of the Word of God, and your willingness to allow that Word to master you! Reflect some time on the dimensions of your current ministry at home, on the job, in the church and the community, and ask the Holy Spirit to show you how your interpretation and application of the Word might enhance some dimension of your life and witness. Ask the Lord to reveal to you some area where the power of his Word must become more real and vital, and be open to changing your attitude or behavior in any particular situation that the Spirit brings to your mind.

We Apply the Word of God in Community With Each Other

*Newbigin has suggested there is only one way the people of God can make the gospel credible: "**the only answer, the only hermeneutic of the gospel**, is a congregation of men and women who believe it and live it . . . they have power to accomplish their purpose only as they are rooted in and lead back to a believing community." These **ecclesia** [church, assembly] of real people, in real places, dealing with real issues, and in touch with human reality, as Calvin said, are the "real" expressions of Christ on earth as the community of God is in heaven.*

~ Gareth Weldon Icenogle. **Biblical Foundations for Small Group Ministry**. (electronic ed.). Downers Grove, IL: InterVarsity Press, 1994.

Counseling and Prayer

God has given us sure and certain promises regarding the power of prayer to transform us, empower us, and supply us with the provision and direction of the Lord. As discussed throughout this lesson, it is simply not possible to understand and apply the Word of God without prevailing prayer, the kind that with deep fervency and contrition asks God to supply us with the necessary wisdom to know and do his Word. Take time with your fellow students to share your requests to the Lord, without anxiety and with thanksgiving, making your requests (and not your demands!) known to God. He has promised that his provision and peace will keep your hearts and minds in Christ Jesus (Phil. 4.6-7). Remember one another during the week, and take note of your requests and those of others, and see how God answers your petitions for wisdom, power, and blessing.

ASSIGNMENTS

Ezra 7.10; Acts 17.11; Psalm 1.1-3

Scripture Memory

To prepare for class, please visit *www.tumi.org/books* to find next week's reading assignment, or ask your mentor.

Reading Assignment

Other Assignments

As in last class session, you will have a quiz on the material covered in this lesson, so make sure that you review carefully the concepts dealt with here. Note, too, that you ought to complete the assigned reading listed above, and as you did last week, please write a brief summary for each reading. Bring these summaries to your next session (please see the "Reading Completion Sheet" at the end of this lesson). Also, now is the time to begin to think about the character of your ministry project, as well as decide what passage of Scripture you will select for your exegetical project. Do not delay in determining either your ministry or exegetical project. The sooner you select, the more time you will have to prepare!

Looking Forward to the Next Lesson

In this lesson we analyzed the *Three-Step Model* of biblical interpretation, a method designed to take seriously the meaning of the Bible in its original and first context, to discover those biblical principles contained in the text, and then to diligently apply those principles in faith and obedience empowered by the Holy Spirit to our lives. Now, in our next lesson, we will turn our attention to the importance of genres, or types of literature, as we employ this model of biblical interpretation to the rich, varied, and remarkable books of our holy library, the Word of God. We will provide a basic overview of the benefits involved in paying attention to genre study, and highlight some of the basic assumptions undergirding this kind of special hermeneutics.

2

Name _____

Date _____

For each assigned reading, write a brief summary (one or two paragraphs) of the author's main point. (For additional readings, use the back of this sheet.)

Reading 1

Title and Author: _____ Pages _____

Reading 2

Title and Author: _____ Pages _____

Biblical Literature
Interpreting the Genres of the Bible

Lesson Objectives

Welcome in the strong name of Jesus Christ! When you have completed your work in this module, we trust that you will be able to:

- Define the term "genre" and its role in biblical interpretation, i.e., that particular kind of literary form which communicates truth and must be interpreted according to the rules of that form.

- Analyze the basic assumptions of genre study of the Scriptures that make it both an essential and worthwhile discipline, including the Bible as a book of literature, as a book which pays attention to literary rules and principles, and the way in which God employed human literary strategies to communicate his Word.

- Lay out some of the more important forms of biblical genre, including the use of narrative (both historical and imaginative), the Law (legal writings), epistles (letters), prophecy, wisdom literature (proverbs, monologues, riddles, fables, parables, allegories, etc.), and poetry.

- Provide the purposes of biblical genres, including to fulfill a particular need, to deepen our understanding of our fundamental human experience, to allow us to image reality in its most concrete from, to display the artistry of the biblical authors as led by the Spirit, and to reveal the richness of the mystery of God and his work in the world.

- Give evidence of the major benefits of careful genre study, including how it will empower us to discover the author's original intention, edify our souls, enrich our appreciation of life, entertain us, and enlighten our minds as we rigorously pursue the meaning of God in the particular form of literature we are exploring.

- Define the term "special hermeneutics," i.e., the rules and procedures that enable us to interpret the literary forms of the Bible.

- Demonstrate a knowledge of narrative form in literature, and the general assumptions of story theology, which include God's providing a record of his work in the story accounts of the Bible, that all theology is reflection on the stories of the Bible, that the stories that refer to historical accounts in

Scripture are reliable and accurate, that the stories are written with artistic skill and mastery, that we can encounter God in the story text, and that God often provides his own commentary on the meaning of the biblical story accounts.

- Lay out the key propositions of story theology: that stories introduce us to sacramental presences, they are more important than facts, they are normative for the Christian community, that Christian traditions evolve and define themselves by stories, and that stories precede and produce community, censure and accountability, and produce theology, ritual, and sacrament. They are history.

- Provide and explain the general elements of narrative in Scripture, including the setting, characters, author's point of view, plot, and theme of the story.

- Explain the general principles underlying prophecy as a genre of biblical interpretation, including how prophecy offers truth about God and the universe, that it flows from the Spirit and is a specific mode of revelation from God which manifests itself in personal and literary modes.

- Define the elements of apocalyptic literature as a biblical genre, including its definition, the types of apocalyptic in the Bible (i.e., Daniel and Revelation), the two main types of Jewish apocalypses, and the most distinctly apocalyptic book in Scripture, the book of Revelation.

- Reproduce the three interpretive principles for the prophetic and apocalyptic genres of Scripture: the need to focus on the person of Jesus Christ, to refer the prophetic messages to the call of the Kingdom of God, and to emphasize the fulfillment of God's sovereign purposes even in the face of evil, suffering and injustice.

Come, Explore the Depth of the Word

Devotion

Ps. 78.1-8 - Give ear, O my people, to my teaching; incline your ears to the words of my mouth! [2] I will open my mouth in a parable; I will utter dark sayings from of old, [3] things that we have heard and known, that our fathers have told us. [4] We will not hide them from their children, but tell to the coming generation the glorious deeds of the Lord, and his might, and the wonders that he has done. [5] He established a testimony in Jacob and appointed a law in Israel, which he commanded our fathers to teach to their children,

[6] that the next generation might know them, the children yet unborn, and arise and tell them to their children, [7] so that they should set their hope in God and not forget the works of God, but keep his commandments; [8] and that they should not be like their fathers, a stubborn and rebellious generation, a generation whose heart was not steadfast, whose spirit was not faithful to God.

What is God's purpose behind so much of the Bible being written in imagery, metaphor, symbol, and story? Why would God write and speak to us in the form of parables and metaphors, and not merely in the plain, straightforward kind of language that is better understood and not so greatly misinterpreted? Is God deliberately trying to mislead us, make it more difficult for us to know his will and Word?

Of course not! Our devotional text explains why David spoke in terms of the parable and "dark sayings from of old," those things which God revealed to his people from ancient times. The purpose is not to hide from us, for verse four makes it directly plain that God's intention is not to hide his meaning from us, nor should our intention be to hide the meaning of the words of God from our children. Rather, we are given pictorial language, parable and story, allegory and poetry, symbol and metaphor to invite us to learn, to explore, to seek God in such a way that his wonders and works can be comprehended well by his people and their children.

How then does the parable, the story, the metaphor, or the picture invite us to come and explore? First, through the image or picture God shows us his meaning rather than merely telling us. By pointing to the lilies of the field and his care for them, he can provide us with a concrete picture of what it means to be cared for by him. Second, images, stories, and pictures involve our imaginations and emotions as well as our intellects. God wants us not merely to know ideas but to be affected by them, to feel the truth, so to speak. Finally, communicating through parable and story invites the hungry to continue to search for the meaning of the genre. Through the image, picture, and story God, in essence, invites us to come and explore further and deeper his meaning. For those who were looking for diamonds on the surface of the text, they will be disappointed. The Scriptures everywhere speak of the fruitfulness of the hungry heart to explore and seek wisdom like treasure in order to receive his deepest and best insights.

> Prov. 2.1-5 - My son, if you receive my words and treasure up my commandments with you, [2] making your ear attentive to wisdom and inclining your heart to understanding; [3] yes, if you call out for insight and

raise your voice for understanding, [4] if you seek it like silver and search for it as for hidden treasures, [5] then you will understand the fear of the Lord and find the knowledge of God.

1 Kings 3.9 - Give your servant therefore an understanding mind to govern your people, that I may discern between good and evil, for who is able to govern this your great people?

Ps. 25.4-5 - Make me to know your ways, O Lord; teach me your paths. [5] Lead me in your truth and teach me, for you are the God of my salvation; for you I wait all the day long.

Ps. 119.34 - Give me understanding, that I may keep your law and observe it with my whole heart.

Prov. 3.6 - In all your ways acknowledge him, and he will make straight your paths.

Prov. 8.17 - I love those who love me, and those who seek me diligently find me.

Luke 11.13 - If you then, who are evil, know how to give good gifts to your children, how much more will the heavenly Father give the Holy Spirit to those who ask him!

James 1.5 - If any of you lacks wisdom, let him ask God, who gives generously to all without reproach, and it will be given him.

This is in fact the reason why the Lord spoke in parables. For those who had no intention of seeking the will and mind of the Lord, the parable was a kind of end game, a word which neither moved nor spurred on to further investigation. For those who were in fact hungry for the truth, the parable was a invitation to explore the meaning of the Lord, and to dig deeper into the work of God. For those who are unwilling to explore, the word of imagery is a word that frustrates and closes down insight, as noted in the NT citation of Psalm 78 in the teaching of the Lord Jesus:

Matt. 13.13 - This is why I speak to them in parables, because seeing they do not see, and hearing they do not hear, nor do they understand.

Matt. 13.34-35 - All these things Jesus said to the crowds in parables; indeed, he said nothing to them without a parable. [35] This was to fulfill what was spoken by the prophet: "I will open my mouth in parables; I will utter what has been hidden since the foundation of the world."

Mark 4.34 - He did not speak to them without a parable, but privately to his own disciples he explained everything.

The Bible is a world of imagery with every parable, story, symbol, and metaphor representing an invitation to explore the mind of the Lord in regard to the truth. Come, join the adventure and seek the truth of the Lord in the midst of the world of imagery.

Nicene Creed and Prayer

After reciting and/or singing the Nicene Creed (located in the Appendix), pray the following prayer:

God of mercy, you promised never to break your covenant with us. Amid all the changing words of our generation, speak your eternal Word that does not change. Then may we respond to your gracious promises with faithful and obedient lives; through our Lord Jesus Christ. Amen.

~ Presbyterian Church (U.S.A.) and Cumberland Presbyterian Church. The Theology and Worship Ministry Unit. **Book of Common Worship**. Louisville: Westminister/John Knox Press, 1993. p. 91.

Quiz

Put away your notes, gather up your thoughts and reflections, and take the quiz for Lesson 2, *Biblical Hermeneutics: The Three-Step Model*.

Scripture Memorization Review

Review with a partner, write out and/or recite the text for last class session's assigned memory verses: Ezra 7.10; Acts 17.11; and Psalm 1.1-3.

Assignments Due

Turn in your summary of the reading assignment for last week, that is, your brief response and explanation of the main points that the authors were seeking to make in the assigned reading (Reading Completion Sheet).

The Word Is the Word, Isn't It?

Many believe that the Word of God should not be over complicated, and that the plain, literal sense for any and every text is sufficient. Many who hold this position feel that attention to the types of literature and the rules for each can actually make the Word of God inaccessible to anybody except those who are experts in the rules of literature and the definitions of genre. The most compelling part of their

argument is their open claim of their faith in the profit of the Word of God for all, beginner, intermediate, and mature believer. 2 Tim. 3.16-17, "All Scripture is breathed out by God and profitable for teaching, for reproof, for correction, and for training in righteousness, [17] that the man of God may be competent, equipped for every good work." How can we so use our understanding of the rules of literature as to improve our knowledge of the Word of God, and not make it impossible for all but the experts to tell us what the text actually means?

Old Fashioned Ways

Around the turn of the century, many evangelical scholars paid more attention to the types of the Bible. A type is a prefiguring of Christ in the OT that is revealed in the NT. For instance, Melchizedek is a type of Christ, for Christ is the high priest of the Church. Manna is seen as a type of Christ, who is the bread of life (John 6), the serpent that Moses placed on the pole in the wilderness that God provided for the healing of the people is a type (John 3.14-15). This form of looking for Christ in the OT images, characters, and pictures (e.g., the Tabernacle, the Levitical priesthood, and the sacrifices recorded in the OT), is now seen as less effective and unimportant by many scholars. Because of exaggerations and misinterpretations of many who used this method, now the focus on the connection between the OT pictures and stories and the person of Jesus is not as popular. Do you think that this may still be a valid method, or has this phase of biblical hermeneutics ended? What should we do with all of the stories, pictures, metaphors and symbols of Scripture as they relate to Jesus Christ?

Which Came First: the Story of the Doctrine?

With such a modern focus upon doctrine, ideas, concepts, and knowledge, many preachers have lost interest in the power of story. Although a new discipline of story-oriented theology is finding a new home in the academy (called "narrative theology"), most preachers and teachers still prefer the simple, direct summary statement that makes clear what a story, an event, or a symbol is about. With little time in their pulpits or in the classroom, many preachers and teachers must go to the around-30 minute format of presentation, which barely allows for enough time to read a text and then summarize what they believe it means in a direct statement. This form of teaching may have its problems, however, for many are seeing that the story is the more foundational form of revelation in the Bible. In other words, when

God wants to communicate to us about the nature of a truth or event, he usually tells stories, either those in history or those invented for illustration and analysis. Which form of biblical study is more foundational to you: the story or doctrinal teaching? Is it necessary to spend a lot of time studying the ways of the story, and seeking God's meaning in the story, or simply going to the portions of Scripture where God's mind is directly and clearly explained (e.g., the Epistles)? Which should come first, the story or the doctrine?

CONTENT **Biblical Literature: Interpreting the Genres of the Bible**

Segment 1: General Principles of Interpretation

Rev. Dr. Don L. Davis

Summary of Segment 1

The term "genre" (pronounced JOHN-ruh) refers to that particular kind of literary form which communicates truth and must be interpreted according to the rules of that form. The study of genres is critical for effective biblical interpretation because the Bible itself as a book of literature is filled with different literary types, all of which function according to specific rules and principles. God has communicated to us using the human literary strategies of genres to communicate his Word. These include the use of narrative (both historical and imaginative), the Law (legal writings), epistles (letters), prophecy, wisdom literature (proverbs, monologues, riddles, fables, parables, allegories, etc.), and poetry. The types of literary presentation differ because of the impulse to fulfill a particular need in a given context, to deepen our understanding of our fundamental human experience, to allow us to image reality in its most concrete form, to display the artistry of the biblical authors as led by the Spirit, and to reveal the richness of the mystery of God and his work in the world. The study of genre can greatly enrich and empower us as we seek to understand the meaning of God's Word.

Our objective for this segment, *General Principles of Interpretation*, is to enable you to see that:

- The term "genre" (pronounced JOHN-ruh) refers to that particular kind of literary form which communicates truth and must be interpreted according to the rules of that form.

- The interpretation of the Bible according to genres must begin with a careful understanding of the basic assumptions of genre study, which affirms the fact that the Bible itself is a book of literature, one which is ordered and governed by attention to literary rules and principles like other works of literature, and that God employed genres and human literary strategies to communicate his Word to us.

- There are many significant forms and types of literature in the Scriptures. These include the use of narrative (both historical and imaginative), the occurrence of the Law (legal writings), epistles (letters), prophecy (including apocalyptic literature), the wisdom literature of Scripture (including proverbs, monologues, riddles, fables, parables, allegories, etc.), and the presence of poetic works.

- Genres occur because of the particular literary purpose of the authors to address particular needs and issues to their respective audiences, as well as to deepen our understanding of our fundamental human experience. Genre study also allows us to comprehend the truth by seeing it *imaged forth* in its most concrete from, as well as to display the artistry of the biblical authors as led by the Spirit, and to reveal the richness of the mystery of God and his work in the world.

- Careful attention to the genres and the rules to interpret them can provide us with major benefits in our biblical interpretation; genre study can empower us to discover the author's original intention, edify us as we identify the meaning of Scripture for our lives, enrich and entertain us in the beauty of the Scripture itself, and enlighten us in the knowledge of the purpose and will of God.

The Importance of Genre in Bible Study

Why is it important to classify biblical texts according to their literary form? First, the literary form of a text is often a clue to its meaning. For example, how we interpret Genesis 1-3 depends on whether it is read as a creation myth, allegory, or scientific history. The meaning we see in a text often derives from our prior judgment about its literary form. Second, the literary form is often a clue to its life setting. If we recognize that a text is in the form of a hymn, this allows us to relate it to the liturgical setting out of which it arose. Third, properly recognizing a literary form enables us to compare the text with similar literary forms in both biblical and nonbiblical writings. Such comparison often enables us to see things in a text we would otherwise miss.

~ Carl R. Holladay. "Biblical Criticism." **Harper's Bible Dictionary**.
P. J. Achtemeier, ed. (1st ed.) Harper & Row: San Francisco, 1985. p. 131.

I. Overview of the "Genre" Concept

    A. Definitions

        1. "A category of artistic composition, as in music or literature, marked by a distinctive style, form, or content" (*American Heritage Dictionary of the English Language*)

        2. Biblical genres = "Those different types and kinds of writing found within the books of the Bible, each sharing their common source and inspiration in God, but revealing truth and his will in different, yet complimentary modes of communication"

        3. "Genre" is the literary term for a type or kind of writing . . . "A literary approach to the Bible is based on the awareness that literature itself is a genre" (Leland Ryken).

        4. "A class or category of artistics endeavor having a particular form, content, and technique" (*Webster's Unabridged*)

        5. *A biblical genre is a particular kind of literary form which communicates truth and must be interpreted according to the rules of that form.*

    B. Basic assumptions

        1. The Bible is literature: each book of the Bible is carefully constructed by the divine and human authors.

3

a. The authors selected from a store of possible experiences they could have written about, John 21.24-25 - This is the disciple who is bearing witness about these things, and who has written these things, and we know that his testimony is true. [25] Now there are also many other things that Jesus did. Were every one of them to be written, I suppose that the world itself could not contain the books that would be written.

b. The writers function as editors, 2 Chron. 24.27, "annotations on the book of the kings"; writer of 2 Chronicles refer to writings of Nathan and Ahijah (9.29), Shemaiah (12.15), Jehu (20.34), and two different books by Iddo (9.29 and 13.22) as part of the sources from which he constructed his book.

c. Things were placed together to communicate the truth in the most assuring and effective way possible, Luke 1.1-4.

2. The Bible uses language in a literary manner (not merely as descriptive reporting or prose).

a. *Metaphors and similes* – the Kingdom of God is like a merchant looking for pearls, like a mustard seed, like a net, etc.

b. *Images and symbols* – an image is a word that names a concrete thing, and a symbol is an object that stands for something over and above its concrete meaning (oil, fire, water, household, fruit, head).

c. *Types and archetypes* – archetypes are the universal elements of human experience (sun, family, weeds, lion), i.e., they are universal symbols. Types are events, persons, and places in salvation history that becomes a pattern of something to occur in the future (i.e., Joseph is a type of Jesus: he is sold for 30 pieces of silver, saves his family, is vindicated by God and elevated to power at the right hand of the Pharaoh).

3. Genres suggest that God's truth can be communicated in various forms of literary text, all of which, in spite of their differences, are inspired by God and communicate his message in Christ.

II. Forms of Biblical Genres – What Are Some of the Most Important Forms of Biblical Genre We Can Study?

Literary Criticism Focuses on the Study of Genres in Biblical Study

Literary criticism also recognizes the existence of a variety of literary forms or genres in which a biblical text may be written. In some instances, entire books belong to a single genre, such as historical narrative (1 Samuel), poetry (Psalms), wisdom (Job), prophetic oracle (Amos), Gospel (Matthew), letter (Romans), or apocalypse (Revelation). Yet within these larger works are found smaller literary forms: creation myths; genealogies; narratives relating the stories of individual figures, such as Abraham or Joseph; legal codes; testaments; psalms; proverbs; prophetic oracles; miracle stories; parables; prayers; hymns; exhortations; and warnings. This list is not comprehensive, but it does suggest that the Bible, rather than being a single literary genre, contains many genres and subgenres.

~ R. Holladay. "Biblical Criticism." **Harper's Bible Dictionary**. P. J. Achtemeier, ed. (1st ed.) Harper & Row: San Francisco, 1985, p. 131.

A. *Narrative* – stories of the events and characters in the Bible, either historical or imaginative

1. Types of narrative

a. Historical Narrative – e.g., OT stories, Acts, the Gospels, the Resurrection Narratives

b.   Imaginative Narrative – e.g., the Parables, i.e., the Prodigal Son

  2. Characters – Who is acting or being acted upon?

  3. Setting – Where is the acting taking place?

  4. Theme – What is the overall theme of this story about

  5. Plot – How does the story line unfold in the narrative?

  6. Principle(s) – What truths can be drawn out of the story that have universal appeal and relevance?

Narratives (the telling of stories) is the heart of God's communication with us, and is meant not merely to tell abstract information, but to involve us in the complexity and richness of human experience, and thus give us insight into our own.

B. *Law (legal writings)* – commandments and codes in Scripture detailing the demands, prohibitions, and conditions of God's will in a particular context

  1. Types of laws

    a. Imperative laws ("Do this")

    b. Prohibitive laws ("Don't do this")

      c.   Conditional laws ("If you do this, then . . .")

2.   Old Testament "Torah" – Exodus-Deuteronomy and "The Law and the Prophets"

      a.   The Covenantal Code – Exodus

      b.   The Deuteronomic Code – Deuteronomy 12-25

      c.   The Holiness Code – Leviticus 17-26

      These laws involve legal issues, including civil and criminal law, murder and assault, theft, negligence and damage, moral and religious offense, family matters, slavery, international law, and most importantly, laws related to personal and corporate holiness before God.

3.   New Testament "nomos" – The "Law" of Christ and its meaning in the apostolic writings

      a.   Reference to the Hebrew Scriptures, the Sinai covenant, and the law of God as the expression of God's will

      b.   Reference to law as governing principle of faith and practice

      c.   The "Royal Law" as fulfilling OT law (e.g., Rom. 13.10)

      d.   Law vs. Gospel – Conflicting principles of approach to God and living out the Christian life, Rom. 11.6

3

e. The Law of Christ – Gal. 6.2; John 13.34-35

C. *Epistles (letters)* – Letters written by the Apostles to Christian churches to encourage the truths of the Gospel and resolve particular challenges they were facing in their setting and time

1. Epistles are the "heritage of all literature peoples" (cf. to the examples of them in the OT, e.g., 2 Sam. 11; 2 Kings 5; Isa. 37).

2. Balance between theological concern and personal and corporate need

3. Pauline epistles – Corinthians, Galatians, Philippians, Thessalonians, Ephesians, Colossians, Romans, Hebrews(?), Philemon, Timothy, Titus

4. Petrine epistles – 1 and 2 Peter

5. Johannine epistles – 1, 2, and 3 John

6. General epistles – James, Hebrews, Jude

Epistles are rhetorical (writing with a point), personal (given to people known), spiritual (highlighting key spiritual themes), doctrinal (dealing with theological issues), occasional (focused on addressing particular needs), and practical (aimed at challenging and encouraging believers in their walk with God and others).

D. *Prophecy* – those writings in the OT and NT which display God's acute awareness and insight into our lives in every dimension (past, present, and future), and his foresight into this world in its coming destiny

1. *Forth-telling* – the communication of God's present Word for a person or people in a particular situation in the form of warnings, encouragements, and challenges (e.g., Nathan and David)

2. *Foretelling* – the communication of God's perspective and vision for a person or people concerning the future (e.g., Isaiah 11)

3. The prophetic office and prophecy are throughout the Scriptures.

   a. Moses as the exemplar prophet (cf. Deut. 18.15-19)

   b. OT – the "major" and the "minor" prophets, Saul, Balaam

   c. NT – Christ, the apostles, Anna, Agabus, Caiaphas

4. Characteristics of prophecy

   a. Richly symbolic

   b. Interweaving of history and prediction

   c. Heavily focused on God's moral blessing or indictment

d. Extremely complex and difficult because of linguistic and symbolic distance

5. Prophetic *forth-telling* reveals God's moral vision and heart.

6. Prophetic *foretelling* displays God's mind and will as ruler of history.

E. *Wisdom Literature* – "a family of literary genres common in the Ancient Near East in which instructions for successful living are given or the perplexities of human existence are contemplated" (cf. *New Bible Dictionary*, pp. 1257-58)

1. *Proverbs* – concise, pithy statements summarizing collective insight on special topics of practical concern

2. *Monologues* or *Dialogues* – communications designed to explore the meanings of the deepest human questions, dilemmas, and concerns related to God and humankind

3. Psalms, Proverbs, Job, Ecclesiastes, and Song of Solomon make up the wisdom literature in the OT.

4. Characteristics of wisdom literature

a. Categorical in its tone

b. Probing in analysis

c. Designed to be memorized and transferred to others

d. Richly poetic

e. Does not seek to resolve all ambiguity and questions

f. Affirms our fundamental human limitation in comprehending final things

g. Celebrates mystery

5. Includes a broad amount of materials and writings

a. Riddles

b. Proverbs

c. Fables

d. Parables

e. Allegories

f. Poetry

3

Wisdom literature is dramatically important because it wrestles with the issues that are of ultimate concern in our lives without resolving all of the tensions and problems associated with them. It is designed to raise our spirits in the midst of life, not give final answers to the issues of life.

F. *Poetic works* – that form of biblical genre which usually appears in the form of song, sonnet, or hymn, and is designed to image forth reality in its most concrete sense to move and inspire us

1. Closely associated with the music tradition of the Hebrew peoples

2. Meter, rhythm, and pace are important for the poems as artistic pieces.

3. How the songs were written is also important in terms of what was written.

4. Psalms are the richest mine of poetry to be found in the OT, but it occurs throughout, especially in the Wisdom Literature.

5. Songs were a significant part of Hebrew life and culture (e.g., Song of the Well, Num. 21.17-18; Gen. 31.27; Jer. 7.34, etc.).

6. Many poems were accompanied by instrumental music (Exod. 15.20; Isa. 23.16).

7. Hebrew poetry was a recited form of communication, highlighting vowel accents and stresses (this is the key to its meter).

8. Characteristics of biblical poetry

    a. Imagery and Action – focus is made on concreteness and movement, not abstraction (e.g., Ps. 1.1-3)

    b. Parallelism – restating in the second line what was stated in the first (e.g., Ps. 59.1)

    c. Reinforcement – a particular message or theme is reinforced in every line and phrase (Ps. 55.6)

    d. Contrasts – opposites set beside one another (e.g., Ps. 1.6)

III. Purpose – Why Do Different Biblical Genres Exist, and Why Is the Study of Biblical Genres Important?

A. To fulfill a particular need (contextual or occasional nature of all literature)

Every part of the Bible was written in a particular context to speak to a particular audience who had particular needs and issues that the text was designed to address.

1. To *inform*: Romans (prose), Proverbs (proverbs or sayings), Acts, historical works

2. To *legislate*: Leviticus, Deuteronomy

3. To *warn*: Prophetic books

3

4. To *inspire*: Shadrach, Meshach, and Abed-nego (narratives)

5. To *entertain*: David and Goliath (narrative); Sermon on the Mount (speck and the beam metaphor)

6. To *question*: Ecclesiastes, Job

7. To *persuade*: Revelation of St. John, Gospel of John

Both narrative and prophecy have characteristics that allow them to address many of these purposes simultaneously.

B. To deepen our understanding of our own fundamental human experience

The Bible focuses in depth on the fundamental experiences and questions that human beings live and encounter throughout their lives.

1. Feeling, participation, and emotion are the purpose of biblical study, not merely the search for abstract information.

2. To use the biblical characters as mirrors of fundamental human experience

3. Allows us to wrestle with the *big questions*: who are we, where did we come from, where are we going, where do we go when we die, etc.

C. To allow us to image reality in its most concrete form

1. Genre study is "show and tell": to display in verbal form the reality of human life

2. To exhibit "the way life is" within the story and teachings of the biblical characters

3. To force us to recognize ourselves within that reality

4. To engage our imaginations and emotions as we experience their stories as our own

5. Genre study unfolds three main themes:

   a. What is *really real*? (The realm of life as it is)

   b. What is really *good or evil*? (The realm of what is moral)

   c. What is *really worthwhile*? (The realm of value, meaning, and purpose)

D. To display the artistry of the biblical authors, as led by the Holy Spirit

   1. Genres are characterized by literature purposely done in various forms to enhance the art of writing and language usage.

   2. Genre writing = beauty, craftsmanship, and technique

3

3. Not only WHAT is said, but also HOW it is said

4. Ryken: elements of artistic form and design (common to all artistry)

    a. Pattern or design

    b. Theme or central focus

    c. Organic unity

    d. Coherence

    e. Balance

    f. Contrast

    g. Symmetry

    h. Repetition

    i. Unified progression

E. To reveal the richness of the biblical mystery of God and his work in the world

1. God employs language, but God is beyond language; he employs difference to make his glory even more rich and thick.

2. The literature of the Bible employs special language.

   a. Metaphor – You cow!

   b. Simile – You smell like a cow!

   c. Irony – Only Bessie, the Jersey, knew how bad cows smelled!

   d. Personification – O, cow of the morning, how I have desired to milk you, to alleviate your pain and pressure . . . !

3. No amount of explanation can capture the richness and depth of God.

4. God's use of genre is an attempt to reveal the richness of mystery, without reducing himself or his work down to a prose sentence.

IV. Benefits of Biblical Genre Study

A. It will *empower* us to discover what the author's originally intended to communicate both through their words as well as their forms.

B. It will *edify* our souls: God causes us to grow by making imaginative connections between our world (the known) and God's truth (the unknown).

C. It will *enrich* our appreciation of life: God draws us into "vicarious living," our experiencing of the concrete human experience of others, and asks us to participate within their struggles, hopes, and challenges ("You are there").

D. It will *entertain* our hearts: God stretches and refreshes us with the beauty and artistry of the literary conventions.

E. It will *enlighten* our minds: God challenges us to recognize his Word in a form very different from our natural ways of thinking and being in the world, and through genres calls us to a rigorous study of the Bible.

As we engage the texts in the forms in which the Holy Spirit gave them to us, we will find that God is the God of infinite wisdom, always going beyond our attempts to put him in a box or concept we build for him!

Conclusion

» Genre (pronounced JOHN-ruh) refers to that particular kind of literary form which communicates truth and must be interpreted according to the rules of that form.

» As a book of literature, the Bible must be understood on its own terms, according to the rules which the Holy Spirit allowed the various portions and sections of the Bible to be written.

Please take as much time as you have available to answer these and other questions that the video brought out. A major element in effective biblical interpretation is training in and attention to the rules and elements related to genre study. The Bible is a book of literature, and understanding how literature functions can enhance greatly our appreciation of the mastery of the biblical authors, as well as our comprehension of the meaning of Scripture itself. Answer the following questions about genres and its relevance for biblical interpretation in light of its importance for developing a valid hermeneutic of Scripture. Be thorough in your answers.

Segue 1

Student Questions and Response

1. What is the definition of the term "genre" and how does this relate to the understanding of literature in general? Why might this definition help us understand the role of genre for biblical studies?

2. What are some of the major assumptions that undergird a valid understanding of the use of genre in biblical interpretation? Why is it so important to recognize the Bible as a book of literature, and what difference does this make in our handling of the texts, in all of its different types and kinds?

3. How do we know that God chose to use these kinds of human literary strategies to communicate his Word to us? Why should this fact encourage us to discover the rules and strategies of genres as they are included in the holy Scriptures?

4. List some of the significant forms and types of literature in the Scriptures. What kind of information do we gain from the Bible by seeing such a wide variety of literary types of material in the Bible?

5. In your assessment of the different genres of the Bible, do you think that there are some types that are more important than others, and if so, which ones are they and why?

6. How might we explain the presence of so many different genres or types of literature contained in the Bible? In what ways do the study of genres help us to better understand the various dimensions of "fundamental human experience?"

7. Someone has said that literature tells the truth by *showing it forth*. How does genre study help us to comprehend the truth by seeing it *imaged forth* in its most concrete form?

8. Why might it be important for biblical students to appreciate the artistry of the biblical authors as *writers* who are under the influence and leading of the Holy Spirit? How, too, does genre study reveal the richness of the mystery of God and his work in the world?

9. List out the major benefits of genre study in biblical interpretation. Of all the benefits covered in this segment, which one do you believe will motivate your own study of the Bible in the most direct way? Explain.

Biblical Literature: Interpreting the Genres of the Bible

Segment 2: Interpreting Narrative and Prophecy Genres in Scripture

Rev. Dr. Don L. Davis

3

"Special hermeneutics" refers to those special rules and procedures that enable us to interpret the literary forms of the Bible. Such a hermeneutic is important, especially as we begin to use these rules in our interpretation of the various types of biblical literature. Narrative is a particular type of study, and is the foundation of story theology, which argues that God has provided a record of his work in the story accounts of the Bible. Story theologians recognize the significance of story, how (among other things) they introduce us to sacramental presences, are normative for the Christian community, and produce theology, ritual, and sacrament. Prophecy is another genre of biblical interpretation, which offers truth about God and the universe, and manifests itself in personal and literary modes. Apocalyptic literature is a sub-genre of prophecy, an element seen in the two main types of Jewish apocalypses, in the OT book of Daniel, and the most distinctly apocalyptic book in Scripture, the book of Revelation. We will interpret prophecy and apocalyptic genres of Scripture well if we focus on the person of Jesus Christ, refer the prophetic messages to the call of the Kingdom of God, and emphasize the fulfillment of God's sovereign purposes even in the face of evil, suffering and injustice.

Our objective for this segment, *Interpreting Narrative and Prophecy Genres in Scripture*, is to enable you to see that:

- "Special hermeneutics" refers to those specific rules and procedures that enable us to interpret the literary forms of the Bible.

- Narrative is the most common form of genre in Scripture, and includes stories and story accounts which are either historical or imaginative.

- Story theologians focus on narrative accounts in Scripture, and begin their work of interpretation with general assumptions of story theology, which include the idea that God's primary way of recording his person and work is in light of story accounts in Scripture. Other assumptions include the idea that all theology is reflection on the stories of the Bible, that biblical stories that refer to historical accounts are reliable and accurate, that stories are written with artistic skill and mastery, that we encounter God in the story

Summary of Segment 2

text, and that God often provides his own commentary on the meaning of the biblical story accounts.

- Story theology is built on the foundation of key propositions about stories, the Bible, and the Church. These include the concept that stories introduce us to sacramental presences, are more important than facts, and are normative for the Christian community. Christian traditions evolve and define themselves by stories, which also precede and produce community, and produce censure, accountability theology, ritual, and sacrament in the Church. Stories, too, are history.

- Like other literature, the general elements of narrative in Scripture include the setting, characters, author's point of view, plot, and theme of the stories.

- Prophecy is another main genre of Scripture, a literary type which offers truth about God and the universe, flows from the Spirit, and is itself a specific mode of revelation from God which comes either in persons or written forms.

- Apocalyptic is a sub-genre of prophecy, and includes the two main types of Jewish apocalypses, the OT book of Daniel, and the most distinctly apocalyptic book in Scripture, the book of Revelation.

- In order to rightly interpret both prophecy and apocalyptic genres of Scripture we must first focus on the person of Jesus Christ, refer the prophetic messages to the call of the Kingdom of God, and seek to emphasize the fulfillment of God's sovereign purposes even in the face of evil, suffering and injustice.

- -

The Diversity of Scripture

In the midst of Scripture's unity, we must not lose sight of its diversity . . . This takes several forms. The books of the Bible are written by different authors, in different times and places, to different audiences in distinct circumstances, using various literary genres. Each book thus displays unique purposes and themes. In some instances, different portions of Scripture are so closely parallel that we can postulate a literary relationship between them and assume that their differences are intentional: sometimes theologically motivated; sometimes merely for stylistic variation. Deuteronomy consciously updates various laws of Exodus and Leviticus for more settled life in the Promised Land. Chronicles retells significant portions of the Deuteronomistic history, adding, omitting and rewording to highlight its focus on the southern kingdom, its kings, the temple and the priestly service. Each of the four Gospels clearly has its own slant on the identity of Jesus and the nature of his ministry, while 2 Peter seems to have revised and supplemented Jude to combat a new group of false teachers in a new context.

~ C. L. Blomberg. "The Unity and Diversity of Scripture."
The New Dictionary of Biblical Theology.
T. D. Alexander, ed. (electronic ed.).
Downers Grove, IL: InterVarsity Press, 2001.

. . . .

I. Special Hermeneutics and the Definition of Narrative

Video Segment 2
Outline

A. Special hermeneutics

(1.) "Special hermeneutics": *the rules and procedures that enable us to interpret the literary forms of the Bible*

2. The Three-Step Model applies to *every text of Scripture you seek to interpret.*

1. a. Understand the original situation.

2. b. Draw out general principles for life.

3. c. Apply these principles to your own life situation.

3. *A biblical genre is a particular kind of literary form which communicates truth and must be interpreted according to the rules of that form.*

4. Special hermeneutics is that branch of biblical interpretation committed to _understanding and applying the specific rules of interpretation_ that _relate to each form as it seeks to communicate its message._

B. Narrative (stories) in literature

1. A narrative in its literary form is distinguished by "the presence of a story and a storyteller" (Robert Scholes and Robert Kellogg, *The Nature of Narrative*, London: Oxford University Press, 1966, p. 4).

2. "A story . . . [is] an account of characters and events in a plot moving over time and space through conflict toward resolution" (Gabriel Fackre, "Narrative Theology").

3. Narratives are *stories*, whether historical (*stories about things that actually happened*) or imaginative (*fictional stories that God or people in Scripture tell, usually to illustrate a spiritual truth or challenge with a spiritual lesson*). Parables are the prime example.

C. General assumptions of *Story Theology*

1. God has provided a record of his character and acts primarily in the story accounts of the Bible.

a. The majority of the text in his Word is in the form of story.

b. An understanding of the ways that stories function can help and increase our knowledge of the Bible, and through it, the God of the Bible.

2. All theology is reflection on the stories of the Bible, and is a "third-order" discipline.

a. *First order*: God acting in history

b. *Second order*: God superintended the recording of his acts in history in the form of story in the Word of God.

c. *Third order*: our reflection upon the Word to grasp the meaning of God's character and acts

d. Theology is reflecting on the meaning of God's acts in history captured in the stories of the Bible.

3. While stories are crafted pieces of literature, the stories of the Bible are reliable and accurate when referring to historical accounts.

a. Types of story

(1) *Historical narratives* which testify accurately to actual occurrences that took place, e.g., Jesus' birth, Luke 2.1-7

(2) *Imaginative narratives* are invented stories created by the author for illustration and teaching, e.g., Nathan's story to David, 2 Sam. 12.1-7.

b. The *accuracy of the historical reporting* in biblical historical narrative: the prologues of the Luke-Acts corpus, Luke 1.1-4

4. The authors of the Scriptures write their stories with artistic skill as master storytellers.

5. The intent of engaging and studying the sacred story is to encounter God in the text, and respond in faith and obedience to that encounter, James 1.22-25.

a. They show God's acts in history and show us how he will also relate to us today.

b. *Analogy of faith*: "As God was with them there-and-then, so he is and will always be with us here-and-now."

c. Story is for *encounter*: correlating the story with our story is the key to a narrative approach of the Bible.

6. God often provides his own commentary on the meaning of his stories within the story itself.

D. Key propositions of *Story Theology*

William J. Bausch lists ten propositions related to story theology that help us understand the significance and importance of the study of stories and the understanding of Bible and theology. (William J. Bausch, *Storytelling and Faith*. Mystic, Connecticut: 23rd Publications, 1984.)

1. Stories introduce us to *sacramental presences.*

2. Stories are always *more important than facts.*

3. Stories remain *normative* (authoritative) for the Christian community of faith.

4. *Christian traditions* evolve and define themselves through and around stories.

5. The stories of God *precede, produce, and empower* the community of God's people.

6. Community story implies *censure, rebuke, and accountability.*

7. Stories produce *theology.*

8. Stories produce *many theologies.*

9. Stories produce *ritual and sacrament.*

10. Stories are *history.*

II. General Elements in Interpreting a Narrative (Story)

As we engage the imaginative stories and historical accounts of the Scriptures, we should be aware of the various literary elements which make up storytelling, and discover their usage and interaction in the texts we are studying.

A. Acknowledge the *Setting* of the story.

    1. Who is telling the story, to whom, where, and for what reasons?

    2. What are the physical surroundings of the story?

    3. What is the cultural-religious-historical-interpersonal situation where the story is being told?

B. Identify the *Characters* of the story.

    1. Who is the "hero?" Who is the "villain?" How do their encounters and interactions affect one another in the story?

    2. How are the characters shown to us?

        a. Direct descriptions of the characters (descriptions and accounts of their attitudes, actions, and appearances)

        b. Indirect characterization (i.e., appearance, by the words that they say, thoughts and attitudes they take, by the effect they have on others, by their actions [virtuous or vice-ridden])

    3. How are the characters tested, and what choices do they make?

    4. Did the characters progress and grow in their development within this the story?

3

C. Watch for the *Author's Point-of View and Voice.*

    1. What are the author's comments about the character's actions and words?

    2. What person is the story being written in?

        a. The view of the Spirit (in literature, the omniscient view)

        b. The First-Person view (telling one's own story: Nehemiah)

        c. The Third-Person narrator

    3. What "voice" is it being written in: "Voice is the attitude toward everything observed" (John Leggett).

D. Detect the underlying *Plot Development* within the story.

    1. Try to outline the basic development of the story (beginning, middle, ending).

    2. Note the classic elements of Plot structure — John Leggett

        a. *Doormat* — how does the story introduce itself?

b. *Complications* — what are the specific conflicts and problems the characters are confronting in the story?

c. *Climax* — what is the peak and turning point of the action, the moment when someone in the conflict "wins", gives in, gets by, gets over?

d. *Denouement* — how does the story finally settle its issues, dispose of its problems, and bring to resolution the issues introduced earlier?

e. *End* — Finis!

E. Note the *Theme of the Story* (God's principles and truths).

1. What "commentary on living" does the story provide?

a. Its view of "*reality*," (What is the world like and who are we in it?)

b. Its view of "*morality*," (What constitutes the good and the bad?)

c. Its understanding of "*value*," (What is the ultimate concern?)

2. What truths about God and ourselves do we glean from our engagement with this story?

The Unity *AND* the Diversity of the Scriptures

In short, the unity and diversity of Scripture must be acknowledged and held in a delicate balance. More liberal scholarship tends to focus so much on diversity that the unity disappears. More conservative scholarship tends to focus so much on unity that the diversity disappears. Without a recognition of the unity of Scripture, the canon in its entirety cannot function as the authoritative foundation for Christian belief and practice as historically it has done. Without an appreciation of the diversity that comes from hearing each text, book and author on its own terms, one risks misinterpreting Scripture and not discerning what God intended to say to his people at any given point in their history. Theologically, the unity of Scripture marks out clear limits of thought and behavior beyond which individuals or 'churches' may not legitimately be called Christian. On the other hand, the diversity of Scripture demonstrates how no one sect or ecclesiastical tradition has a monopoly of the truth. One can become heretical by being either too broad-minded or too narrow-minded!

~ C. L. Blomberg. "The Unity and Diversity of Scripture."
The New Dictionary of Biblical Theology. T. D. Alexander, ed. (electronic ed.).
Downers Grove, IL: InterVarsity Press, 2001.

3

III. Prophecy as a Genre of Biblical Literature

A. Prophecy offers truth about God and the universe.

1. It deals with central questions of human existence and life.

2. It deals with the nature of creation and the universe.

 3. It flows from a transcendent view of the world (i.e., a triune God working his will in the world).

4. It provides a distinctive claim on truth above and beyond human reason, philosophy, and scientific enquiry.

    a.   1 Cor. 1.18-3.20

    b.   Col. 2.1-10

    c.   2 Pet. 1.20-21

B. Prophecy flows from *the Holy Spirit of God*.

   1. The gift of prophecy is a "gift" of the Spirit, Rom. 12.6; 1 Cor. 12.10, 28; Eph. 4.8; 1 Thess. 5.19.

   2. The prophet is often identified as a person "of the Spirit," 1 Cor. 14.37 with Hos. 9.7; see also 1 Sam. 19.20; 2 Kings 2.15; Neh. 9.30.

   3. The prophetic promise of the Kingdom: the Spirit poured out on all flesh

    a.   Moses' hope: "all the Lord's people are to be prophets," Num. 11.16, 29 cf. Luke 10.1.

    b.   Joel's prophetic oracle: "God will pour out his Spirit on all flesh," Joel 2.28.

    c.   Fulfillment: the day of Pentecost (see Matt. 3.11 with Acts 2.16, 33)

3

C. Prophecy is a *specific mode of the revelation* of God.

1. Varieties of divine revelation exist: Jer. 18.18 (see Isa. 28.7; 29.10, 14) (e.g., the law from the priest, counsel from the wise, word from the prophet).

2. Who were the prophets?

   a. They might live together in guilds, schools, or communities, (e.g., 2 Kings 2.3ff; 6.1).

   b. Some were attached to the temple, and could have served as priests, (e.g., Samuel, Elijah, Ezekiel [1.3], and Jeremiah [1.1]).

   c. Priests had a prophetic function to interpret, transcribe, update, and apply the Law (cf. Isa. 28.7, also Ezra's example).

   d. Wisdom teachers were also regarded in Israel as prophetically gifted (see Gen. 41.38f; 2 Sam. 14.20, 16.23; 1 Kings 3.9, 12, 28).

D. Prophecy manifests itself in various *personal and literary modes*.

1. Recognized in Judaism and early Christianity as having many different forms (cf. Josephus, *Against Apion* I, 38-42 with Mark 12.36; Acts 2.30; 7.37)

2. Oracles in Scripture, Isa. 1.1ff.

3. Preachings in the Church, 1 Cor. 12-14

4. Statements, exhortations of the apostles, Acts 2

5. Revelatory teaching of inspired persons, 1 Cor. 14.6

6. The totality of divine revelation in written form, 2 Pet. 1.19-21 (cf. Luke 11.50-51, Acts 2.16ff, James 5.10-11)

E. Characteristics of biblical prophecy

1. Collections of oracles delivered orally or portrayed physically in events and actions

2. Rich in symbols, images, metaphors, and allegories, cf. Amos 4.1 and Isa. 44.23

3. Often delivered and/or written in poetic form

a. Makes the prophetic word memorable

b. Use of parallelism

c. Imaging forth truth, or enacting it in order to deliver God's message

4. May be delivered to conceal truth as well as reveal God's person and mind, Num. 12.6-8

5. The prophet cannot be the final judge of his or her message's validity.

    a. Prophets and their messages in both the OT and NT were contested and conflicted (see 1 Kings 22; Jer. 23; 28; and 2 Cor. 11.4, 13; 1 John 4.1-3).

    b. Prophetic utterances were tested :

        (1) For their prophetic character, 1 Cor. 14.29

        (2) For its agreement with the teaching of Moses, Deut. 13.1-5

        (3) For its fulfillment of history, Jer. 23

        (4) For its consistency with the person and teaching of Jesus, Matt. 7.15; 24.11; 2 Pet. 2.1

        (5) And received once proven true, 1 Thess. 5.19-21

IV. Apocalyptic as a Biblical Genre of Scripture

A. Definition of apocalyptic literature

    1. Derives from the term "apocalypse" a·poc·a·lypse (-pk-lps) n. "unveiling"

    2. Portions of Daniel and the book of Revelation.

3

3. Any number of anonymous Jewish or Christian texts from around the second century B.C. to the second century A.D. containing prophetic or symbolic visions, (especially of the imminent destruction of the world and the salvation of the righteous.)

4. Great or total devastation; doom: *the apocalypse of nuclear war*; a prophetic disclosure; a revelation

5. Apocalyptic literature deals largely with eschatology (study of the last things) (which tends to be emphasized during times of intense crisis, persecution, or upheaval.)

B. Types of apocalyptic literature

1. True apocalyptic in the OT: Daniel, cf. Daniel 2; 7

2. Great age of Jewish apocalyptic: 2nd century BC to 2nd century AD (various books)

   1 Enoch, 2 Baruch, 4 Ezra (known in the English Apocrypha as 2 Esdras), 3 Baruch, The Apocalypse of Abraham, 2 Enoch, The Apocalypse of Zephaniah

3. Traits of Jewish apocalypses

   a. Revelations of heavenly mysteries

   b. Usually deal with a list of spiritual themes

      (1) The nature of the cosmos

3

(2) The content of the heavens

(3) The vision of the heavenly throne-room

(4) The realms of the dead

(5) The problem of human suffering and theodicy

c. Written under a pseudonym (a different name than the author's real name) usually a great character of the biblical past (e.g., Enoch, Ezra)

d. Given usually through dreams, visions, or special revelations in which rich symbolic representations are interpreted to the "seer" (i.e., the recipient of the vision) by an angel

4. Two main types of Jewish apocalypses

a. *Cosmological apocalypses* – concentrate on the secrets of the cosmos and the heavens which are revealed in other-worldly journeys

b. *Historical-eschatological apocalypses* – (cf. Daniel) – focus on God's purposes in history, covering summaries of human history where God has ordained certain periods

(1) They focus on the coming of the end of human history.

(2) They speak of God's coming victory over the evil powers and nations destroying and oppressing people.

(3) They talk of God's utter destruction of all results of the demonic powers, evil, and suffering associated with the fall.

(4) They address God's establishment of his everlasting Kingdom, including the resurrection from the dead, the judgment of the wicked and unrepentant, and the coming blessedness of the universe and the righteous.

3

A Message Leading to the Person of Jesus Christ

The Bible did not originate in one piece as a doctrinal handbook or a manual of ethics. Rather, made up of diverse literary genres, it is a record of the history of special revelation, a history of which its own production (inscripturation . . .) is a part. This long history begins as early as the garden of Eden and, after the fall, continues as God's ongoing redemptive activity, accompanied by his own attesting and interpreting word, primarily in his covenantal dealings with Israel, until its culmination in the person and work of Christ. Biblical revelation, then, is essentially redemptive, or covenantal-historical, and the concern of biblical theology is to explore and clarify this historically progressive and differentiated character of special revelation.
~ R. B. Gaffin "New Testament Theology." *New Dictionary of Theology.* Sinclair B. Ferguson, David Wright, eds. (electronic ed.). Downers Grove, IL: InterVarsity Press, 1988, p.463.

C. NT apocalyptic: the book of Revelation

1. The only true apocalypse in the NT (cf., *Shepherd of Hermas*, written by a Christian prophet)

2. Belongs to the historical-eschatological tradition of Jewish apocalypses

3. Deals with God's intent to alert his Church to the events about to take place, Rev. 1.1-3

4. Gives comprehensive revelation of the person and work of Jesus Christ, Rev. 1.7-18

5. Addresses the issues of judgment at the end of human history, Rev. 20.11-15

6. Employs mystical and imagistic language of metaphor, symbol, and fantasy, Rev. 12.14-16

7. Focuses on the importance of numbers and numbered sets to both structure and communicate the content of the message, e.g., Rev. 13.18; 21.12-14; 4.2-8

V. Three Interpretative Principles for the Prophetic and Apocalyptic Genre

A. Principle One: *Focus on the person of Jesus Christ.*

1. The testimony of Jesus is the very spirit (i.e., inner motive and rationale) for all prophetic interpretation, Rev. 19.10.

2. Christ is the center of biblical interpretation, and therefore historical foretellings (i.e., prophecy as applied to historical future events) find their ultimate integrating point in him (cf. Luke 24.27, 44-48).

3. Three-fold sense of historical prophetic fulfillment (Walter Kaiser, *An Introduction to Biblical Hermeneutics*)

    1   a. *The predicted word* that proceeds the event referred to

    2   b. *The historic means by which God kept that predicted word alive for succeeding generations* (i.e., the down payments that connects the first announcement with its climatic fulfillment)

    3.   c. The ultimate fulfillment in the NT of the prophetic prediction given in the OT referred to either in the First or Second Advent of Jesus Christ.

B. Principle Two: Refer prophetic messages to the call to the Kingdom – *adopt a kingdom lifestyle in the face of future coming events.*

1. New resolve to prepare and make ready for Christ's return, 1 Pet. 1.10-13

2. Absolute certain assurance of the events yet to come, 2 Pet. 1.19-21

3. Call to holiness and godliness in light of the certain judgment on all things, 2 Pet. 3.10-14

C. Principle Three: Emphasize the fulfillment of *God's sovereign purpose even in the face of evil, suffering, and injustice.*

1. God's kingdom reign will ultimately crush all worldly substitutes, Dan. 2.44.

2. God's sovereign purpose will finally be accomplished in all dimensions of the universe, all for his glory and name's sake, Dan. 4.34-37.

3. God will ultimately render to every human being according to their works, whether good or bad, Rev. 22.8-16.

3

Conclusion

» In the study of biblical genres, perhaps no others are as prominent and significant for study as narrative and prophecy.

» As we discover the rules of the various kinds of genre in Scripture, we will be better able to understand and apply the rules of the form in order to discover the truth of God in his marvelous Word.

Segue 2

Student Questions and Response

The following questions were designed to help you review the material in the second video segment. In this section we looked at the role of "special hermeneutics" in two distinct types of literature, narrative and prophecy. Narrative accounts serve as the foundation of story theology, and prophecy offers truth about God and the universe in both personal and literary modes. As you become better at interpreting genres, your own enrichment and edification from the Word will grow, and so will your ability to teach and preach the Scriptures with power and clarity. Answer the following questions, reviewing carefully the central concepts surrounding the special hermeneutics of both narrative and prophecy, including apocalyptic literature.

1. What is the definition of "special hermeneutics," and how do its rules and procedures help us interpret the various literary forms of the Bible?

2. What is narrative, and how prominent is it within the Bible itself? What is the distinction between narrative materials that are "historical" versus those that are "imaginative?"

3. How do narrative or story theologians relate to the narrative accounts in Scripture? Recite the general assumptions that give shape and substance to the idea of story theology.

4. Of all the assumptions of story theologians, which one(s) do you believe are most important for all of us who seek to take the stories of the Bible seriously, as history as well as revelations of God?

5. What is the relationship of our interpretation of a story and the commentary and meaning that God gives us through the comments of the author in the biblical story accounts? Explain your answer.

6. List out the key propositions about stories, the Bible, and the Church included in this section. Of all the propositions, which one(s) do you believe are most important for us to recognize as we seek to take seriously the role of narrative in biblical interpretation? Explain your answer.

7. What are the general elements of narrative in Scripture, and how do they relate as elements to other stories told elsewhere in novels, short stories, or other kinds of literature?

8. Define prophecy as a main genre of Scripture. What do we know to be true about prophecy as it relates to our knowledge of God, the universe, and his work in the world?

9. What is "apocalyptic literature," what books of our Bible are of this sub-genre of prophecy, and why is the study of the apocalyptic genre so important for effective biblical interpretation?

10. What three principles and perspectives are significant if we are ever to rightly interpret both prophecy and apocalyptic genres of Scripture?

CONNECTION

Summary of Key Concepts

This lesson focuses upon the role and uses of genre in biblical interpretation. The concepts below summarize the major insights covered in this segment on the significance of genres in special hermeneutics.

- ☛ The term "genre" (pronounced JOHN-ruh) refers to that particular kind of literary form which communicates truth and must be interpreted according to the rules of that form.

- ☛ The interpretation of the Bible according to genres must begin with a careful understanding of the basic assumptions of genre study, which affirms the fact that the Bible itself is a book of literature, one which is ordered and governed by attention to literary rules and principles like other works of literature, and that God employed genres and human literary strategies to communicate his Word to us.

- ☛ There are many significant forms and types of literature in the Scriptures. These include the use of narrative (both historical and imaginative), the occurrence of the Law (legal writings), epistles (letters), prophecy (including apocalyptic literature), the wisdom literature of Scripture (including proverbs, monologues, riddles, fables, parables, allegories, etc.), and the presence of poetic works.

- ☛ Genres occur because of the particular literary purpose of the authors to address particular needs and issues to their respective audiences, as well as to deepen our understanding of our fundamental human experience. Genre study also allows us to comprehend the truth by seeing it *imaged forth* in its most concrete from, as well as to display the artistry of the biblical authors as led by the Spirit, and to reveal the richness of the mystery of God and his work in the world.

- ☛ Careful attention to the genres and the rules to interpret them can provide us with major benefits in our biblical interpretation; genre study can empower us to discover the author's original intention, edify us as we identify the meaning of Scripture for our lives, enrich and entertain us in the beauty of the Scriptures, and enlighten us in the knowledge of the purpose and will of God.

- ☛ Special hermeneutics refers to those specific rules and procedures that enable us to interpret the literary forms of the Bible.

⊷ Narrative is the most common form of genre in Scripture, and includes stories and story accounts which are either historical or imaginative.

⊷ Story theologians focus on narrative accounts in Scripture, and begin their work of interpretation with general assumptions of story theology, which include the idea that God's primary way of recording his person and work is in light of story accounts in Scripture. Other assumptions include the idea that all theology is reflection on the stories of the Bible, that biblical stories that refer to historical accounts are reliable and accurate, that stories are written with artistic skill and mastery, that we encounter God in the story text, and that God often provides his own commentary on the meaning of the biblical story accounts.

⊷ Story theology is built on the foundation of key propositions about stories, the Bible, and the Church. These include the concept that stories introduce us to sacramental presences, are more important than facts, and are normative for the Christian community. Christian traditions evolve and define themselves by stories, which also precede and produce community, and produce censure, accountability theology, ritual, and sacrament in the Church. Stories, too, are history.

⊷ Like other literature, the general elements of narrative in Scripture include the setting, characters, author's point of view, plot, and theme of the stories.

⊷ Prophecy is another main genre of Scripture, a literary type which offers truth about God and the universe, flows from the Spirit, and is itself a specific mode of revelation from God which comes either in persons or written forms.

⊷ Apocalyptic is a sub-genre of prophecy, and includes the two main types of Jewish apocalypses, the OT book of Daniel, and the most distinctly apocalyptic book in Scripture, the book of Revelation.

⊷ In order to rightly interpret both prophecy and apocalyptic genres of Scripture we must first focus on the person of Jesus Christ, refer the prophetic messages to the call of the Kingdom of God, and seek to emphasize the fulfillment of God's sovereign purposes even in the face of evil, suffering and injustice.

Student Application and Implications

As a student of the Word of God, you will need to wrestle with the rules, procedures, and processes to fully understand and apply this lesson's teachings on genres and the Bible. Your ability to comprehend this concept and apply it in your study will influence all of your walk and ministry, especially your preaching and teaching, and your personal Bible study. Now you ought to focus on those questions about genre that have lingered in your mind throughout the discussions and investigations of this material. Use the questions below to help you form and clarify those areas of concern and interest that continue to remain in your comprehension of the role of genres in biblical interpretation.

* Are you now convinced that the Bible cannot be properly interpreted without a careful understanding of the genres of the Bible? Are you convinced that because the Bible itself is a book of literature, you must therefore seek to interpret it according to the literary rules and principles like other works of literature? Explain your answer.

* Of the genres listed in this lesson, which have been the greatest challenge for you to understand, apply, and teach to others? (Remember, these include narrative, Law, epistles, prophecy [including apocalyptic literature], wisdom literature, and poetic works).

* Have you spent much time in genre study? What were your overall impressions then? Has this lesson made any difference in how you see the role of genre study in your own study of the Bible? Explain.

* Why is it important to use the *Three-Step Model* in conjunction with your study of specific genres, and their rules to interpret them? Are there genres that the *Three-Step Model* does not apply to? Explain.

* How much time do you spend studying both the stories and prophecies of the Bible? Given the fact that these two genres make up the vast majority of the biblical content, are you saying that you are ignoring or concentrating on this material in your present study of the Bible?

* Is there a certain genre of the Bible that you tend to focus on? Why would you say you place your focus on this kind of material–is it easier to understand, more interesting, another reason(s)?

* How much time do you spend studying the Gospels and the parables within them? Do you think that if you understood better "how narrative works" you would actually spend more time in the Gospels and Acts, and other story accounts?

3

* In looking at the propositions included in this lesson on story theology, are there propositions that seem overstated or untrue to you? Explain your answer. If so, how would you reword the proposition to be more in line with what you believe?

* Have you ever studied the materials of prophecy and apocalyptic in a thorough way before? What would need to happen before you would tackle a study of this kind of literature in the Bible–where are your gaps in knowing *how* to study them?

Too Many Rules

CASE STUDIES

1

In looking at the diversity of literary material in the Bible (i.e., poems, prose, songs, hymns, stories, metaphors, symbolic literature, prophecy, allegory, parable, etc.) some become extremely discouraged at genre study. You can clearly understand why. Who could possibly spend enough time to learn all of the genres of the Bible in order to gain a pretty good understanding of them all? Isn't such a task impossible? Aren't there scholars who have spent decades of time pouring over a particular genre, and still confess that they barely understand any of it? How are we, neither expert in the biblical languages nor the genres themselves, ever to use these rules as the basis for our Bible study? Doesn't a genre-oriented approach to the Bible offer us simply too many rules to know and master before we can begin to glean some of the fresh understanding that the Word of God offers us?

Stories Are for the Children's Sermon

2

The children's sermon in many churches is quite simply a story time. This is not without interest or significance. Usually armed with an object in hand to serve as the introduction to the sermon, the children each week are given insight into the will of God invariably through a story that has been carefully selected to deal with an issue usually related to how the children ought to think, speak, behave, or choose. The story provides an illustration for the main truth, the moral of the story, which the story serves to illustrate. For many, this kind of elementary use of story is its primary and most direct application. Frankly put, many believe that stories are for children, specifically for the children's Sunday School, children's sermon, or the vacation Bible school. At the heart of this belief is the notion that story is a more elementary and simple form of religious truth, and that doctrine is the deeper, clearer, and more adult approach to the Scriptures. This view is being challenged more and more in many Christian quarters. Story and narrative theologians today argue that stories are the most foundational and important vehicle for communicating the truth of God, as shown in our Lord's use of parable, metaphor, and symbol in his teaching. Whose view is more correct in your opinion, those believing that stories are essentially for the children's sermon, or those who believe that stories are the most foundational and important element in God's written Word?

Three Points, a Poem, and a Prayer?

One of the key homiletical strategies being taught in seminaries everywhere is the "rule of three," three points, three concepts, three exhortations to help structure our preaching and teaching presentations. This method is not intended to be applied woodenly and unthinkingly, yet it does tend to reduce presentation down to sharing a few clear points, using a Scripture reference for each, and illustrating each point with an object lesson or example from experience. Few would embrace the idea that essentially all preaching and teaching should be a mastery of the art of storytelling, whether the Story of God in Scripture which comes to its climax in the story of Jesus of Nazareth, or sharing the stories of those whom we know and those which we live each day. If you were in a position to instruct a new generation of modern preachers and teachers in a communication strategy that you believed would be effective in the city, what would yours be? Would you be more focused on presenters learning to study, preach, and communicate stories, or would you place more emphasis on the traditional forms of homiletics and teaching: "three points, a poem, and a prayer?"

Bitten by the "Prophecy Bug"

Many Christians today are ignorant of the genre of prophecy. One of the most ignored segments of the Word of God, many preachers and teachers today avoid the use of the prophetic Scriptures. They do not teach it systematically in their sermons, they ignore it in their Sunday School units, and avoid using it in sharing the Good News in evangelism. The province of prophetic literature, often times becomes the domain of fringe teachers who, armed with the newspaper in one hand and the prophetic Scriptures in the other, make predictions about the latest events in the world backing them up with references to the prophetic Word. Because of these tendencies, many believers grow up spiritually without a healthy exposure and meditation upon the prophetic Scriptures. What kinds of changes in attitude, style, and schedule must we make in order to truly embrace and rightly divide the prophetic Scriptures in our churches? Why might a new and fresh interpretation of the word of prophecy prove an important and powerful discovery within the spiritual walks of urban churches?

Restatement of the Lesson's Thesis

The term "genre" (pronounced JOHN-ruh) refers to that particular kind of literary form which communicates truth and must be interpreted according to the rules of that form. Genre study begins certain assumptions about the Bible as literature, ordered and governed by rules and principles like other works of literature, rules that God employed to communicate his Word to us.

There are many significant forms and types of literature in the Scriptures. These include the use of narrative (both historical and imaginative), the occurrence of the Law (legal writings), epistles (letters), prophecy (including apocalyptic literature), the wisdom literature of Scripture (including proverbs, monologues, riddles, fables, parables, allegories, etc.), and the presence of poetic works. Genres address particular needs of respective audiences, deepens our view of our fundamental human experience, images forth reality, reveals the artistry of the biblical authors, and reveals the richness of the mystery of God and his work in the world.

Special hermeneutics refers to those specific rules and procedures that enable us to interpret the literary forms of the Bible. Narrative, Scripture's most common genre, deals with subject matter that is either historical or imaginative. Story theologians highlight story as God's primary way of revealing his person and work in Scripture, and contend that all theology is reflection on the stories of the Bible, which historically are reliable and accurate, and show the artistry and skill of the authors, and meaning of the Lord in his own commentary on them. Narrative theology affirms that stories introduce us to sacramental presences, are more important than facts, and are normative for the Christian community. Christian traditions evolve and define themselves by stories, which also precede and produce community, produce censure and accountability, and theology, ritual, and sacrament in the Church. Like other literature, the general elements of narrative in Scripture include the setting, characters, author's point of view, plot, and theme of the stories. Prophecy the next major genre of Scripture, is a literary type dealing with God and his relationship to his people, the nations, and creation. Apocalyptic is a sub-genre of prophecy, and includes the two main types of Jewish apocalypses, the OT book of Daniel, and the most distinctly apocalyptic book in Scripture, the book of Revelation. Three broad principles can help us rightly interpret prophetic and apocalyptic genres: focus on the person of Jesus Christ, refer the prophetic messages to the call of the Kingdom of God, and seek to emphasize the fulfillment of God's sovereign purposes even in the face of evil, suffering and injustice.

Resources and Bibliographies

If you are interested in pursuing some of the ideas of *Biblical Literature: Interpreting the Genres of the Bible*, you might want to give these books a try:

Adler, Mortimer, and Charles Van Doren. *How to Read a Book*. New York: Simon and Schuster, 1972.

Ryken, Leland. *Words of Delight: A Literary Introduction to the Bible*. 2nd ed. Grand Rapids: Baker Book House, 1992.

------. *How to Read the Bible as Literature*. Grand Rapids: Zondervan, 1984.

Ministry Connections

Opening yourself to the Bible as literature can do wonders on every facet of your preaching, teaching, and communication of the Word of God. Not only will you begin to see things that typically you would have missed in your study, but the imagery of the world of Scripture will awaken your imagination in such a way as to rediscover the "native tongue" of the Bible. Rather than merely focusing on ideas, concept, and propositions, you will begin to live in the world of imagination, storytelling, and faith, and this will enable you to "stretch your wings" in the way in which you share Christ in the various dimensions of your ministry, at home, on the job, and through your church. Be open to ways in which the Holy Spirit might want you to incorporate these approaches in every dimension of our witness and ministry, and spend good time this week meditating on the power of the imagination and story in your life and work. As you consider your ministry project for this module, you can possibly use it to connect to these truths in a practical way.

Counseling and Prayer

Seek the face of the Lord regarding your own understanding and application of the principles related to genres in biblical interpretation, and do not hesitate to find a partner in prayer who can share the burden and lift up your requests to God. Ask your instructor for counsel and direction as you pursue the lessons and insights gained from this session in your own life and study. Above all, be open to the Lord

3

to lead you in new directions, and ask your colleagues to pray for you as he leads you in new directions in your own study and application of the Word of God.

ASSIGNMENTS

2 Timothy 3.14-17

Scripture Memory

To prepare for class, please visit *www.tumi.org/books* to find next week's reading assignment, or ask your mentor.

Reading Assignment

As usual you ought to come with your reading assignment sheet containing your summary of the reading material for the week. Also, you must have selected the text for your exegetical project, and turn in your proposal for your ministry project.

Other Assignments

In this lesson we explored the nature of genre study in biblical interpretation. We saw how such study recognizes the diverse materials making up the literature of the Bible, and argued that these forms must be interpreted according to the rules of literature itself. Genre study begins with certain assumptions about the Bible as literature, ordered and governed by rules and principles like other works of literature, rules that God employed to communicate his Word to us. We looked in particular at both narrative and prophecy, and saw how careful attention to certain rules can deepen our view of our fundamental human experience, and reveal the richness of the mystery of God and his work in the world.

Looking Forward to the Next Lesson

In our next lesson, we will conclude this module with a focus upon the role of scholarly tools and resources as we attempt to understand the meaning of the text. Many remarkable written and digital tools exist to enhance the learning of the aspiring student of the Word of God, and in our next lesson we will discuss the availability, purpose, and benefits of these tools in effective biblical interpretation.

For each assigned reading, write a brief summary (one or two paragraphs) of the author's main point. (For additional readings, use the back of this sheet.)

Reading 1

Title and Author: _____ Pages _____

Reading 2

Title and Author: _____ Pages _____

Biblical Studies
Using Study Tools in Bible Study

Lesson Objectives

Welcome in the strong name of Jesus Christ! After your reading, study, discussion, and application of the materials in this lesson, you will be able to:

- Identify and understand the role of scholarly tools in our attempt to understand the meaning of the text.

- Recite the purpose of using tools in biblical interpretation, including their ability to help us bridge the various gaps between the biblical world and our own contemporary world, to take advantage of the explosion of remarkable tools that have emerged in our day, and their value in helping us be more faithful to the Word of God by enabling us to reconstruct their meaning in its original context.

- Recognize and explain what are considered the basic and elemental tools to all biblical interpretation including a good translation of the Bible, Greek and Hebrew lexicons keyed to the Strong's numbering system, a solid Bible dictionary, a concordance, and credible exegetical commentaries which focus on the biblical meanings of the passage.

- Recognize and explain those tools which can provide additional insight into the meaning of biblical texts, including several different translations of the Bible, a Bible atlas and handbook, a topical Bible, a dictionary of theology, and finally theological commentaries which focus on the larger theological context of the passage.

- Explain the three languages in which the Bible was written (Hebrew, Aramaic, and Greek), and identify the particular challenges associated with making good translations, including the difficulties of word usage, cultural distinctions, contextual considerations, and differences among the translators themselves.

- Explain the meaning of concordances, lexicons, dictionaries, and commentaries, and show how to use the particular tools in the context of biblical interpretation, as well as offer a suggestion for each that could enhance our exegesis of Scripture.

4

- Define the role of cross-reference aids in biblical exegesis (e.g., topical bibles, cross-reference bibles, and topical guides and concordances), define their benefits for study, and lay out some of the major cautions we should be aware of when we use such tools.

- Lay out the reasons for employing Bible dictionaries, encyclopedias, atlases, and handbooks dealing with customs and history, identifying the benefits of such tools, as well as the caution of what wrong use or over-reliance on them can produce in our own interpretation.

- Cite the definition, benefits, and cautions associated with the use of Bible handbooks, study Bibles, and guides to biblical imagery, demonstrating their usefulness and our caution in employing them in our study.

- Outline the major kinds of commentaries that exist as aids to our interpretation (i.e., devotional, doctrinal, exegetical, and homiletic), and carefully articulate the major benefits and cautions associated with their use.

- Summarize the "best use" protocol for using extra-biblical tools in our biblical interpretation, including our attempt to help us bridge the gap between the two worlds of the text and our contemporary world.

- Articulate the limits of the tools, i.e., how in the final analysis, all claims are to be rigorously tested against the claims of the Scriptures themselves, and nothing is to be accepted that is found to contradict the plain confession of the Scriptures about the person of Christ and his work of redemption.

4

The Spirit Most Noble

Devotion

Acts 17.10-12 - The brothers immediately sent Paul and Silas away by night to Berea, and when they arrived they went into the Jewish synagogue. [11] Now these Jews were more noble than those in Thessalonica; they received the word with all eagerness, examining the Scriptures daily to see if these things were so. [12] Many of them therefore believed, with not a few Greek women of high standing as well as men.

In our quest to understand the purpose and plan of God through our interpretation of the Scriptures, it is easy to get lost on side issues and less important trails, to major on minors and to miss the heart and soul of what God seeks to communicate to us. What is the most important thing in our study of the Word of God? Are we to seek to impress others with the breadth of knowledge we have attained from all the hours we have poured over the Scriptures? Do we like to correct others in their wrong interpretation because they do not understand the meaning of the original languages, or their making of a historical or grammatical blunder which we are only too happy to bring to their attention? Do we enjoy having the reputation of being a person of profound knowledge and insight, someone that others deeply respect and seek to consult because of our vast knowledge of the Word? Do we want others to swoon over the depth and genius of our teaching, and the way in which we stun audiences by our remarkable insight into the deeper things of God?

This kind of warped desire is ever present in our study of the Word of God, and it is wonderful that the Scriptures themselves give to us a clue of the proper kind of attitude and approach we need when it comes to technical competence in our knowledge of the Word of God. Rather than seeking to impress others or outdo them in our knowledge and study of the text, we must above all else be oriented to the Bible itself. In other words, in regard to all questions about the claims of Christ and his Kingdom, we must respectfully submit to the discipline of going to the Bible itself for our answers. We must play no favorites, create no false or phony factions, not follow in the wake of cult personalities, or be impressed with the outward show of others. In all matters spiritual, we must seek answers from a firsthand investigation of the Scriptures themselves.

This kind of orientation is seen vividly in the example of the Bereans who heard the preaching and teaching of Paul and Silas after they had a fruitful ministry in Thessalonica as recorded in Acts 17.1-9. After a fairly open response from many devout Greeks and a few leading women in Thessalonica, Paul and Silas were hunted down by members of the Jewish faction of that city that rejected their teaching. When Paul and Silas could not be found, the crowd took its frustration out on Jason and others of Paul's companions, accusing them of turning the world upside down and continuing their ministry of disruption there (17.6ff.). Our text speaks of the open reception the proclamation of the Word concerning Jesus had in Berea, and Luke, speaking under the influence of the Holy Spirit, suggests that the Bereans had a more noble spirit than those in Thessalonica. What precisely was the character of this Berean nobility?

It is plainly indicated in the text, in Acts 17.11. "Now these Jews were more noble than those in Thessalonica; they received the word with all eagerness, examining the Scriptures daily to see if these things were so." The Bereans were eager students of the Word concerning Jesus and the Kingdom of God. They received the Word of God with all eagerness, with full hunger and interest and receptivity, and rather

4

than merely taking the word of Paul and Silas about the Scriptures and Jesus at face value they engaged in their own rigorous study of the Scriptures daily for the purpose of "to see if these things were so." Rather than evaluating their verifying orientation as either doubt-filled or disobedient, God saw their spirit as noble, eager, hungry, and praiseworthy. What is plain here is that no authority, not even apostles, are to be consulted and believed unless verified by the testimony of the Scriptures themselves.

How does this relate to our task of biblical interpretation? Thankfully, many thousands of excellent biblical scholars have spent entire lifetimes researching virtually every dimension of the Word of God, from the original languages in which it was written to volumes on virtually every kind of subject matter covered within it. These come in all forms, written, digital, online, audio, video—the entire technological circle. While we must thank God for the immeasurable value of such works and aids, we, like the Bereans, must never allow others to do our verifying of the Scriptures for us. Furthermore, it is never wrong to verify the claims and teaching of any spiritual authority, especially if the purpose is to see if the things in which they are teaching actually match up with the direct teaching of the Bible itself. In God's mind, this verifying work is noble, the most noble spirit of all.

While you work diligently to understand the broad range of excellent tools for Bible study that are available to us, make certain that you reserve the right to check, double-check, and triple-check all claims made about the Scriptures against the direct teaching of the Scriptures themselves. This is noble and praiseworthy, and will always find the approval and blessing of the Lord. Verifying the word of an apostle with a daily study of Scripture is dubbed "noble" by the Lord. Let's live out that nobility as often as we can, all for the sake of verifying the truth that sets us free in the Word of the Lord (John 8.31-32).

Nicene Creed and Prayer

After reciting and/or singing the Nicene Creed (located in the Appendix), pray the following prayer:

O God, by your Spirit tell us what we need to hear, and show us what we ought to do, to obey Jesus Christ our Savior.

~ Presbyterian Church (U.S.A.) and Cumberland Presbyterian Church. The Theology and Worship Ministry Unit. **Book of Common Worship**. Louisville: Westminister/John Knox Press, 1993. p. 60.

Quiz

Put away your notes, gather up your thoughts and reflections, and take the quiz for Lesson 3, *Biblical Literature: Interpreting the Genres of the Bible.*

Scripture Memorization Review

Review with a partner, write out and/or recite the text for last class session's assigned memory verse: 2 Timothy 3.14-17.

Assignments Due

Turn in your summary of the reading assignment for last week, that is, your brief response and explanation of the main points that the authors were seeking to make in the assigned reading (Reading Completion Sheet).

Tools Suitable for the Hungry Heart

Those who hold to a simplistic view of the Bible (i.e., tend to ignore the Bible's identity as literature, and therefore subject to the rules and norms of literature) find focus on genre study and the use of scholarly tools too cumbersome and on the brink of being elitist, being only for a few people who can understand all the literary rules and can afford all the scholarly tools. They rightly are concerned about the Bible being pushed away from the ordinary person who simply loves and believes in the Lord Jesus as his disciple, and who seeks to read the Word of God with the intent to believe and obey it. They are not Greek scholars, and will never understand all the principles and rules of the Bible as literature. They do not have access to the latest lexicons or Bible dictionaries. They have relied on their own humility and openness to the Holy Spirit to help them understand the Word of God, and have submitted joyfully to the leadership of their church pastor as he has ministered the Word in their midst. Isn't this kind of open, humble, devout use of the Scriptures sufficient for the Christian leader as well? Doesn't a focus on tools and resources make our interpretation of the Bible dependent on our access to tools that are too expensive and impossible for millions to obtain and/or understand? What then might be the usefulness of scholarly tools in biblical interpretation, and how do we go about using them in the right way?

Individual Use of Tools vs. Official Teaching Gifts in the Church

While scholarship and scholarly tools can greatly enhance our ability to understand many difficult and hard sayings of the text, we must ask whether or not tools are as significant as the living gifts of the Spirit in the midst of the Church to discover the meaning of the Word of God. For many Protestant Christians today, the Bible is a private book, a book of their own individual study and devotional appropriation. Oftentimes Christians will conceive of the Bible as a Word severed from the gifts and the Church. They do not rely heavily on the gifted men and women in their own churches, but select tools, resources, and references that essentially teach what they already believe. It is also common to identify those teachers in the public sphere that focus on the kinds of subjects and interpretations that we believe in, and we become experts on what "X" or "Y" says about salvation, redemption, healing, or whatever subject is "hot" at the time. Some who are more oriented around interpretations provided by official church authority even suggest that the use of tools independent from the pastoral authority of the church can actually fuel division, schism, and even heresy. They argue that if every single Christian is his own authority for interpretation, how can we ever truly make sense of what Christian belief really is? What do you make of the use of tools versus the recognition of official gifted teachers of a church or community? What is most helpful—our own individual study or our place in a local congregation?

Modern Translations Polluted

Even in our day of the accessibility of many reliable translations based on the best manuscripts we have available, a significant number of Christians still have a deep distrust in many of the latest translations. Seeing the kinds of social issues that influence the translators, these individuals and groups believe that the Word of God has actually been tampered with by these newer translations. It is their belief that an over concern on issues of gender equality, cultural sensitivity, and a host of modern ethical controversies have actually polluted the translations, forcing the translators to subtlety change the meaning of the text to fit the sensibility of the day. While many of these accusations are overstated, it does seem that these claims do accurately capture what many seem to suggest about these translations. Do you feel that too much attention has been given to issues of political correctness in many of the modern translations, or are they simply updating the Word of God in a way that postmodern readers can understand it?

CONTENT

Biblical Studies: Using Study Tools in Bible Study

Segment 1: The Basic Tools

Rev. Dr. Don L. Davis

Summary of Segment 1

Thanks to the works of hundreds of dedicated scholars who cherish and love the Scriptures, we have access to a remarkable array of scholarly tools which can enable us to understand the meaning of the biblical text. The essential purpose of our use of scholarly tools is to help us bridge the various gaps between the biblical world and our own contemporary world. This bridging helps the diligent biblical interpreter to be more faithful to the Word of God by enabling him or her to reconstruct the meaning in its original context. The basic tools of biblical interpretation include a good translation of the Bible, Greek and Hebrew lexicons keyed to the Strong's numbering system, a solid Bible dictionary, a concordance, and credible exegetical commentaries which focus on the biblical meanings of the passage. Used in their proper place and times, these tools can prove invaluable in bridging the gap between the biblical world and our understanding of that world.

Our objective for this segment, *The Basic Tools*, is to enable you to see that:

- As a result of hundreds of dedicated biblical scholars and new technologies, we now have access to a vast array of solid scholarly tools which can greatly enhance our ability to understand, apply, and teach others on the meaning of biblical texts.

- Three purposes of using scholarly tools in biblical interpretation are their ability to help us bridge the various gaps between the biblical world and our own contemporary world, their ability to expose us to the vast explosion of remarkable tools that have emerged in our day, and their value in helping us be more faithful to the Word of God by enabling us to reconstruct their meaning in its original context.

4

- The key to understanding the various tools for biblical interpretation is recognizing how and in what way a particular tool helps us to overcome the gaps between our culture and that of the biblical authors and their audiences.

- The basic tools of biblical interpretation include a good translation of the Bible, Greek and Hebrew lexicons keyed to the Strong's numbering system, a solid Bible dictionary, a concordance, and credible exegetical commentaries which focus on the biblical meanings of the passage.

- The Bible was written in three languages (Hebrew, Aramaic, and Greek), and therefore we need a good translation of the Scriptures in our own native tongue. Because of differences in language, word meaning and grammar, cultural distinctions and historical distance, and differing approaches and philosophies among translators, translations differ greatly.

- Most of our modern translations are based on strong manuscript evidence and data, and are well-documented, well-researched, and reliable for the biblical student.

- Among the basic tools, concordances list all the words of the Bible and where they are found in alphabetical order, and lexicons give the definitions (usages) of words as given in a particular verse of Scripture. Expository dictionaries add comments to explain the relationship between word meanings and biblical doctrines.

- Bible dictionaries list historical, geographical, cultural, scientific, and theological information about people, places, animals, events, and physical objects found in the Bible, as well as summaries on each book of the Bible.

- Exegetical commentaries share expert opinion on the actual meaning of the words in the original text, including issues of grammar, word meanings, and the findings of biblical criticism. They also include information on historical facts and cultural insights from the biblical world which may influence the interpretation of a text.

- Regardless of the tool, we ought to use the references liberally, yet always mindful that their right use will *make plain* the meaning of the text, and not *deny* or *downplay* its significance.

Video Segment 1
Outline

**Always the Need
for Interpretation**

*An acceptance of the
claims of Scripture
concerning its own
truthfulness does not
guarantee true
interpretations.
Human interpreters
can make, and have
made, mistakes. Thus
the meaning of
Scripture has been
disputed in many
important and less
important areas.
~ E. J. Schnabel.
"Scripture." New
Dictionary of Biblical
Theology*. T. D.
Alexander, ed.
(electronic ed.).
InterVarsity Press:
Downers Grove, IL:
InterVarsity Press, 2001.

I.   The Importance of Tools in Biblical Interpretation

A. Their *purpose*: to help *bridge the gap* between the biblical world and our contemporary world

1. The *Three-Step Model* is rooted in connecting the ancient world and our contemporary world.

2. In order for the model to work correctly, we must strive to understand the meaning of the biblical authors in their original context.

3. Tools in biblical interpretation are invaluable in connecting us with the idioms, cultures, languages, and historical events connected with the biblical world (i.e., "You Are There").

B. Their *occasion*: an explosion of biblical resources has occurred since the 1950s.

C. Their *benefit: fidelity to the message of the Word of God on its own terms*

1. Understanding of the original context

2. Better able to identify and discover the meanings of the text as *the original audience would have understood the message*

3. Less susceptible to make historical, grammatical, and cultural blunders as we seek to interpret the Word of God for our own lives

4

The Bible's Central Message

The Bible's central message is the story of salvation, and throughout both Testaments three strands in this unfolding story can be distinguished: the bringer of salvation, the way of salvation and the heirs of salvation. This could be reworded in terms of the covenant idea by saying that the central message of the Bible is God's covenant with men, and that the strands are the mediator of the covenant, the basis of the covenant and the covenant people. God himself is the Savior of his people; it is he who confirms his covenant mercy with them. The bringer of salvation, the Mediator of the covenant, is Jesus Christ, the Son of God. The way of salvation, the basis of the covenant, is God's grace, calling forth from his people a response of faith and obedience. The heirs of salvation, the covenant people, are the Israel of God, the Church of God.

~ F. F. Bruce. "Bible." **New Bible Dictionary**. D. R. W. Wood, ed. (3rd ed). (electronic ed.). Downers Grove, IL: InterVarsity Press, 1996, pp. 137-138.

II. The Tools in Biblical Interpretation

A. The *Basic Tools*

1. A good translation of the Bible in your own tongue

2. Greek and Hebrew lexicons keyed to Strong's numbering system

3. A Bible dictionary

4. A concordance with Strong's numbering system

5. Exegetical commentaries

B. The *Additional Tools*

1. Several different English translations of the Bible

2. Bible atlas

3. Bible handbook

4. Topical Bible

5. Dictionary of theology

6. Theological commentaries

III. Using the *Basic Tools*: Obtain a Good Translation of the Bible

The key to understanding various tools for biblical interpretation is our desire as Bible students to overcome the gap between our culture and that of the biblical authors and audiences. The first and most important step of biblical interpretation is bridging the distance between these two worlds and peoples.

A "translation," by definition, is the first step to bridging the various gaps between the biblical world and our own. A translation of the Bible is one that has been translated directly from the Hebrew and Greek manuscripts. (This is different from a "paraphrase" which is a rewording of an existing translation in order to make it more understandable to a particular modern audience).

4

A. The Bible was written in three languages.

1. Hebrew (the Old Testament)

   a. An *ancient* language (The roots of the language have been traced back to 2400 BC or about 4,400 years ago.)

      (1) From our perspective it reads "backwards" (from right to left).

      (2) Has its own, different alphabet

   b. Concrete and pictorial (uses images to stand for concepts such as "horn" for strength)

   c. An *economical* language

      (1) One root word may stand for many different meanings and applications.

      (2) In Hebrew, Psalm 23 is only 55 words while the KJV in English uses 119 words.

2. Aramaic

   a. Has the longest continuous usage of any language known. It was spoken during the time of Abraham and is still spoken by a few groups today.

   b. A secondary Old Testament language; used in Genesis 31.47; Ezra 4.8-6.18, 7.12-26; Jer. 10.11; Dan. 2.4b-7.28

c. It was commonly spoken by Jews in Jesus' day and was quite possibly the language spoken by Jesus in common speech. It was preferred by Jews because it had Semitic roots (it resembled Hebrew) but was commonly understood by many others. In Jesus' day, it was common to read the Scriptures in the Synagogue in Hebrew and then read them in Aramaic so that non-Hebrew speakers could understand. Beginning around 200 B.C. portions of the Hebrew Scriptures began being written down in Aramaic in individual portions called "Targums."

3. Greek

a. Koine dialect - ("street Greek") different from the classical grammar kind of Greek, is simpler and more accessible

b. Simple, popular speech, the common language of commerce and government in the widespread Roman empire

c. Septuagint - a translation of the Old Testament Scriptures into Greek by 70 Jewish scholars. (It is often referred to by the abbreviation LXX which is the Roman number for 70.)

B. The challenge of language translation: why is translation difficult to do?

1. Overcoming the differences in word meaning, use, and grammar

a. Translation is about the receiving culture; but what if the receiving culture has fewer or different options than those listed in the Scriptures?

4

What about translating the Bible into a language that only has five colors. How do you translate the word "purple," as when the soldiers put a purple robe on Jesus? More importantly, how does the translation keep the original meaning, since all NT readers understood that the color purple stood for royalty and that the soldiers were making fun of Jesus' claim to kingship? What if some other color stands for royalty? What if purple stands for merchants? Is it okay for a translator to substitute that word, even though its not the word that the Scriptures used?

b. *Cases not conjunctions*: Greek does not have the common English word "of."

c. *Multiple words for a singular concept*: English only has one word for love, Greek has several.

d. *Different gender for words with meanings for them*: many languages have masculine, feminine and neuter forms, English does not.

2. Linguistic and cultural distinctions make translation necessary.

a. *Farming, ancient symbolism*: some cultures have never seen sheep but they do keep pigs in much the same way as the Hebrews kept sheep. Is it okay to use an animal from their culture when translating?

b. *The absence of concepts in some cultures.* In some cultures, it is believed that only people who are lying mention that they are not lying. How would you then translate Paul's statement in Romans 9.1 - "I speak the truth—I am not lying, my conscience confirms it in the Holy Spirit."

C. Translation challenges: being faithful both to the message of Scripture *and* to the language and cultural norms of the receiving culture

1. Translators select different approaches in their translation philosophies.

    a. *Literal Translation* - exact words (as literal as possible), as close as possible to the original grammatical structure

    b. *Dynamic Equivalence* - exact meaning using whatever words can be found to carry that meaning

2. *The Translators themselves* are very different from one another (i.e., they hold different beliefs about the reliability of Scripture).

    a. The editors of the Dartmouth Bible felt free to edit the Scriptures, only preserving what they saw as non-repetitive and most necessary.

    b. The Jehovah's Witnesses have published their own version of the Bible because parts of it seems to disagree with their doctrine. Therefore, they have changed those parts.

    c. The Jerusalem Bible is a very fine Catholic translation but the notes that accompany the Bible interpret the text from a traditional Catholic perspective.

3. Translators *work alone or on a committee* (i.e., groups of scholars tend to have more total skills and must be more balanced in order for everyone's viewpoint to be heard).

4

4. Translators *use different types of language* and styles in their translations.

a. They use different *dialects*.

(1) *British* - KJV, Jerusalem Bible, J.B. Phillips

(2) *American* - RSV, NASB

(3) *Combination* - NIV

b. They use different *styles of language*.

(1) *Formal* styles: KJV, NKJV, RSV

(2) *Moderately formal* styles: NIV, NRSV, TEV

(3) *Informal* styles: Phillips, LB, CEV

c. Special cases also exist.

(1) *Paraphrases*. Paraphrases are versions of the Bible that have not been translated from the original languages. Instead an existing translation has been reworded in an attempt to make it clearer or more accessible.

(2) *Amplified Version*. The Amplified Version gives all possible meanings for key words used in the text.

(3) *Jewish translation*. In the 20th century some very important Jewish translations of the Bible have been published. *The Holy Scriptures according to the Masoretic Text: A New Translation*, and *The Complete Jewish Bible*.

D. Choosing a good translation

1. *Solid foundation of scholarship for modern translations*. The many discoveries of ancient manuscripts in our times have confirmed how

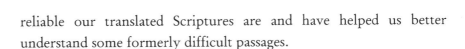

reliable our translated Scriptures are and have helped us better understand some formerly difficult passages.

a. The Dead Sea Scrolls discovered in the 1940's and 50's give us an OT text dating back to before AD 70. That is about 1000 years older than any texts we had before that time.

b. In 1898, 35 new manuscripts of the NT were found in Egypt. In the 20th century, nearly 100 manuscripts with portions of the NT have been discovered.

2. Superb scholarly foundations undergird the work of our modern translations.

3. Many translations today are well-documented, well-researched, and reliable.

4. Choose a translation and become familiar with it. *Any of the following will serve as a reliable basic translation for Bible study.*

a. English Standard Version - ESV

b. New King James Version (or King James Version) - NKJV or KJV

c. New International Version - NIV

d. New Revised Standard Version (or Revised Standard Version) - NRSV or RSV

4

e.   New American Standard Bible - NASB

    f.   Revised English Bible (or New English Bible) - REB or NEB

5.   Know why you chose the translation and take that into account as you study.

6.   Compare translations as you read a verse of Scripture.

    a.   Know which readings are most common. If many versions translate in similar ways, that should be taken seriously.

    b.   Think about the implications of a different reading.

    c.   Explore differences using other study tools.

IV. A Concordance (with Strong's Numbering System)

A. Definition: a concordance is a book which lists all the words of the Bible and where they are found in alphabetical order.

1.   Use to trace a *particular word* (Hebrew or Greek) through a testament (Old or New)

2.   Find a particular verse with which you are unfamiliar by a word with which you are familiar.

3.   Gather verses on a particular topic for study or preaching.

B.   The use of a good concordance: comparing Scripture with Scripture

1.   Perhaps the most essential skill in all biblical interpretation: comparing Scripture with Scripture

2.   As you study a passage, a concordance allows you to quickly find other places in Scripture where the same words and ideas occur.

3.   By using the numbering system in a concordance, you can identify the exact Hebrew or Greek word that is used in a passage you are studying and study it further in a Hebrew or Greek lexicon or compare it with other parts of Scripture.

4.   We advocate the Strong's concordance and its numbering system (*Strong's Exhaustive Concordance of the Bible* [Word Publishing]).

V.   Greek and Hebrew Lexicons

A.   Definition of the tool: A lexicon gives the definitions of words. Many lexicons used for the study of the Bible also show which meaning is used in a particular verse of Scripture. Expository Dictionaries add comments to explain the relationship between word meanings and biblical doctrine.

B.   Use of the tool: A lexicon allows you to examine the full meaning of a Hebrew or Greek word and gain insight into the meaning of that word for a particular text.

4

C. Useful basic tools for Hebrew and Greek word usage

    1. Strong's Dictionaries of the Hebrew and Greek Bible

    2. *Vine's Expository Dictionary of Old and New Testament Words*

D. Treasury of tools using the Strong's numbering system

    1. Greek

        a. *Vine's Complete Expository Dictionary of Old and New Testament Words*, W. E. Vine, Merrill F. Unger, and William White, Jr. (Nashville: Thomas Nelson Publishers, 1996).

        b. *The Complete Word Study Dictionary — New Testament*, Spiros Zodhiates, Rev. ed. (Chattanooga: AMG Publishers, 1993).

        c. *Thayer's Greek-English Lexicon of the New Testament: Coded With the Numbering System from Strong's Exhaustive Concordance of the Bible*, Joseph Thayer. (Peabody, MA: Hendrickson 1997).

        d. *The New International Dictionary of New Testament Theology*, Colin Brown, ed. 4 Volumes. (Grand Rapids: Zondervan, 1971).

4

2. Hebrew

    a. *Vine's Complete Expository Dictionary of Old and New Testament Words*, W. E. Vine, Merrill F. Unger, and William White, Jr. (Nashville: Thomas Nelson Publishers, 1996).

    b. *The Brown-Driver-Briggs Hebrew and English Lexicon: With an Appendix Containing the Biblical Aramaic: Coded With the Numbering System from Strong's*, F. Brown, S. Driver and C. Briggs. (Peabody, MA: Hendrickson Publishers, 1996).

    c. *Theological Wordbook of the Old Testament*, R. Laird Harris, Gleason L. Archer, Jr. and Bruce K. Waltke, 2 Volumes. (Chicago: Moody Press, 1980).

    d. *New Wilson's Old Testament Word Studies*, William Wilson. (Grand Rapids: Kregel Publishing, 1987)

    e. *New International Dictionary of Old Testament Theology and Exegesis*, by Willem A. Vangemeren. (Grand Rapids: Zondervan, 1997) [Keyed to Goodrick/Kohlenberger as well as Strong].

VI. A Good Bible Dictionary

A. Definition of the tool

1. A Bible dictionary lists historical, geographical, cultural, scientific, and theological information about people, places, animals, events, and physical objects found in the Bible.

2. It also has a listing for each book of the Bible (such as Romans) which often outlines the book, gives information about the date, the author and the original audience and lists historical or cultural information that is important for understanding the author's message.

B. Use of the tool

1. *Introductory materials and info*: This is one possible starting point for finding out who wrote the book, when it was written, and what the concerns of the author and the original audience were.

2. Most "nouns" (persons, places, or things) that you come across while reading a Scripture verse can be looked up in the Bible dictionary to give you further insight into where they were, what they meant, or how they were used during biblical times.

C. Choice of a tool: *The New Bible Dictionary* (Eerdmans Publishing Co.)

VII. Exegetical Commentaries

A. Definition of the tool

1. An aid to Bible interpretation which gives insight into the meaning of the Scriptures by sharing expert opinion on grammar, word meanings, higher and lower critical issues

2. Exegetical commentaries also provide understanding of the ways in which historical facts and cultural insights from the biblical world might influence our understanding of a text.

B. Use of the tool

    1. Enables you as a biblical interpreter to read the language and grammar of the text more clearly

    2. Fosters a better discovery of historical events and cultural perspectives that may influence the way the original audience would have understood the text

C. Choice of the tool

    1. *The New Bible Commentary* (InterVarsity Press)

    2. *The Expositor's Bible Commentary* (Zondervan)

    3. *Tyndale Old Testament Commentaries* (InterVarsity Press)

    4. *Tyndale New Testament Commentaries* (InterVarsity Press)

    5. *The New International Commentary on the New Testament* (Eerdmans)

Conclusion

» The basic group of tools for biblical interpretation can help bridge the distance between our understanding of the ancient text and our own application of it today.

» With a relatively small investment, the student of Scripture can obtain and use these tools to learn the historical, cultural, linguistic, and social gaps that block our understanding of the text.

Please take as much time as you have available to answer these and other questions that the video brought out. Because of the dedicated work of scores of biblical scholars, we now have the ability to use a remarkable array of scholarly tools designed to give insight into the world of the biblical text. Our essential commitment to such scholarly tools is to bridge the gap between our world and the ancient biblical world, and thus to be better able to rightly interpret the Word in our reconstruction of the meaning in its original context. Make sure that you understand the role and usage of the basic tools and how they can enhance our study of the text as you review the following questions.

1. What is the current state of availability to the general public of scholarly biblical tools, and what kind of possibilities do such tools open up for those of us interested in bridging the gap between our knowledge of this world and the ancient world?

2. Explain the meaning of the statement: "the tools in biblical interpretation are designed to help us bridge the various gaps between the biblical world and our own contemporary world." Why is bridging the distance between these two worlds so central in rightly interpreting the Word of God and understanding its significance for us today?

3. Why is it so important to evaluate a tool according to how in particular it helps us identify a way in which we can overcome a particular gap in language, culture, or knowledge between our culture and that of the biblical authors and their audiences?

4. List out what were considered to be the "basic tools of biblical interpretation" in this segment. Of all of these basic tools, which do you believe is most essential and fundamental in all biblical interpretation? Explain.

5. In what ancient languages was the Bible written, and why therefore do we need a translation of these languages? What are some the reasons why it is so difficult to create a translation that will be sufficient for *all believers*? Explain.

6. How much confidence can we have in most of the modern translations of the Scriptures? How do we know that they are reliable translations of the original languages?

7. What is a concordance, a lexicon, and a expository dictionary, and how do they function in terms of enhancing our understanding of the biblical text? How ought they be used, and what cautions should we be aware of as we employ them?

8. What are exegetical commentaries, and how might they help in our efforts at interpreting the text of Scripture?

9. What particular principle must we keep in mind as we seek to liberally use the basic tools available to us? What must we always be careful of as we employ these tools in our Bible study?

Biblical Studies: Using Study Tools in Bible Study

Segment 2: Additional Theological Tools

Rev. Dr. Don L. Davis

Summary of Segment 2

In addition to the basic tools of biblical interpretation (i.e., a good translation of the Bible, Greek and Hebrew lexicons, Bible dictionary, concordance, and credible exegetical commentaries), there are additional tools which can enrich our understanding of the Word of God. These include several different translations of the Bible, a Bible atlas and handbook, a topical Bible, a dictionary of theology, and theological commentaries. Each of these tools focus on a particular challenge of biblical interpretation, from issues of language, culture, history, and theology. As with any tool, we must be careful to use them to enhance our knowledge of the text, neither denying nor downplaying the essential message of the Bible as it speaks to our salvation in the person of Jesus Christ.

Our objective for this segment, *Additional Theological Tools*, is to enable you to see that:

- In addition to the basic tools of biblical interpretation (i.e., a good translation of the Bible, Greek and Hebrew lexicons, Bible dictionary, concordance, and credible exegetical commentaries), there are more tools which can enrich our understanding of the Word of God.

- The additional tools we ought to learn how to use include several different translations of the Bible, a Bible atlas and handbook, a topical Bible, a dictionary of theology, and theological commentaries.

4

- Cross-reference aids focus on the relationship of various texts and passages which share a common topic or thematic center in biblical exegesis (e.g., topical Bibles, cross-reference Bibles, and topical guides and concordances). While these help us associate texts together on a given subject, we must be careful not to make contextual errors as we connect verses, and always be mindful that editors may make associations which are neither legitimate nor defensible.

- Certain tools provide background into the history, culture, social customs, peoples, and physical environment of the biblical world, and these include Bible dictionaries, Bible encyclopedias, Bible atlases and handbooks, and works dealing with biblical history and customs. These tools can provide an amazing amount of information on the world of the text, but must be carefully read to distinguish *historical data* with *interpretation on the validity of the text itself.*

- Other tools are especially useful to obtain background information on the author, date, and circumstances on the book, and certain uses of special language in interpretation and exegesis (symbol, metaphor, figurative language, etc.). These tools include Bible handbooks, study Bibles, and guides to biblical imagery. We ought to be careful in weighing the views contained in such resources as expressions of *the commentators own views* and not the text *itself.*

- Commentaries are aids to help interpret the meaning of a particular book of Scripture from the vantage point of a pastor, scholar, or biblical interpreter. There are four major kinds of commentaries as aids to our study: devotional, doctrinal, exegetical, and homiletical (i.e., aids specifically designed for preachers and teachers to deliver sermons and prepare Bible lessons). While commentaries can enhance greatly our knowledge of the text, they ought never be substituted for our own firsthand study of the text itself.

- We rightly use these basic and additional tools when we use them to help us bridge the gap between the two worlds: the world of the text and our contemporary world. No explanation or speculation from any interpreter should be accepted that denies or contradicts the testimony of the Scriptures themselves. Nothing in any tool is to be accepted that is found to contradict the plain confession of the Scriptures about the person of Christ and his work of redemption through the cross.

"Higher" and "Lower" Criticism of the Bible: What is the Difference?

[Higher criticism is] that portion of biblical studies that attempts to assess compositional features such as date of writing, authorship, destination, sources used in writing (oral, written, etc.), and general literary form (including comparison with contemporary non-biblical literary features and styles); done constructively and with a high view of the integrity of Scripture, this area of study can make important contributions; done without a high regard for Scripture it can be a destructive influence; hence, the term is sometimes used for rationalistic approaches to the Bible over the last hundred years that tended to treat it solely as a human work, not as an integrated revelation from God; [compare this to] lower criticism (= textual criticism), which deals with establishing the best text of Scripture to work with.

~ Paul Karleen. **The Handbook to Bible Study**. (electronic ed.). New York: Oxford University Press, 1987.

Video Segment 2 Outline

I. **Cross-reference Aids, Topical Bibles, Cross Reference Bibles, and Topical Concordances**

A. Cross-reference aids (helpful in the *Finding General Principles stage*)

1. Definition: *Cross-reference aids help us tap into the interconnections between texts of the Bible on the same or related themes by comparing Scripture with Scripture.*

2. Recommended cross-reference aids

a. *The New Treasury of Scriptural Knowledge*, Jerome H. Smith, ed. (Thomas Nelson 1997)

4

b. *Thompson Chain-Reference Bible*

     c. *Holman Topical Concordance*

     d. *The New Torrey's Topical Textbook*

3. Benefits: *help us associate texts together on a given subject, theme, or issue*

4. Cautions

     a. Can encourage a tendency to gloss over the text under discussion for the sake of finding new associations

     b. The editors may organize the associations in ways that are not entirely legitimate or defensible.

B. Topical Bibles

1. Definition: *a topical Bible lists a topic and then shows Scripture verses related to those topics underneath.*

2. Recommended topical Bibles and topical concordances

     a. *Baker Topical Guide to the Bible*, Walter A. Elwell, Gen. ed. (Baker, 2000).

     b. *Nave's Topical Bible*, Orville J. Nave. (Zondervan, 1999).

3. Benefits: *extraordinary time saver in hunting down relevant texts on a similar topic*

4. Cautions: *over-dependence on these can make one's analysis a little disjointed and itemized (the focus on parts and not on whole Bible themes and books)*

Analogy of Faith: Interpret the Scriptures by Scripture

Each book proceeded from the same divine mind, so the teaching of the Bible's sixty-six books will be complementary and self-consistent. If we cannot yet see this, the fault is in us, not in Scripture. It is certain that Scripture nowhere contradicts Scripture; rather, one passage explains another. This sound principle of interpreting Scripture by Scripture is sometimes called the analogy of Scripture or the analogy of faith.
~ J. I. Packer. *Concise Theology: A Guide to Historic Christian Beliefs*. (electronic ed.). Wheaton, IL: Tyndale House, 1995.

II. Bible Dictionaries, Bible Encyclopedias, Bible Atlases, and Bible History and Customs Reference Works

A. Bible dictionary, Bible encyclopedia

1. Definition: *to provide background on the history, culture, social customs, peoples, topography, and related matters of the biblical periods*

2. Fantastic aids to bridge the historical and cultural gap between our world and the ancient world

a. These tools are the single most important tools for shortening the distance between our world and the world of the Bible!

b. Numerous, excellent, and accessible volumes and software

3. Useful to identify information on critical biblical concepts

a. *People* (Abraham, Sennacherib, Ruth)

b. *Places* (Ur, Bethlehem, Goshen, Sea of Galilee, Assyria)

4

    c.   *Things* (Urim and Thummim, Tabernacle, Pillar, Denarius)

    d.   *Topics and Concepts* (Diseases, Canaanite Religions, Language of the Old Testament, Prayer, Perfection, Evil, Prayer, Praise)

4.   Bible dictionaries and encyclopedias also provide helpful background information on the specific books of the Bible (i.e. date, author, audience, purposes, etc.).

5.   Most Bible dictionaries try to be as comprehensive as possible concerning the first three categories.

6.   Benefits: *these tools unlock treasures of the Bible backgrounds of various interest and importance.*

7.   Caution: *over-reliance on the explanations contained within these tools can blunt one's rigorous wrestling with the text FIRST.*

8.   Recommended Bible dictionaries and encyclopedias

    a.   *New Bible Dictionary*, 3rd edition. I. H. Marshall & others, eds. (InterVarsity Press, 1996)

    b.   *Baker Encyclopedia of the Bible* (2 volumes), Walter A. Elwell, ed. (Baker 1988)

    c.   *International Standard Bible Encyclopedia* (4 volumes), Geoffrey W. Bromiley, Gen. ed., Revised edition. (Eerdmans, 1979)

B. Bible atlas

1. Definition: *use to establish the setting of biblical narratives and events, and find background information about places and regions*

2. Recommended Bible atlases

a. *The NIV Atlas of the Bible*, Carl G. Rasmussen. (Zondervan, 1989)

b. *The Macmillan Bible Atlas*, Revised 3rd edition Yohanan Aharoni, Michael Avi-Yonah, A. Rainey and Z. Safrai. (Macmillan, 1993)

C. Historical and socio-cultural reference works

1. Definition: *references which provide insight into the nature of particular social, cultural, and religious customs or historical events which can shed much light on the meaning of the text in its own context*

2. The usual brief invitation in America, and the ready acceptance of it would be considered in the East entirely undignified. In the East the one invited must not at first accept, but is expected rather to reject the invitation. He must be urged to accept (*Manners and Customs of Bible Lands*).

3. What might be the implications of understanding this in the following texts?

a. Luke 14.23 - And the master said to the servant, "Go out to the highways and hedges and compel people to come in, that my house may be filled."

b. Acts 16.15 - And after she was baptized, and her household as well, she urged us, saying, "If you have judged me to be faithful to the Lord, come to my house and stay." And she prevailed upon us.

4. Recommended reference works

a. *New Manners and Customs of Bible Times*, Fred Wight and Ralph Gower. (Moody, 1987)

b. *Life and Times of Jesus the Messiah*, Alfred Edersheim. (Hendrickson, 1997)

c. *Ancient Israel: Its Life and Institutions* (Biblical Resource Series), by Roland De Vaux, David Noel Freedman, ed. (Eerdmans, 1997)

D. Historical resources

1. *Cities of the Biblical World*, LaMoine F. DeVries. (Hendrickson, 1997)

2. For the Old Testament

a. *Israel and the Nations: The History of Israel from the Exodus to the Fall of the Second Temple*, David F. Payne and F. F. Bruce. (InterVarsity Press, 1998)

    b. *Old Testament Survey: The Message, Form, and Background of the Old Testament*, William Sanford La Sor; David Allan Hubbard, and Frederick William Bush. (Grand Rapids: William B. Eerdmans Publishing, 1985)

  3. New Testament

    a. *New Testament History*, F. F. Bruce. (Anchor, 1972)

    b. *Jerusalem in the Time of Jesus*, Joachim Jeremias. (Fortress, 1979)

III. Bible Handbooks, Study Bibles, and Guides to Biblical Imagery

A. Bible handbooks

  1. Definition: *Bible handbooks and study Bibles are useful for obtaining information about author, date, and circumstances in which book was written (Their World).*

  2. Example: *Halley's Bible Handbook* (Grand Rapids: Zondervan)

B. Study Bibles

  1. Definition: *study Bibles offer in-the-context commentary from a scholar or group of interpreters connected to a particular translation of the Scriptures.*

4

2. Convenience: commentary on critical texts are usually in the footnotes or appendices of the translation itself.

3. Caution: *the view contained within study Bibles express the commentator's own understanding of the text and theological commitments.*

4. Examples

   a. *Harper Study Bible, New American Standard Bible.* (Grand Rapids: Zondervan) (These can be obtained usually in various translations.)

   b. *Oxford Study Bible, Revised English Bible.* (New York: Oxford University Press)

C. Guides to biblical imagery

1. Definition: *these tools help the biblical interpreter determine how the Bible develops certain images, symbols, and motifs, usually in both Old and New Testaments,* with an eye toward literary convention and spiritual application.

2. These tools are invaluable in understanding the message of the Bible in the form and idiom of the biblical authors (i.e., the world of the ancient east is a world filled with imagery, symbol, metaphor, and storytelling).

3. Recommended guides to biblical imagery

   a. *Dictionary of Biblical Imagery,* Leland Ryken and others. (InterVarsity Press, 1998)

b. *A Dictionary of Bible Types*, Walter L. Wilson. (Hendrickson, 1999)

IV. Commentaries

A. Purpose: *Commentaries are aids to interpretation which give us the testimony, findings, and insights of a particular book of Scripture from the vantage point of a pastor, scholar, or biblical interpreter.*

1. Aids to interpretation: *commentaries are not a substitute for interpretation.*

2. Gives us testimony, findings, and insights of a particular book of Scripture: *commentary is analysis of the text based on the commentator's knowledge and experience.*

3. From the vantage point of a pastor, scholar, or biblical interpreter: *commentaries are collections of informed opinions.*

B. Types of commentaries

1. Single volume versus multi-volume sets: *The New Bible Commentary is a superb single volume commentary.*

2. Devotional commentaries

a. Purpose: *to provide daily help for one's reading of Scripture and walk with God*

4

    b.   William Barclay, *Daily Study Bible Series* (devotional not a scholarly commentary)

3.   Doctrinal (theological) commentaries

    a.   Purpose: *provide interpretation on the major teachings of the books of Scripture, with a view toward a systematic treatment of theology*

    b.   Calvin's *Commentaries*

    c.   Denominations and groups may commission scholars from within their tradition to provide an authoritative read of Scripture with their positions in view (*Broadman's Bible Commentary*–Southern Baptist connection).

4.   Exegetical commentaries

    a.   Purpose: *commentaries designed to give helpful information on the language, history, culture, and grammar of the text for the purpose of good exegesis*

    b.   *The Tyndale Old Testament Commentaries, The Tyndale New Testament Commentaries, The New International Commentary of the New Testament*

    c.   Scholarly, rigorous, difficult for those beginning in the Scriptures

4

5. Homiletic (pulpit) commentaries

    a. Purpose: *to give the busy preacher or teacher the resources to prepare and deliver sermons and/or Bible lessons based on the texts of Scripture*

    b. Lawrence O. Richards, *The Teacher's Commentary, Matthew Henry's Commentaries.*

C. Use of commentaries

  1. Cautions

    a. Commentaries should never be substituted for study of the text. *Never begin your study with reference to commentaries.*

    b. Understand that all commentaries are operating from a vantage point, according to a *particular perspective.*

    c. Use the exegetical commentaries as the first type when engaged in your own study.

    d. Never take any commentary's assessment as truth without seeking to verify for yourself its claims directly from the text, and the larger teaching of Scripture.

4

2. Use

    a.   Learn who the person/people are who sponsored and/or wrote the commentary you are referencing.

    b.   Postpone use of the commentary until after you have done your study, and drawn your own principles (the *second stage*).

    c.   Use the commentaries to check and double-check your ideas as you shape your ideas and opinions.

    d.   Allow the ideas of the commentator to point you in new directions for further study.

V. Final Word about Tools

Remember that the Bible is Inspired of God:
Use the Tools Appropriately

According to 2 Tim. 3.16, what is inspired is precisely the biblical writings. Inspiration is a work of God terminating, not in the men who were to write Scripture (as if, having given them an idea of what to say, God left them to themselves to find a way of saying it), but in the actual written product. It is **Scripture—graphe**, *the* **written** *text—that is God-breathed. The essential idea here is that all Scripture has the same character as the prophets' sermons had, both when preached and when written (cf. 2 Pet. 1.19–21, on the divine origin of every 'prophecy of the Scriptures'; see also Jer. 36; Isa. 8.16–20). That is to say, Scripture is not only man's word, the fruit of human thought, premeditation and art, but also, and equally, God's word, spoken through man's lips or written with man's pen. In other words, Scripture has a double authorship, and man is only the secondary author; the primary author, through whose initiative, prompting and enlightenment, and under whose superintendence, each human writer did his work, is God the Holy Spirit.*

~ J. I. Packer. "Inspiration." **New Bible Dictionary**. D. R. W. Wood, ed. (3rd ed). (electronic ed.). Downers Grove, IL: InterVarsity Press, 1996. p. 507.

A. Use tools to help you bridge the gap between the two worlds: *the world of the text and the world in which you live and work.*

B. Substitute no word of man for the undying Word of the Living God.

    1. In the end, let all speculation against the Lord be rejected.

        a. Rom. 3.4

        b. Deut. 32.4

        c. Ps. 100.5

        d. Ps. 119.160

        e. Ps. 138.2

        f. Titus 1.2

    2. *Accept nothing against the testimony of Scripture*: no matter how scholarly, expert, or experienced the commentator. If they disagree with the teachings of Scripture, they are wrong!

        a. Acts 17.11

        b. Ps. 119.100

4

c. Isa. 8.20

3. *Test everything: hold fast that which is good* (i.e., that which conforms to the Word of God), 1 Thess. 5.21.

Conclusion

» In addition to the basic tools of biblical interpretation, many other historical, theological, and exegetical tools exist that can greatly enrich our understanding of the Word of God.

» Regardless of what tools we use, not one of them is meant to serve as a substitute for our own disciplined, prayerful, and obedient study of the Word of God.

» However, if we are cautious and use these tools correctly, i.e., as a means to understand the biblical world, these tools can revolutionize our study of the Word.

» Not only will we be better fed, but, through them, we will be able to preach the good news of the Kingdom and feed the flock of God as Christ has commanded us to do.

» May God give us the passion and energy to be workmen and work women who study to prove ourselves diligent laborers in the Word of God, handling accurately his perfect Word of truth!

The following questions were designed to help you review the material in the second video segment. This particular teaching session focused on some of the additional tools in biblical interpretation that can greatly enhance our study of the Word of God. These included the obtaining of several different translations of the Bible, a Bible atlas and Bible handbook, a topical Bible, a dictionary of theology, and commentaries of various kinds. All of these tools can provide us with invaluable help in bridging the distance between our world and the world of the authors and their audience. Review the following facts about these tools, concentrating especially on what rules and principles we ought to be aware of in order to use them correctly in our own biblical interpretation.

Segue 2

Student Questions and Response

1. For sake of review, restate those biblical resources considered to be the "basic tools of biblical interpretation." Again, restate why these tools are so fundamental to our own credible approach to the Word, especially as those entrusted with responsibility to lead and feed others in the Church.

2. What are the additional tools we considered in this segment which are designed to enhance our ability to bridge the gap between the biblical world and our own. Of these additional tools, which one(s) do you believe are more essential than others, especially for urban leaders in their responsibility to care for the souls of urban disciples? Explain your answer.

3. What are some of the major *cross-reference aids* for biblical exegesis, and what specifically do such aids enable us to do in regards to the text? How specifically do these helps deepen our understanding of the passage's or book's meaning? What cautions must be kept in mind as we employ them in our study?

4. What are those specific reference works which concentrate on supplying us insight into the history, culture, social customs, peoples, and physical environment of the biblical world? What are the main benefits of integrating these tools into our study of the text? What kinds of things must we keep in mind as we seek to take advantage of the sound research contained within them?

5. What are the biblical tools that are especially useful in helping us obtain background information on the author, date, and circumstances of the book, and certain uses of special language in the Bible (e.g., symbol, metaphor, figurative language, etc.)? What are the kinds of cautions we should be mindful of as we use these resources in our study?

6. Why are commentaries a unique kind of reference tool, compared to many of the other tools mentioned above? What are the four main types of commentaries available to us today, and how does each one function specifically?

7. While commentaries are invaluable aides in providing helpful and thorough understandings of passages and books of the Bible, how ought they never be used? Can any commentary series, however useful or brilliant, ever take the place of our own firsthand study of the text itself? Explain.

4

8. If you had to give a single statement of the "right use" of tools of biblical interpretation, what would it be? Why ought we to accept no explanation of any tool which would deny or contradict the testimony of the Scriptures themselves? Explain.

9. In light of the Bible's purpose to make us "wise for salvation through faith in Christ Jesus" (cf. 2 Tim. 3.15), why in our use of all the tools should nothing be accepted that calls into question the plain confession of the Scriptures about the person of Christ and his work of redemption? Explain.

CONNECTION

**Summary of
Key Concepts**

This lesson focuses upon the goal of bridging the gap between two worlds, the world of the biblical text and our own contemporary world, and the remarkable set of tools and resources designed to help us accomplish this task. In one sense, all effective biblical interpretation is designed to help us understand the nature of that lost world better, in order that we may not make historical, theological, grammatical, or cultural blunders as we seek to understand the meaning of the biblical texts we study. Listed below are the major themes and concepts associated with the right use of both the basic and additional tools of biblical interpretation. As you review these concepts keep in mind always the purpose of these tools, and how their right use can transform our study of the Scriptures.

☞ As a result of hundreds of dedicated biblical scholars and new technologies, we now have access to a vast array of solid scholarly tools which can greatly enhance our ability to understand, apply, and teach others on the meaning of biblical texts. The basic purpose of these tools is to help us bridge the various gaps between the biblical world and our own contemporary world.

☞ The key to understanding the various tools for biblical interpretation is recognizing how and in what way a particular tool helps us to overcome the gaps between our culture and that of the biblical authors and their audiences.

☞ The basic tools include a good translation of the Bible, Greek and Hebrew lexicons keyed to the Strong's numbering system, a solid Bible dictionary, a concordance, and credible exegetical commentaries which focus on the biblical meanings of the passage.

☛ The Bible was written in three languages (Hebrew, Aramaic, and Greek), and therefore we need a good translation of the Scriptures in our own native tongue. *Translations* are difficult, largely because of differences in language, cultural distinctions, historical distance, and differing approaches and philosophies among translators.

☛ *Concordances* list all the words of the Bible and where they are found in alphabetical order, and *lexicons* give the definitions (usages) of words as given in a particular verse of Scripture. Expository dictionaries add comments to explain the relationship between word meanings and biblical doctrines.

☛ *Bible dictionaries* list historical, geographical, cultural, scientific, and theological information about people, places, animals, events, and physical objects found in the Bible, as well as summaries on each book of the Bible.

☛ *Exegetical commentaries* share expert opinion on the actual meaning of the words in the original text, including issues of grammar, word meanings, the findings of biblical criticism, and historical and cultural insights which may influence the interpretation of a text.

☛ Regardless of the tool, we ought to use the references liberally, yet always mindful that their right use will *make plain* the meaning of the text, and not *deny* or *downplay* its significance.

☛ The *additional tools* we ought to learn how to use include several different translations of the Bible, a Bible atlas and handbook, a topical Bible, a dictionary of theology, and theological commentaries.

☛ *Cross-reference aids* focus on the relationship of various texts and passages which share a common topic or thematic center in biblical exegesis (e.g., topical bibles, cross-reference bibles, and topical guides and concordances). These aids must be carefully used to avoid contextual errors as well as biases of editors to make associations which are neither legitimate nor defensible.

☛ The tools which provide background into the history, culture, social customs, peoples, and physical environment of the Bible are Bible dictionaries, Bible encyclopedias, Bible atlases and handbooks, and works dealing with Bible history and customs. They must be carefully read so as to distinguish *historical data* from *interpretation on the validity of the text itself.*

4

↪ *Bible handbooks, study Bibles, and guides to biblical imagery* provide background information on the author, date, and circumstances on the book, and certain uses of special language in interpretation and exegesis (symbol, metaphor, figurative language, etc.). Care should be used to distinguish between *the commentators own views* and the *text itself.*

↪ *Commentaries* help interpret the meaning of a particular book of Scripture from the vantage point of a pastor, scholar, or biblical interpreter. There are four major kinds of commentaries: devotional, doctrinal, exegetical, and homiletical. While invaluable in understanding the text, they are no substitute for our own firsthand study of the text itself.

↪ We rightly use these basic and additional tools as aids to help us bridge the gap between the two worlds: the world of the text and our contemporary world. No explanation or speculation from any interpreter should be accepted that denies or contradicts either the testimony of the Scriptures themselves, or the plain confession of the Scriptures about the person of Christ and his work of redemption through the Cross.

Now is the time for you to discuss with your fellow students your questions about the use of tools in biblical interpretation. Thank God for such a rich and abundant amount of tools to aid us in our study of the Bible. We must be careful, however, never to substitute these tools for our study of the text itself. You must carefully assess your own use of tools in your personal use of the Bible, and seek to discover the right appropriation of them for your own growth's sake. Use the questions below to assess how you currently employ these tools in your own study and use of the Bible.

Student Application and Implications

* How many of the basic tools do your currently own in your personal library? Of them, which tool do you use most often in your own study of the Scriptures?

* How would you rate your awareness of the gap between the biblical world and our own contemporary world; how would you further grade yourself in overcoming that gap through your use of tools?

* Do you understand how the various tools *function*, in other words, how and in what way each tool provides knowledge to help you overcome some knowledge gap between our culture and that of the biblical authors and their audiences?

* Of the basic tools, which do you use least of all, and why? Correspondingly, of the additional tools, which do use most and least of all, and why?

* Which commentary series do you use most? Are you aware of their particular commitments and ideas that they are committed to? How does this influence your uses of them?

* What translation of the Bible do you use most often? How many translations of the Bible do you own, and how do you use them in your study of the Word? How do they help you capture the meaning of different passages of Scripture?

* When do you find time most often to actually study the Bible-do you have any regular habits, or do you study when you can? Do you study the Bible in a small group, with a friend or mentor, with the pastor, or at the church? What kinds of changes in your schedule will you need to make in order to ensure a steady, focused study of the Bible?

* How do you record the fruits of your study-on computer, on hand written notes, some other way? How do you store your notes, and do you have a system to retrieve them, once you have finished a study?

* Is your first impulse when you encounter a hard saying or difficult passage of the Bible to go to other Scriptures to understand it, or immediately to commentaries and dictionaries? Is this a good habit, or not? Explain.

* What is the one attitude you need to acquire if you are going to use the tools more effectively in your own personal study of the Bible? Explain.

 CASE STUDIES

From the Page to the Pulpit

(Based on a True Story). Recently in a growing urban church, a pastor was relieved of his position as senior pastor because it was found that he was actually in large measure merely reading his sermons from a book, with virtually no edit, citation, or communication that he was doing so! The elder board was so deeply troubled at this, that they felt it necessary to suspend his ministry in the church, not so much because of academic issues but because of spiritual issues. What does it suggest of a spiritual leader, they argued, who can virtually word-for-word recite someone else's ideas as his own, without giving the congregation and the people the freshest, best, and most candid word he has received from the Lord for them? What do you think of this situation—has reliance on the tools and resources of others made many Christian leaders lazy, incapable of reflecting afresh on the Word of God in such a way that they can deliver a new Word from the Lord to their congregations? Has the explosion in availability of tools made it easier for Christian leaders to relax their own standards of study and discipline, and simply become those who regurgitate up the same kind of food they have received from others?

Knowledge Puffs Up

Who has not encountered the story of a dear, humble, and sweet young person who was on fire for the Lord and hopeful to be used of him, who joyfully was accepted at a far away seminary or graduate school? After four to five years, they return for service, only to communicate with an entirely different spirit and emphasis. Rather than focus on the things he used to emphasize (e.g., love for God, love for souls, seeking the presence of God in worship, enjoying the depth and power of the Word of God, etc.), he now wants to discuss difficult theological concepts. Using terms and phrases that only the most literate of the congregation knows, his teaching is not filled with tears and longing for God but with controversies over theological issues that seem trite and unimportant. What happened to our brother? In what way does an over-focus on tools, resources, knowledge, and expertise puff up the person who is exposed to that focus? How can one enjoy and be empowered by the many biblical tools available without being puffed up and rendered boring and unfruitful in the process?

You Are Not Liberated Because You Do Not Know the Truth

Recently, a member of a local urban church was accosted by three members of the local Kingdom Hall of Jehovah's Witnesses who were canvassing the neighborhood. After a few moments of cordial conversation, they launched into one of the stock issues, the denial of the deity of Jesus Christ. Your member, a person fully knowledgeable in his copy of the Scriptures, defended as best he could his understanding of the divinity of Jesus. The three Witnesses, however, constantly referred to the Greek of John 1.1, which they argued was missing the definite article of the Greek, making most of the renderings in our modern English translations false. Frustrated and flustered, the member has asked the pastor for an introductory class on Greek, so he can defend his beliefs about Jesus with greater confidence and better evidence. What is the answer to answering the claims of groups like these Witnesses, who argue that most Christian belief is not rooted in knowledge, but superstition, tradition, and false knowledge about the Bible? Should we endeavor to help all believers gain a better knowledge of the language of the Bible, or focus more on issues of growth and spiritual maturity? What role should use of language and theological tools play in equipping our members with the ability to rightly divide and nobly defend the Word of truth as it is in Scripture?

A Little Knowledge Is Worse than None?

Many of us have been the victim of a conversation with a person who is out to correct us in all that we have come to believe. Upon asking us whether or not we have ever heard of the renown biblical scholar, "Dr. X," they begin to tell us with great intensity and energy how they have been changed by his "new revelation" into the Word of God. Whatever the subject matter "Dr. X" had mastered and spoke about, it now represents to our friend the definitive word on the subject. Just the fact that we have never heard of Dr. X and his life-changing teaching on this subject suggests a kind of isolation and ignorance on your part to the latest and best teaching of the Lord on this theme. After hearing for some time the ideas of Dr. X, you politely end the conversation as friendly as possible. Upon further reflection, it occurs to you that one of the problems with the expansion of knowledge is the very real possibility that new heresies, sects, and oddball emphases are rapidly growing as well. With so many now claiming God's own leading and blessing, thousands of teachers and preachers all carrying official titles such as "Elder So and So" and "Bishop Such and Such" preach their new revelations in churches and across the airwaves. The vast majority of many of these new teachers are utterly independent, not subject to any kind of spiritual authority or association that might protect them from themselves or from error. How do we remedy this current state of affairs, with so many claiming their own independent Word from the Lord, all being their own resources for spiritual authority and teaching?

Thanks to the works of hundreds of dedicated scholars who cherish and love the Scriptures, we have access to a remarkable array of scholarly tools which can enable us to understand the meaning of the biblical text. The essential purpose of our use of scholarly tools is to help us bridge the various gaps between the biblical world and our own contemporary world. This bridging helps the diligent biblical interpreter to be more faithful to the Word of God by enabling him or her to reconstruct the meaning in its original context. The basic tools of biblical interpretation include a good translation of the Bible, Greek and Hebrew lexicons keyed to the Strong's numbering system, a solid Bible dictionary, a concordance, and credible exegetical commentaries which focus on the biblical meanings of the passage. Used in their proper place and times, these tools can prove invaluable in bridging the gap between the biblical world and our understanding of that world.

In addition to the basic tools of biblical interpretation (i.e., a good translation of the Bible, Greek and Hebrew lexicons, Bible dictionary, concordance, and credible exegetical commentaries), there are additional tools which can enrich our understanding of the Word of God. These include several different translations of the Bible, a Bible atlas and handbook, a topical Bible, a dictionary of theology, and theological commentaries. Each of these tools focus on a particular challenge of biblical interpretation, from issues of language, culture, history, and theology. As with any tool, we must be careful to use them to enhance our knowledge of the text, neither denying nor downplaying the essential message of the Bible as it speaks to our salvation in the person of Jesus Christ.

Restatement of
the Lesson's Thesis

If you are interested in pursuing some of the ideas of *Biblical Studies: Using Study Tools in Bible Study*, you might want to give these books a try:

Resources and
Bibliographies

Bruce, F. F. *New Testament History*. New York: Doubleday, 1969.

Penney, Russell, and Mal Couch. eds. *An Introduction to Classical Evangelical Hermeneutics: A Guide to the History and Practice of Biblical Interpretation*. Grand Rapids: Kregel Books, 2000.

Sire, James W. *Scripture Twisting: Twenty Ways the Cults Misread the Bible*. Downers Grove, IL: InterVarsity, 1980.

Stott, John. *The Contemporary Christian: Applying God's Word to Today's World*. Downers Grove, IL: InterVarsity, 1992.

Ministry Connections

Understanding the ways in which these tools can better help you understand the ancient world, will make you a better minister of the Word of God in this world. Nothing will affect every dimension of your ministry like a mastery of the Word of God. Our goal should be consistent with the Word of the Lord from Paul to Timothy in 2 Tim. 4.1-2: "I charge you in the presence of God and of Christ Jesus, who is to judge the living and the dead, and by his appearing and his kingdom: preach the word; be ready in season and out of season; reprove, rebuke, and exhort, with complete patience and teaching." Nothing is wasted in the man or woman of God who will discipline themselves in the Word of God, to be ready to preach, teach, speak, counsel, and pray for others at any time God may direct, regardless of place or condition. This is our dream and mandate.

You now have the privilege to share the insights you have learned in this module in a practicum that you and your mentor agree to. What will be important will be to find a venue where you can share the rich insights you have learned and applied in this module– whether with the members of your family, in a venue at your church, at work, or wherever God may lead. What you will want to concentrate upon is how this teaching has connected with your life, work, and ministry. The ministry project is designed for this, and in the next days you will have the opportunity to share these insights in real-life, actual ministry environments. Pray that God will give you insight into his ways as you share your insights in your projects.

Counseling and Prayer

Now that you are at the end of this module, reflect on whether or not there are any remaining issues, persons, situations, or opportunities that need to be prayed for as a result of your studies in this lesson. Ask the Lord, the Holy Spirit, to bring to your mind any applications or changes he desires to see in your life as a result of these studies, and take the time to pray with and for your colleagues in their areas of concern. Remember, prayer provides us with the necessary support we need to confidently and courageously follow through on those areas that our Lord desires change and growth.

4

No assignment due.

No assignment due.

Your ministry project and your exegetical project should now be outlined, determined, and accepted by your instructor. Make sure that you plan ahead, so you will not be late in turning in your assignments.

The final will be a take home exam, and will include questions taken from the first three quizzes, new questions on material drawn from this lesson, and essay questions which will ask for your short answer responses to key integrating questions. Also, you should plan on reciting or writing out the verses memorized for the course on the exam. When you have completed your exam, please notify your mentor and make certain that they get your copy.

Please note: Your module grade cannot be determined if you do not take the final exam and turn in all outstanding assignments to your mentor (ministry project, exegetical project, Scripture memory verses, reading completion sheets, quizzes, and the final exam).

In this lesson we have considered the kinds of tools we have access to which can enhance our interpretation of the Bible. We have considered the need for biblical interpretation, and our own preparation of our hearts, our minds, and our wills to engage the eternal Word of the Living God. We have examined the theme of the Bible's inspiration and the claims of modern biblical scholarship, and saw how the Word of God is inspired by God, for the authors were carried along by the Holy Spirit and the Scriptures they wrote therefore are the very inspired words of the living God. Our *Three-Step Model* has provided us with an effective model to understand the meaning of the Bible in its own context, to draw out biblical principles and to apply its meaning in practical ways in our lives under the Spirit's direction and leading.

In addition to these insights, we have also defined the importance of genre study in biblical interpretation, and looked at the importance of both narrative and prophecy in biblical interpretation. Finally, we examined a group of tools, both basic and otherwise, designed to help us bridge the distance between our understanding of the ancient text and our own application of it today. Regardless of what methods or tools we employ, nothing can serve as well as our own disciplined, prayerful, and obedient study of the Word of God. Apart from the aid and leading of the Spirit, we are simply unable to comprehend the meaning of the Scriptures. Yet, if we are humble and diligent, the truth of the Word will come into our lives and transform us as we serve our Lord as disciples of the Kingdom. Not only will such study transform us, but God will also use us as vessels to communicate his Word, both in the Church and in the world, all to his glory.

May God give us the passion and energy to be workmen and work women who study to prove ourselves diligent laborers in the Word of God, handling accurately his perfect Word of truth, in order that we may know Christ and make him known, all for his greater glory.

Amen and amen!

4

Appendices

APPENDIX 1

The Nicene Creed

Memory Verses ⇩

Rev. 4.11 (ESV) *Worthy are you, our Lord and God, to receive glory and honor and power, for you created all things, and by your will they existed and were created.*

John 1.1 (ESV) *In the beginning was the Word, and the Word was with God, and the Word was God.*

1 Cor.15.3-5 (ESV) *For what I received I passed on to you as of first importance: that Christ died for our sins according to the Scriptures, that he was buried, that he was raised on the third day according to the Scriptures, and that he appeared to Peter, and then to the Twelve.*

Rom. 8.11 (ESV) *If the Spirit of him who raised Jesus from the dead dwells in you, he who raised Christ Jesus from the dead will also give life to your mortal bodies through his Spirit who dwells in you.*

1 Pet. 2.9 (ESV) *But you are a chosen race, a royal priesthood, a holy nation, a people for his own possession, that you may proclaim the excellencies of him who called you out of darkness into his marvelous light.*

1 Thess. 4.16-17 (ESV) *For the Lord himself will descend from heaven with a cry of command, with the voice of an archangel, and with the sound of the trumpet of God. And the dead in Christ will rise first. Then we who are alive, who are left, will be caught up together with them in the clouds to meet the Lord in the air, and so we will always be with the Lord.*

We believe in one God, *(Deut. 6.4-5; Mark 12.29; 1 Cor. 8.6)*
    the Father Almighty, *(Gen. 17.1; Dan. 4.35; Matt. 6.9; Eph. 4.6; Rev. 1.8)*
    Maker of heaven and earth *(Gen 1.1; Isa. 40.28; Rev. 10.6)*
    and of all things visible and invisible. *(Ps. 148; Rom. 11.36; Rev. 4.11)*

We believe in one Lord Jesus Christ, the only Begotten Son of God,
    begotten of the Father before all ages,
    God from God, Light from Light, True God from True God,
    begotten not created,
    of the same essence as the Father, *(John 1.1-2; 3.18; 8.58; 14.9-10; 20.28; Col. 1.15, 17; Heb. 1.3-6)*
    through whom all things were made. *(John 1.3; Col. 1.16)*

Who for us men and for our salvation came down from heaven
    and was incarnate by the Holy Spirit and the virgin Mary
    and became human. *(Matt. 1.20-23; John 1.14; 6.38; Luke 19.10)*
    Who for us too, was crucified under Pontius Pilate,
    suffered, and was buried. *(Matt. 27.1-2; Mark 15.24-39, 43-47; Acts 13.29; Rom. 5.8; Heb. 2.10; 13.12)*
    The third day he rose again
    according to the Scriptures, *(Mark 16.5-7; Luke 24.6-8; Acts 1.3; Rom. 6.9; 10.9; 2 Tim. 2.8)*
    ascended into heaven,
    and is seated at the right hand of the Father. *(Mark 16.19; Eph. 1.19-20)*
    He will come again in glory
    to judge the living and the dead,
    and his Kingdom will have no end.
      (Isa. 9.7; Matt. 24.30; John 5.22; Acts 1.11; 17.31; Rom. 14.9; 2 Cor. 5.10; 2 Tim. 4.1)

We believe in the Holy Spirit, the Lord and life-giver,
    (Gen. 1.1-2; Job 33.4; Ps. 104.30; 139.7-8; Luke 4.18-19; John 3.5-6; Acts 1.1-2; 1 Cor. 2.11; Rev. 3.22)
    who proceeds from the Father and the Son, *(John 14.16-18, 26; 15.26; 20.22)*
    who together with the Father and Son
    is worshiped and glorified, *(Isa. 6.3; Matt. 28.19; 2 Cor. 13.14; Rev. 4.8)*
    who spoke by the prophets. *(Num. 11.29; Mic. 3.8; Acts 2.17-18; 2 Pet. 1.21)*

We believe in one holy, catholic, and apostolic Church.
    (Matt. 16.18; Eph. 5.25-28; 1 Cor. 1.2; 10.17; 1 Tim. 3.15; Rev. 7.9)

We acknowledge one baptism for the forgiveness of sin, *(Acts 22.16; 1 Pet. 3.21; Eph. 4.4-5)*
    And we look for the resurrection of the dead
    And the life of the age to come. *(Isa. 11.6-10; Mic. 4.1-7; Luke 18.29-30; Rev. 21.1-5; 21.22-22.5)*

Amen.

APPENDIX 2

We Believe: Confession of the Nicene Creed (8.7.8.7. meter*)

Rev. Dr. Don L. Davis, 2007. All Rights Reserved.

* This song is adapted from the Nicene Creed, and set to 8.7.8.7. meter, meaning it can be sung to tunes of the same meter, such as: *Joyful, Joyful, We Adore Thee; I Will Sing of My Redeemer; What a Friend We Have in Jesus; Come, Thou Long Expected Jesus*

Father God Almighty rules, the Maker of both earth and heav'n.
All things seen and those unseen, by him were made, by him were giv'n!
We believe in Jesus Christ, the Lord, God's one and only Son,
Begotten, not created, too, he and our Father God are one!

Begotten from the Father, same, in essence, as both God and Light;
Through him by God all things were made, in him all things were giv'n life.
Who for us all, for our salvation, did come down from heav'n to earth,
Incarnate by the Spirit's pow'r, and through the Virgin Mary's birth.

Who for us too, was crucified, by Pontius Pilate's rule and hand,
Suffered, and was buried, yet on the third day, he rose again.
According to the Sacred Scriptures all that happ'ned was meant to be.
Ascended high to God's right hand, in heav'n he sits in glory.

Christ will come again in glory to judge all those alive and dead.
His Kingdom rule shall never end, for he will rule and reign as Head.
We worship God, the Holy Spirit, Lord and the Life-giver known;
With Fath'r and Son is glorified, Who by the prophets ever spoke.

And we believe in one true Church, God's holy people for all time,
Cath'lic in its scope and broadness, built on the Apostles' line!
Acknowledging that one baptism, for forgiv'ness of our sin,
And we look for Resurrection, for the dead shall live again.

Looking for unending days, the life of the bright Age to come,
When Christ's Reign shall come to earth, the will of God shall then be done!
Praise to God, and to Christ Jesus, to the Spirit—triune Lord!
We confess the ancient teachings, clinging to God's holy Word!

APPENDIX 3

The Story of God: Our Sacred Roots

Rev. Dr. Don L. Davis

The LORD God is the source, sustainer, and end of all things in the heavens and earth. All things were formed and exist by his will and for his eternal glory, the triune God, Father, Son, and Holy Spirit, Rom. 11.36.

The Alpha and the Omega	Christus Victor	Come, Holy Spirit	Your Word Is Truth	The Great Confession	His Life in Us	Living in the Way	Reborn to Serve
THE TRIUNE GOD'S UNFOLDING DRAMA — God's Self-Revelation in Creation, Israel, and Christ				**THE CHURCH'S PARTICIPATION IN GOD'S UNFOLDING DRAMA** — Fidelity to the Apostolic Witness to Christ and His Kingdom			
The Objective Foundation: The Sovereign Love of God — God's Narration of His Saving Work in Christ				The Subjective Practice: Salvation by Grace through Faith — The Redeemed's Joyous Response to God's Saving Work in Christ			
The Author of the Story	*The Champion of the Story*	*The Interpreter of the Story*	*The Testimony of the Story*	*The People of the Story*	*Re-enactment of the Story*	*Embodiment of the Story*	*Continuation of the Story*
The Father as Director	Jesus as Lead Actor	The Spirit as Narrator	Scripture as Script	As Saints, Confessors	As Worshipers, Ministers	As Followers, Sojourners	As Servants, Ambassadors
Christian Worldview	Communal Identity	Spiritual Experience	Biblical Authority	Orthodox Theology	Priestly Worship	Congregational Discipleship	Kingdom Witness
Theistic and Trinitarian Vision	Christ-centered Foundation	Spirit-Indwelt and -Filled Community	Canonical and Apostolic Witness	Ancient Creedal Affirmation of Faith	Weekly Gathering in Christian Assembly	Corporate, Ongoing Spiritual Formation	Active Agents of the Reign of God
Sovereign Willing	Messianic Representing	Divine Comforting	Inspired Testifying	Truthful Retelling	Joyful Excelling	Faithful Indwelling	Hopeful Compelling
Creator True Maker of the Cosmos	**Recapitulation** Typos and Fulfillment of the Covenant	**Life-Giver** Regeneration and Adoption	**Divine Inspiration** God-breathed Word	**The Confession of Faith** Union with Christ	**Song and Celebration** Historical Recitation	**Pastoral Oversight** Shepherding the Flock	**Explicit Unity** Love for the Saints
Owner Sovereign Disposer of Creation	**Revealer** Incarnation of the Word	**Teacher** Illuminator of the Truth	**Sacred History** Historical Record	**Baptism into Christ** Communion of Saints	**Homilies and Teachings** Prophetic Proclamation	**Shared Spirituality** Common Journey through the Spiritual Disciplines	**Radical Hospitality** Evidence of God's Kingdom Reign
Ruler Blessed Controller of All Things	**Redeemer** Reconciler of All Things	**Helper** Endowment and the Power	**Biblical Theology** Divine Commentary	**The Rule of Faith** Apostles' Creed and Nicene Creed	**The Lord's Supper** Dramatic Re-enactment	**Embodiment** Anamnesis and Prolepsis through the Church Year	**Extravagant Generosity** Good Works
Covenant Keeper Faithful Promisor	**Restorer** Christ, the Victor over the powers of evil	**Guide** Divine Presence and Shekinah	**Spiritual Food** Sustenance for the Journey	**The Vincentian Canon** Ubiquity, antiquity, universality	**Eschatological Foreshadowing** The Already/Not Yet	**Effective Discipling** Spiritual Formation in the Believing Assembly	**Evangelical Witness** Making Disciples of All People Groups

APPENDIX 4

The Theology of Christus Victor

A Christ-Centered Biblical Motif for Integrating and Renewing the Urban Church

Rev. Dr. Don L. Davis

	The Promised Messiah	The Word Made Flesh	The Son of Man	The Suffering Servant	The Lamb of God	The Victorious Conqueror	The Reigning Lord in Heaven	The Bridegroom and Coming King
Biblical Framework	Israel's hope of Yahweh's anointed who would redeem his people	In the person of Jesus of Nazareth, the Lord has come to the world	As the promised king and divine Son of Man, Jesus reveals the Father's glory and salvation to the world	As Inaugurator of the Kingdom of God, Jesus demonstrates God's reign present through his words, wonders, and works	As both High Priest and Paschal Lamb, Jesus offers himself to God on our behalf as a sacrifice for sin	In his resurrection from the dead and ascension to God's right hand, Jesus is proclaimed as Victor over the power of sin and death	Now reigning at God's right hand till his enemies are made his footstool, Jesus pours out his benefits on his body	Soon the risen and ascended Lord will return to gather his Bride, the Church, and consummate his work
Scripture References	Isa. 9.6-7￼ Jer. 23.5-6￼ Isa. 11.1-10	John 1.14-18￼ Matt. 1.20-23￼ Phil. 2.6-8	Matt. 2.1-11￼ Num. 24.17￼ Luke 1.78-79	Mark 1.14-15￼ Matt. 12.25-30￼ Luke 17.20-21	2 Cor. 5.18-21￼ Isa. 52.53￼ John 1.29	Eph. 1.16-23￼ Phil. 2.5-11￼ Col. 1.15-20	1 Cor. 15.25￼ Eph. 4.15-16￼ Acts. 2.32-36	Rom. 14.7-9￼ Rev. 5.9-13￼ 1 Thess. 4.13-18
Jesus' History	The pre-incarnate, only begotten Son of God in glory	His conception by the Spirit, and birth to Mary	His manifestation to the Magi and to the world	His teaching, exorcisms, miracles, and mighty works among the people	His suffering, crucifixion, death, and burial	His resurrection, with appearances to his witnesses, and his ascension to the Father	The sending of the Holy Spirit and his gifts, and Christ's session in heaven at the Father's right hand	His soon return from heaven to earth as Lord and Christ: the Second Coming
Description	The biblical promise for the seed of Abraham, the prophet like Moses, the son of David	In the Incarnation, God has come to us; Jesus reveals to humankind the Father's glory in fullness	In Jesus, God has shown his salvation to the entire world, including the Gentiles	In Jesus, the promised Kingdom of God has come visibly to earth, demonstrating his binding of Satan and rescinding the Curse	As God's perfect Lamb, Jesus offers himself up to God as a sin offering on behalf of the entire world	In his resurrection and ascension, Jesus destroyed death, disarmed Satan, and rescinded the Curse	Jesus is installed at the Father's right hand as Head of the Church, Firstborn from the dead, and supreme Lord in heaven	As we labor in his harvest field in the world, so we await Christ's return, the fulfillment of his promise
Church Year	Advent	Christmas	Season after Epiphany￼ Baptism and Transfiguration	Lent	Holy Week￼ Passion	Eastertide￼ Easter, Ascension Day, Pentecost	Season after Pentecost￼ Trinity Sunday	Season after Pentecost￼ All Saints Day, Reign of Christ the King
	The Coming of Christ	*The Birth of Christ*	*The Manifestation of Christ*	*The Ministry of Christ*	*The Suffering and Death of Christ*	*The Resurrection and Ascension of Christ*	*The Heavenly Session of Christ*	*The Reign of Christ*
Spiritual Formation	As we await his Coming, let us proclaim and affirm the hope of Christ	O Word made flesh, let us every heart prepare him room to dwell	Divine Son of Man, show the nations your salvation and glory	In the person of Christ, the power of the reign of God has come to earth and to the Church	May those who share the Lord's death be resurrected with him	Let us participate by faith in the victory of Christ over the power of sin, Satan, and death	Come, indwell us, Holy Spirit, and empower us to advance Christ's Kingdom in the world	We live and work in expectation of his soon return, seeking to please him in all things

APPENDIX 5

Christus Victor

An Integrated Vision for the Christian Life

Rev. Dr. Don L. Davis

For the Church

- The Church is the primary extension of Jesus in the world
- Ransomed treasure of the victorious, risen Christ
- *Laos:* The people of God
- God's new creation: presence of the future
- Locus and agent of the Already/Not Yet Kingdom

For Theology and Doctrine

- The authoritative Word of Christ's victory: the Apostolic Tradition: the Holy Scriptures
- Theology as commentary on the grand narrative of God
- *Christus Victor* as core theological framework for meaning in the world
- The Nicene Creed: the Story of God's triumphant grace

For Spirituality

- The Holy Spirit's presence and power in the midst of God's people
- Sharing in the disciplines of the Spirit
- Gatherings, lectionary, liturgy, and our observances in the Church Year
- Living the life of the risen Christ in the rhythm of our ordinary lives

For Gifts

- God's gracious endowments and benefits from *Christus Victor*
- Pastoral offices to the Church
- The Holy Spirit's sovereign dispensing of the gifts
- Stewardship: divine, diverse gifts for the common good

Christus Victor

*Destroyer of Evil and Death
Restorer of Creation
Victor o'er Hades and Sin
Crusher of Satan*

For Worship

- People of the Resurrection: unending celebration of the people of God
- Remembering, participating in the Christ event in our worship
- Listen and respond to the Word
- Transformed at the Table, the Lord's Supper
- The presence of the Father through the Son in the Spirit

For Evangelism and Mission

- Evangelism as unashamed declaration and demonstration of *Christus Victor* to the world
- The Gospel as Good News of kingdom pledge
- We proclaim God's Kingdom come in the person of Jesus of Nazareth
- The Great Commission: go to all people groups making disciples of Christ and his Kingdom
- Proclaiming Christ as Lord and Messiah

For Justice and Compassion

- The gracious and generous expressions of Jesus through the Church
- The Church displays the very life of the Kingdom
- The Church demonstrates the very life of the Kingdom of heaven right here and now
- Having freely received, we freely give (no sense of merit or pride)
- Justice as tangible evidence of the Kingdom come

APPENDIX 6

Old Testament Witness to Christ and His Kingdom

Rev. Dr. Don L. Davis

Christ Is Seen in the OT's:	Covenant Promise and Fulfillment	Moral Law	Christophanies	Typology	Tabernacle, Festival, and Levitical Priesthood	Messianic Prophecy	Salvation Promises
Passage	Gen. 12.1-3	Matt. 5.17-18	John 1.18	1 Cor. 15.45	Heb. 8.1-6	Mic. 5.2	Isa. 9.6-7
Example	The Promised Seed of the Abrahamic covenant	The Law given on Mount Sinai	Commander of the Lord's army	Jonah and the great fish	Melchizedek, as both High Priest and King	The Lord's Suffering Servant	Righteous Branch of David
Christ As	Seed of the woman	The Prophet of God	God's present Revelation	Antitype of God's drama	Our eternal High Priest	The coming Son of Man	Israel's Redeemer and King
Where Illustrated	Galatians	Matthew	John	Matthew	Hebrews	Luke and Acts	John and Revelation
Exegetical Goal	To see Christ as heart of God's sacred drama	To see Christ as fulfillment of the Law	To see Christ as God's revealer	To see Christ as antitype of divine typos	To see Christ in the Temple *cultus*	To see Christ as true Messiah	To see Christ as coming King
How Seen in the NT	As fulfillment of God's sacred oath	As *telos* of the Law	As full, final, and superior revelation	As substance behind the historical shadows	As reality behind the rules and roles	As the Kingdom made present	As the One who will rule on David's throne
Our Response in Worship	God's veracity and faithfulness	God's perfect righteousness	God's presence among us	God's inspired Scripture	God's ontology: his realm as primary and determinative	God's anointed servant and mediator	God's resolve to restore his kingdom authority
How God Is Vindicated	God does not lie; he's true to his word	Jesus fulfills all righteousness	God's fulness is revealed to us in Jesus of Nazareth	The Spirit spoke by the prophets	The Lord has provided a mediator for humankind	Every jot and tittle written of him will occur	Evil will be put down, creation restored, under his reign

APPENDIX 7

Summary Outline of the Scriptures

Rev. Dr. Don L. Davis

1. GENESIS - Beginnings
   a. Adam
   b. Noah
   c. Abraham
   d. Isaac
   e. Jacob
   f. Joseph

2. EXODUS - Redemption, (out of)
   a. Slavery
   b. Deliverance
   c. Law
   d. Tabernacle

3. LEVITICUS - Worship and Fellowship
   a. Offerings, sacrifices
   b. Priests
   c. Feasts, festivals

4. NUMBERS - Service and Walk
   a. Organized
   b. Wanderings

5. DEUTERONOMY - Obedience
   a. Moses reviews history and law
   b. Civil and social laws
   c. Palestinian Covenant
   d. Moses' blessing and death

6. JOSHUA - Redemption (into)
   a. Conquer the land
   b. Divide up the land
   c. Joshua's farewell

7. JUDGES - God's Deliverance
   a. Disobedience and judgment
   b. Israel's twelve judges
   c. Lawless conditions

8. RUTH - Love
   a. Ruth chooses
   b. Ruth works
   c. Ruth waits
   d. Ruth rewarded

9. 1 SAMUEL - Kings, Priestly Perspective
   a. Eli
   b. Samuel
   c. Saul
   d. David

10. 2 SAMUEL - David
    a. King of Judah
       (9 years - Hebron)
    b. King of all Israel
       (33 years - Jerusalem)

11. 1 KINGS - Solomon's Glory, Kingdom's Decline
    a. Solomon's glory
    b. Kingdom's decline
    c. Elijah the prophet

12. 2 KINGS- Divided Kingdom
    a. Elisha
    b. Israel (N. Kingdom falls)
    c. Judah (S. Kingdom falls)

13. 1 CHRONICLES - David's Temple Arrangements
    a. Genealogies
    b. End of Saul's reign
    c. Reign of David
    d. Temple preparations

14. 2 CHRONICLES - Temple and Worship Abandoned
    a. Solomon
    b. Kings of Judah

15. EZRA - The Minority (Remnant)
    a. First return from exile - Zerubbabel
    b. Second return from exile - Ezra (priest)

16. NEHEMIAH - Rebuilding by Faith
    a. Rebuild walls
    b. Revival
    c. Religious reform

17. ESTHER - Female Savior
    a. Esther
    b. Haman
    c. Mordecai
    d. Deliverance: Feast of Purim

18. JOB - Why the Righteous Suffer
    a. Godly Job
    b. Satan's attack
    c. Four philosophical friends
    d. God lives

19. PSALMS - Prayer and Praise
    a. Prayers of David
    b. Godly suffer; deliverance
    c. God deals with Israel
    d. Suffering of God's people - end with the Lord's reign
    e. The Word of God (Messiah's suffering and glorious return)

20. PROVERBS - Wisdom
    a. Wisdom versus folly
    b. Solomon
    c. Solomon - Hezekiah
    d. Agur
    e. Lemuel

21. ECCLESIASTES - Vanity
    a. Experimentation
    b. Observation
    c. Consideration

22. SONG OF SOLOMON - Love Story

23. ISAIAH - The Justice (Judgment) and Grace (Comfort) of God
    a. Prophecies of punishment
    b. History
    c. Prophecies of blessing

24. JEREMIAH - Judah's Sin Leads to Babylonian Captivity
    a. Jeremiah's call; empowered
    b. Judah condemned; predicted Babylonian captivity
    c. Restoration promised
    d. Prophesied judgment inflicted
    e. Prophesies against Gentiles
    f. Summary of Judah's captivity

25. LAMENTATIONS - Lament over Jerusalem
    a. Affliction of Jerusalem
    b. Destroyed because of sin
    c. The prophet's suffering
    d. Present desolation versus past splendor
    e. Appeal to God for mercy

26. EZEKIEL - Israel's Captivity and Restoration
    a. Judgment on Judah and Jerusalem
    b. Judgment on Gentile nations
    c. Israel restored; Jerusalem's future glory

27. DANIEL - The Time of the Gentiles
    a. History; Nebuchadnezzar, Belshazzar, Daniel
    b. Prophecy

28. HOSEA - Unfaithfulness
    a. Unfaithfulness
    b. Punishment
    c. Restoration

29. JOEL - The Day of the Lord
    a. Locust plague
    b. Events of the future day of the Lord
    c. Order of the future day of the Lord

30. AMOS - God Judges Sin
    a. Neighbors judged
    b. Israel judged
    c. Visions of future judgment
    d. Israel's past judgment blessings

31. OBADIAH - Edom's Destruction
    a. Destruction prophesied
    b. Reasons for destruction
    c. Israel's future blessing

32. JONAH - Gentile Salvation
    a. Jonah disobeys
    b. Other suffer
    c. Jonah punished
    d. Jonah obeys; thousands saved
    e. Jonah displeased, no love for souls

33. MICAH - Israel's Sins, Judgment, and Restoration
    a. Sin and judgment
    b. Grace and future restoration
    c. Appeal and petition

34. NAHUM - Nineveh Condemned
    a. God hates sin
    b. Nineveh's doom prophesied
    c. Reasons for doom

35. HABAKKUK - The Just Shall Live by Faith
    a. Complaint of Judah's unjudged sin
    b. Chaldeans will punish
    c. Complaint of Chaldeans' wickedness
    d. Punishment promised
    e. Prayer for revival; faith in God

36. ZEPHANIAH - Babylonian Invasion Prefigures the Day of the Lord
    a. Judgment on Judah foreshadows the Great Day of the Lord
    b. Judgment on Jerusalem and neighbors foreshadows final judgment of all nations
    c. Israel restored after judgments

37. HAGGAI - Rebuild the Temple
    a. Negligence
    b. Courage
    c. Separation
    d. Judgment

38. ZECHARIAH - Two Comings of Christ
    a. Zechariah's vision
    b. Bethel's question; Jehovah's answer
    c. Nation's downfall and salvation

39. MALACHI - Neglect
    a. The priest's sins
    b. The people's sins
    c. The faithful few

Summary Outline of the Scriptures (continued)

1. MATTHEW - Jesus the King
   a. The Person of the King
   b. The Preparation of the King
   c. The Propaganda of the King
   d. The Program of the King
   e. The Passion of the King
   f. The Power of the King

2. MARK - Jesus the Servant
   a. John introduces the Servant
   b. God the Father identifies the Servant
   c. The temptation initiates the Servant
   d. Work and word of the Servant
   e. Death, burial, resurrection

3. LUKE - Jesus Christ the Perfect Man
   a. Birth and family of the Perfect Man
   b. Testing of the Perfect Man; hometown
   c. Ministry of the Perfect Man
   d. Betrayal, trial, and death of the Perfect Man
   e. Resurrection of the Perfect Man

4. JOHN - Jesus Christ is God
   a. Prologue - the Incarnation
   b. Introduction
   c. Witness of Jesus to his Apostles
   d. Passion - witness to the world
   e. Epilogue

5. ACTS - The Holy Spirit Working in the Church
   a. The Lord Jesus at work by the Holy Spirit through the Apostles at Jerusalem
   b. In Judea and Samaria
   c. To the uttermost parts of the Earth

6. ROMANS - The Righteousness of God
   a. Salutation
   b. Sin and salvation
   c. Sanctification
   d. Struggle
   e. Spirit-filled living
   f. Security of salvation
   g. Segregation
   h. Sacrifice and service
   i. Separation and salutation

7. 1 CORINTHIANS - The Lordship of Christ
   a. Salutation and thanksgiving
   b. Conditions in the Corinthian body
   c. Concerning the Gospel
   d. Concerning collections

8. 2 CORINTHIANS - The Ministry in the Church
   a. The comfort of God
   b. Collection for the poor
   c. Calling of the Apostle Paul

9. GALATIANS - Justification by Faith
   a. Introduction
   b. Personal - Authority of the Apostle and glory of the Gospel
   c. Doctrinal - Justification by faith
   d. Practical - Sanctification by the Holy Spirit
   e. Autographed conclusion and exhortation

10. EPHESIANS - The Church of Jesus Christ
    a. Doctrinal - the heavenly calling of the Church
       A Body
       A Temple
       A Mystery
    b. Practical - The earthly conduct of the Church
       A New Man
       A Bride
       An Army

11. PHILIPPIANS - Joy in the Christian Life
    a. Philosophy for Christian living
    b. Pattern for Christian living
    c. Prize for Christian living
    d. Power for Christian living

12. COLOSSIANS - Christ the Fullness of God
    a. Doctrinal - In Christ believers are made full
    b. Practical - Christ's life poured out in believers, and through them

13. 1 THESSALONIANS - The Second Coming of Christ:
    a. Is an inspiring hope
    b. Is a working hope
    c. Is a purifying hope
    d. Is a comforting hope
    e. Is a rousing, stimulating hope

14. 2 THESSALONIANS - The Second Coming of Christ
    a. Persecution of believers now; judgment of unbelievers hereafter (at coming of Christ)
    b. Program of the world in connection with the coming of Christ
    c. Practical issues associated with the coming of Christ

15. 1 TIMOTHY - Government and Order in the Local Church
    a. The faith of the Church
    b. Public prayer and women's place in the Church
    c. Officers in the Church
    d. Apostasy in the Church
    e. Duties of the officer of the Church

16. 2 TIMOTHY - Loyalty in the Days of Apostasy
    a. Afflictions of the Gospel
    b. Active in service
    c. Apostasy coming; authority of the Scriptures
    d. Allegiance to the Lord

17. TITUS - The Ideal New Testament Church
    a. The Church is an organization
    b. The Church is to teach and preach the Word of God
    c. The Church is to perform good works

18. PHILEMON - Reveal Christ's Love and Teach Brotherly Love
    a. Genial greeting to Philemon and family
    b. Good reputation of Philemon
    c. Gracious plea for Onesimus
    d. Guiltless illustration of Imputation
    e. General and personal requests

19. HEBREWS - The Superiority of Christ
    a. Doctrinal - Christ is better than the Old Testament economy
    b. Practical - Christ brings better benefits and duties

20. JAMES - Ethics of Christianity
    a. Faith tested
    b. Difficulty of controlling the tongue
    c. Warning against worldliness
    d. Admonitions in view of the Lord's coming

21. 1 PETER - Christian Hope in the Time of Persecution and Trial
    a. Suffering and security of believers
    b. Suffering and the Scriptures
    c. Suffering and the sufferings of Christ
    d. Suffering and the Second Coming of Christ

22. 2 PETER - Warning Against False Teachers
    a. Addition of Christian graces gives assurance
    b. Authority of the Scriptures
    c. Apostasy brought in by false testimony
    d. Attitude toward Return of Christ: test for apostasy
    e. Agenda of God in the world
    f. Admonition to believers

23. 1 JOHN - The Family of God
    a. God is Light
    b. God is Love
    c. God is Life

24. 2 JOHN - Warning against Receiving Deceivers
    a. Walk in truth
    b. Love one another
    c. Receive not deceivers
    d. Find joy in fellowship

25. 3 JOHN - Admonition to Receive True Believers
    a. Gaius, brother in the Church
    b. Diotrephes
    c. Demetrius

26. JUDE - Contending for the Faith
    a. Occasion of the epistle
    b. Occurrences of apostasy
    c. Occupation of believers in the days of apostasy

27. REVELATION - The Unveiling of Christ Glorified
    a. The person of Christ in glory
    b. The possession of Jesus Christ - the Church in the World
    c. The program of Jesus Christ - the scene in Heaven
    d. The seven seals
    e. The seven trumpets
    f. Important persons in the last days
    g. The seven vials
    h. The fall of Babylon
    i. The eternal state

APPENDIX 8

From Before to Beyond Time:

The Plan of God and Human History

Adapted from Suzanne de Dietrich. **God's Unfolding Purpose.** *Philadelphia: Westminster Press, 1976.*

I. Before Time (Eternity Past) 1 Cor. 2.7
   A. The Eternal Triune God
   B. God's Eternal Purpose
   C. The Mystery of Iniquity
   D. The Principalities and Powers

II. Beginning of Time (Creation and Fall) Gen. 1.1
   A. Creative Word
   B. Humanity
   C. Fall
   D. Reign of Death and First Signs of Grace

III. Unfolding of Time (God's Plan Revealed Through Israel) Gal. 3.8
   A. Promise (Patriarchs)
   B. Exodus and Covenant at Sinai
   C. Promised Land
   D. The City, the Temple, and the Throne (Prophet, Priest, and King)
   E. Exile
   F. Remnant

IV. Fullness of Time (Incarnation of the Messiah) Gal. 4.4-5
   A. The King Comes to His Kingdom
   B. The Present Reality of His Reign
   C. The Secret of the Kingdom: the Already and the Not Yet
   D. The Crucified King
   E. The Risen Lord

V. The Last Times (The Descent of the Holy Spirit) Acts 2.16-18
   A. Between the Times: the Church as Foretaste of the Kingdom
   B. The Church as Agent of the Kingdom
   C. The Conflict Between the Kingdoms of Darkness and Light

VI. The Fulfillment of Time (The Second Coming) Matt. 13.40-43
   A. The Return of Christ
   B. Judgment
   C. The Consummation of His Kingdom

VII. Beyond Time (Eternity Future) 1 Cor. 15.24-28
   A. Kingdom Handed Over to God the Father
   B. God as All in All

From Before to Beyond Time
Scriptures for Major Outline Points

I. Before Time (Eternity Past)

1 Cor. 2.7 (ESV) - But we impart a secret and hidden wisdom of God, *which God decreed before the ages* for our glory (cf. Titus 1.2).

II. Beginning of Time (Creation and Fall)

Gen. 1.1 (ESV) - *In the beginning*, God created the heavens and the earth.

III. Unfolding of Time (God's Plan Revealed Through Israel)

Gal. 3.8 (ESV) - And the Scripture, foreseeing that God would justify the Gentiles by faith, *preached the Gospel beforehand to Abraham*, saying, "In you shall all the nations be blessed" (cf. Rom. 9.4-5).

IV. Fullness of Time (The Incarnation of the Messiah)

Gal. 4.4-5 (ESV) - *But when the fullness of time had come*, God sent forth his Son, born of woman, born under the law, to redeem those who were under the law, so that we might receive adoption as sons.

V. The Last Times (The Descent of the Holy Spirit)

Acts 2.16-18 (ESV) - But this is what was uttered through the prophet Joel: "'*And in the last days it shall be*,' God declares, 'that I will pour out my Spirit on all flesh, and your sons and your daughters shall prophesy, and your young men shall see visions, and your old men shall dream dreams; even on my male servants and female servants in those days I will pour out my Spirit, and they shall prophesy.'"

VI. The Fulfillment of Time (The Second Coming)

Matt. 13.40-43 (ESV) - Just as the weeds are gathered and burned with fire, *so will it be at the close of the age*. The Son of Man will send his angels, and they will gather out of his Kingdom all causes of sin and all lawbreakers, and throw them into the fiery furnace. In that place there will be weeping and gnashing of teeth. Then the righteous will shine like the sun in the Kingdom of their Father. He who has ears, let him hear.

VII. Beyond Time (Eternity Future)

1 Cor. 15.24-28 (ESV) - Then comes the end, when he delivers the Kingdom to God the Father after destroying every rule and every authority and power. For he must reign until he has put all his enemies under his feet. The last enemy to be destroyed is death. For "God has put all things in subjection under his feet." But when it says, "all things are put in subjection," it is plain that he is excepted who put all things in subjection under him. When all things are subjected to him, then the Son himself will also be subjected to him who put all things in subjection under him, that God may be all in all.

APPENDIX 9
"There Is a River"

Identifying the Streams of a Revitalized Authentic Christian Community in the City[1]

Rev. Dr. Don L. Davis • Psalm 46.4 (ESV) - There is a river whose streams make glad the city of God, the holy habitation of the Most High.

Tributaries of Authentic Historic Biblical Faith			
Recognized Biblical Identity	*Revived Urban Spirituality*	*Reaffirmed Historical Connectivity*	*Refocused Kingdom Authority*
The Church Is **One**	The Church Is **Holy**	The Church Is **Catholic**	The Church Is **Apostolic**
A Call to Biblical Fidelity *Recognizing the Scriptures as the anchor and foundation of the Christian faith and practice*	**A Call to the Freedom, Power, and Fullness of the Holy Spirit** *Walking in the holiness, power, gifting, and liberty of the Holy Spirit in the body of Christ*	**A Call to Historic Roots and Continuity** *Confessing the common historical identity and continuity of authentic Christian faith*	**A Call to the Apostolic Faith** *Affirming the apostolic tradition as the authoritative ground of the Christian hope*
A Call to Messianic Kingdom Identity *Rediscovering the story of the promised Messiah and his Kingdom in Jesus of Nazareth*	**A Call to Live as Sojourners and Aliens as the People of God** *Defining authentic Christian discipleship as faithful membership among God's people*	**A Call to Affirm and Express the Global Communion of Saints** *Expressing cooperation and collaboration with all other believers, both local and global*	**A Call to Representative Authority** *Submitting joyfully to God's gifted servants in the Church as undershepherds of true faith*
A Call to Creedal Affinity *Embracing the Nicene Creed as the shared rule of faith of historic orthodoxy*	**A Call to Liturgical, Sacramental, and Catechetical Vitality** *Experiencing God's presence in the context of the Word, sacrament, and instruction*	**A Call to Radical Hospitality and Good Works** *Expressing kingdom love to all, and especially to those of the household of faith*	**A Call to Prophetic and Holistic Witness** *Proclaiming Christ and his Kingdom in word and deed to our neighbors and all peoples*

---

[1] *This schema is an adaptation and is based on the insights of the **Chicago Call** statement of May 1977, where various leading evangelical scholars and practitioners met to discuss the relationship of modern evangelicalism to the historic Christian faith.*

APPENDIX 10

A Schematic for a Theology of the Kingdom and the Church

The Urban Ministry Institute

The Reign of the One, True, Sovereign, and Triune God, the LORD God, Yahweh, God the Father, Son, and Holy Spirit

The Father	The Son	The Spirit
Love - 1 John 4.8 — Maker of heaven and earth and of all things visible and invisible	Faith - Heb. 12.2 — Prophet, Priest, and King	Hope - Rom. 15.13 — Lord of the Church
Creation — All that exists through the creative action of God.	**Kingdom** — The Reign of God expressed in the rule of his Son Jesus the Messiah.	**Church** — The one, holy, apostolic community which functions as a witness to (Acts 28.31) and a foretaste of (Col. 1.12; James 1.18; 1 Pet. 2.9; Rev. 1.6) the Kingdom of God.

The Father

The eternal God, sovereign in power, infinite in wisdom, perfect in holiness, and steadfast in love, is the source and goal of all things.

O, the depth of the riches and wisdom and knowledge of God! How unsearchable are his judgments, and how inscrutable his ways! For who has known the mind of the Lord, or who has been his counselor? Or who has ever given a gift to him, that he might be repaid? For from him and through him and to him are all things. To him be glory forever! Amen! - Rom. 11.33-36 (ESV) (cf. 1 Cor. 15.23-28, Rev.)

The Son

Rom. 8.18-21 →

Freedom (Slavery)

Jesus answered them, "Truly, truly, I say to you, everyone who commits sin is a slave to sin. The slave does not remain in the house forever; the son remains forever. So if the Son sets you free, you will be free indeed." - John 8.34-36 (ESV)

Rev. 21.1-5 →

Wholeness (Sickness)

But he was wounded for our transgressions; he was crushed for our iniquities; upon him was the chastisement that brought us peace, and with his stripes we are healed. - Isa. 53.5 (ESV)

Isa. 11.6-9 →

Justice (Selfishness)

Behold, my servant whom I have chosen, my beloved with whom my soul is well pleased. I will put my Spirit upon him, and he will proclaim justice to the Gentiles. He will not quarrel or cry aloud, nor will anyone hear his voice in the streets; a bruised reed he will not break, and a smoldering wick he will not quench, until he brings justice to victory - Matt. 12.18-20 (ESV)

The Spirit / Church

The Church is an Apostolic Community Where the Word is Rightly Preached, Therefore it is a Community of:

Calling - For freedom Christ has set us free; stand firm therefore, and do not submit again to a yoke of slavery. - Gal. 5.1 (ESV) (cf. Rom. 8.28-30; 1 Cor. 1.26-31; Eph. 1.18; 2 Thess. 2.13-14; Jude 1.1)

Faith - ". . . for unless you believe that I am he you will die in your sins" . . . So Jesus said to the Jews who had believed in him, "If you abide in my word, you are truly my disciples, and you will know the truth, and the truth will set you free." - John 8 24b, 31-32 (ESV) (cf. Ps. 119.45; Rom. 1.17; 5.1-2; Eph. 2.8-9; 2 Tim. 1.13-14; Heb. 2.14-15; James 1.25)

Witness - The Spirit of the Lord is upon me, because he has anointed me to proclaim good news to the poor. He has sent me to proclaim liberty to the captives and recovering of sight to the blind, to set at liberty those who are oppressed, to proclaim the year of the Lord's favor. - Luke 4.18-19 (ESV) (cf. Lev. 25.10; Prov. 31.8; Matt. 4.17; 28.18-20; Mark 13.10; Acts 1.8; 8.4, 12; 13.1-3; 25.20; 28.30-31)

The Church is One Community Where the Sacraments are Rightly Administered, Therefore it is a Community of:

Worship - You shall serve the Lord your God, and he will bless your bread and your water, and I will take sickness away from among you. - Exod. 23.25 (ESV) (cf. Ps. 147.1-3; Heb. 12.28; Col. 3.16; Rev. 15.3-4; 19.5)

Covenant - And the Holy Spirit also bears witness to us; for after the saying, "This is the covenant that I will make with them after those days, declares the Lord: I will put my laws on their hearts, and write them on their minds," then he adds, "I will remember their sins and their lawless deeds no more." - Heb. 10.15-17 (ESV) (cf. Isa. 54.10-17; Ezek. 34.25-31; 37.26-27; Mal. 2.4-5; Luke 22.20; 2 Cor. 3.6; Col. 3.15; Heb. 8.7-13; 12.22-24; 13.20-21)

Presence - In him you also are being built together into a dwelling place for God by his Spirit. - Eph. 2.22 (ESV) (cf. Exod. 40.34-38; Ezek. 48.35; Matt. 18.18-20)

The Church is a Holy Community Where Discipline is Rightly Ordered, Therefore it is a Community of:

Reconciliation - For he himself is our peace, who has made us both one and has broken down in his flesh the dividing wall of hostility by abolishing the law of commandments and ordinances, that he might create in himself one new man in place of the two, so making peace, and might reconcile us both to God in one body through the cross, thereby killing the hostility. And he came and preached peace to you who were far off and peace to those who were near. For through him we both have access in one Spirit to the Father. - Eph. 2.14-18 (ESV) (cf. Exod. 23.4-9; Lev. 19.34; Deut. 10.18-19; Ezek. 22.29; Mic. 6.8; 2 Cor. 5.16-21)

Suffering - Since therefore Christ suffered in the flesh, arm yourselves with the same way of thinking, for whoever has suffered in the flesh has ceased from sin, so as to live for the rest of the time in the flesh no longer for human passions but for the will of God. - 1 Pet. 4.1-2 (ESV) (cf. Luke 6.22; 10.3; Rom. 8.17; 2 Tim. 2.3; 3.12; 1 Pet. 2.20-24; Heb. 5.8; 13.11-14)

Service - But Jesus called them to him and said, "You know that the rulers of the Gentiles lord it over them, and their great ones exercise authority over them. It shall not be so among you. But whoever would be great among you must be your servant, and whoever would be first among you must be your slave even as the Son of Man came not to be served but to serve, and to give his life as a ransom for many." - Matt. 20.25-28 (ESV) (cf. 1 John 4.16-18, Gal. 2.10)

APPENDIX 11
Living in the Already and the Not Yet Kingdom
Rev. Dr. Don L. Davis

The Spirit: The pledge of the inheritance (***arrabon***)
The Church: The foretaste (***aparche***) of the Kingdom
"In Christ": The rich life (***en Christos***) we share as citizens of the Kingdom

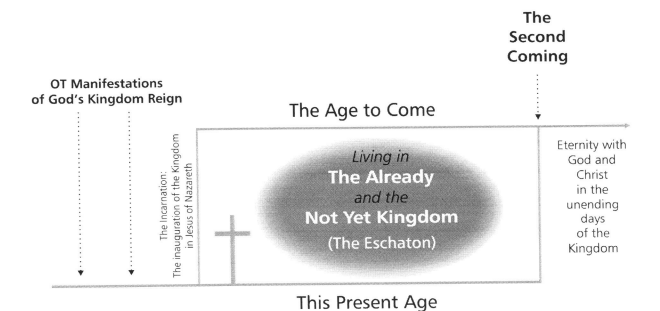

Internal enemy: The flesh (*sarx*) and the sin nature
External enemy: The world (*kosmos*) the systems of greed, lust, and pride
Infernal enemy: The devil (*kakos*) the animating spirit of falsehood and fear

Jewish View of Time

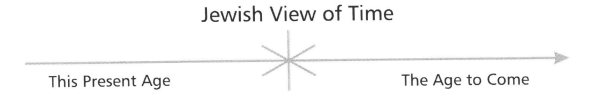

This Present Age   The Age to Come

The Coming of Messiah
The restoration of Israel
The end of Gentile oppression
The return of the earth to Edenic glory
Universal knowledge of the Lord

Jesus of Nazareth: The Presence of the Future

Rev. Dr. Don L. Davis

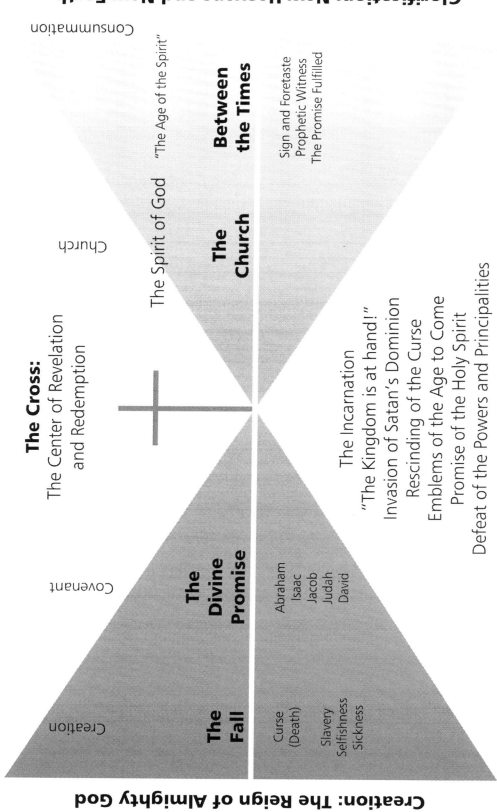

Glorification: New Heavens and New Earth

Consummation

Between the Times

"The Age of the Spirit"

Sign and Foretaste
Prophetic Witness
The Promise Fulfilled

The Church

Church

The Spirit of God

The Cross:
The Center of Revelation and Redemption

The Incarnation
"The Kingdom is at hand!"
Invasion of Satan's Dominion
Rescinding of the Curse
Emblems of the Age to Come
Promise of the Holy Spirit
Defeat of the Powers and Principalities

The Divine Promise

Covenant

Abraham
Isaac
Jacob
Judah
David

The Fall

Creation

Curse
(Death)

Slavery
Selfishness
Sickness

Creation: The Reign of Almighty God

APPENDIX 13

Traditions

(Paradosis)

Dr. Don L. Davis and Rev. Terry G. Cornett

Strong's Definition

Paradosis. Transmission, i.e. (concretely) a precept; specifically, the Jewish traditionary law

Vine's Explanation

denotes "a tradition," and hence, by metonymy, (a) "the teachings of the rabbis," . . . (b) "apostolic teaching," . . . of instructions concerning the gatherings of believers, of Christian doctrine in general . . . of instructions concerning everyday conduct.

1. **The concept of tradition in Scripture is essentially positive.**

   Jer. 6.16 (ESV) - Thus says the Lord: "Stand by the roads, and look, and ask for the ancient paths, where the good way is; and walk in it, and find rest for your souls. But they said, 'We will not walk in it'" (cf. Exod. 3.15; Judg. 2.17; 1 Kings 8.57-58; Ps. 78.1-6).

   2 Chron. 35.25 (ESV) - Jeremiah also uttered a lament for Josiah; and all the singing men and singing women have spoken of Josiah in their laments to this day. They made these a rule in Israel; behold, they are written in the Laments (cf. Gen. 32.32; Judg. 11.38-40).

   Jer. 35.14-19 (ESV) - The command that Jonadab the son of Rechab gave to his sons, to drink no wine, has been kept, and they drink none to this day, for they have obeyed their father's command. I have spoken to you persistently, but you have not listened to me. I have sent to you all my servants the prophets, sending them persistently, saying, 'Turn now every one of you from his evil way, and amend your deeds, and do not go after other gods to serve them, and then you shall dwell in the land that I gave to you and your fathers.' But you did not incline your ear or listen to me. The sons of Jonadab the son of Rechab have kept the command that their father gave them, but this people has not obeyed me. Therefore, thus says the

Traditions (continued)

Lord, the God of hosts, the God of Israel: Behold, I am bringing upon Judah and all the inhabitants of Jerusalem all the disaster that I have pronounced against them, because I have spoken to them and they have not listened, I have called to them and they have not answered." But to the house of the Rechabites Jeremiah said, "Thus says the Lord of hosts, the God of Israel: Because you have obeyed the command of Jonadab your father and kept all his precepts and done all that he commanded you, therefore thus says the Lord of hosts, the God of Israel: Jonadab the son of Rechab shall never lack a man to stand before me."

2. Godly tradition is a wonderful thing, but not all tradition is godly.

Any individual tradition must be judged by its faithfulness to the Word of God and its usefulness in helping people maintain obedience to Christ's example and teaching.[1] In the Gospels, Jesus frequently rebukes the Pharisees for establishing traditions that nullify rather than uphold God's commands.

Mark 7.8 (ESV) - You leave the commandment of God and hold to the tradition of men" (cf. Matt. 15.2-6; Mark 7.13).

Col. 2.8 (ESV) - See to it that no one takes you captive by philosophy and empty deceit, according to human tradition, according to the elemental spirits of the world, and not according to Christ.

3. Without the fullness of the Holy Spirit, and the constant edification provided to us by the Word of God, tradition will inevitably lead to dead formalism.

Those who are spiritual are filled with the Holy Spirit, whose power and leading alone provides individuals and congregations a sense of freedom and vitality in all they practice and believe. However, when the practices and teachings of any given tradition are no longer infused by the power of the Holy Spirit and the Word of God, tradition loses its effectiveness, and may actually become counterproductive to our discipleship in Jesus Christ.

Eph. 5.18 (ESV) - And do not get drunk with wine, for that is debauchery, but be filled with the Spirit.

[1] *"All Protestants insist that these traditions must ever be tested against Scripture and can never possess an independent apostolic authority over or alongside of Scripture." (J. Van Engen, "Tradition,"* **Evangelical Dictionary of Theology,** *Walter Elwell, Gen. ed.) We would add that Scripture is itself the "authoritative tradition" by which all other traditions are judged. See "Appendix A, The Founders of Tradition: Three Levels of Christian Authority," p. 4.*

Gal. 5.22-25 (ESV) - But the fruit of the Spirit is love, joy, peace, patience, kindness, goodness, faithfulness, gentleness, self-control; against such things there is no law. And those who belong to Christ Jesus have crucified the flesh with its passions and desires. If we live by the Spirit, let us also walk by the Spirit.

2 Cor. 3.5-6 (ESV) - Not that we are sufficient in ourselves to claim anything as coming from us, but our sufficiency is from God, who has made us competent to be ministers of a new covenant, not of the letter but of the Spirit. For the letter kills, but the Spirit gives life.

4. **Fidelity to the Apostolic Tradition (teaching and modeling) is the essence of Christian maturity.**

2 Tim. 2.2 (ESV) - and what you have heard from me in the presence of many witnesses entrust to faithful men who will be able to teach others also.

1 Cor. 11.1-2 (ESV) - Be imitators of me, as I am of Christ. Now I commend you because you remember me in everything and maintain the traditions even as I delivered them to you (cf.1 Cor. 4.16-17, 2 Tim. 1.13-14, 2 Thess. 3.7-9, Phil. 4.9).

1 Cor. 15.3-8 (ESV) - For I delivered to you as of first importance what I also received: that Christ died for our sins in accordance with the Scriptures, that he was buried, that he was raised on the third day in accordance with the Scriptures, and that he appeared to Cephas, then to the twelve. Then he appeared to more than five hundred brothers at one time, most of whom are still alive, though some have fallen asleep. Then he appeared to James, then to all the apostles. Last of all, as to one untimely born, he appeared also to me.

5. **The Apostle Paul often includes an appeal to the tradition for support in doctrinal practices.**

1 Cor. 11.16 (ESV) - If anyone is inclined to be contentious, we have no such practice, nor do the churches of God (cf. 1 Cor. 1.2, 7.17, 15.3).

Traditions (continued)

1 Cor. 14.33-34 (ESV) - For God is not a God of confusion but of peace. As in all the churches of the saints, the women should keep silent in the churches. For they are not permitted to speak, but should be in submission, as the Law also says.

6. When a congregation uses received tradition to remain faithful to the "Word of God," they are commended by the apostles.

1 Cor. 11.2 (ESV) - Now I commend you because you remember me in everything and maintain the traditions even as I delivered them to you.

2 Thess. 2.15 (ESV) - So then, brothers, stand firm and hold to the traditions that you were taught by us, either by our spoken word or by our letter.

2 Thess. 3.6 (ESV) - Now we command you, brothers, in the name of our Lord Jesus Christ, that you keep away from any brother who is walking in idleness and not in accord with the tradition that you received from us.

Appendix A

The Founders of Tradition: Three Levels of Christian Authority

Exod. 3.15 (ESV) - God also said to Moses, "Say this to the people of Israel, 'The Lord, the God of your fathers, the God of Abraham, the God of Isaac, and the God of Jacob, has sent me to you.' This is my name forever, and thus I am to be remembered throughout all generations."

1. The Authoritative Tradition: the Apostles and the Prophets (The Holy Scriptures)

Eph. 2.19-21 (ESV) - So then you are no longer strangers and aliens, but you are fellow citizens with the saints and members of the household of God, built on the foundation of the apostles and prophets, Christ Jesus himself being the cornerstone, in whom the whole structure, being joined together, grows into a holy temple in the Lord.

~ The Apostle Paul

Those who gave eyewitness testimony to the revelation and saving acts of Yahweh, first in Israel, and ultimately in Jesus Christ the Messiah. This testimony is binding for all people, at all times, and in all places. It is the authoritative tradition by which all subsequent tradition is judged.

2. The Great Tradition: the Ecumenical Councils and their Creeds[2]

[2] See Appendix B, "Defining the Great Tradition."

What has been believed everywhere, always, and by all.

~ Vincent of Lerins

The Great Tradition is the core dogma (doctrine) of the Church. It represents the teaching of the Church as it has understood the Authoritative Tradition (the Holy Scriptures), and summarizes those essential truths that Christians of all ages have confessed and believed. To these doctrinal statements the whole Church, (Catholic, Orthodox, and Protestant)[3] gives its assent. The worship and theology of the Church reflects this core dogma, which finds its summation and fulfillment in the person and work of Jesus Christ. From earliest times, Christians have expressed their devotion to God in its Church calendar, a yearly pattern of worship which summarizes and reenacts the events of Christ's life.

[3] Even the more radical wing of the Protestant reformation (Anabaptists) who were the most reluctant to embrace the creeds as dogmatic instruments of faith, did not disagree with the essential content found in them. "They assumed the Apostolic Creed–they called it 'The Faith,' Der Glaube, as did most people." See John Howard Yoder, Preface to Theology: Christology and Theological Method. Grand Rapids: Brazos Press, 2002. pp. 222-223.

3. Specific Church Traditions: the Founders of Denominations and Orders

The Presbyterian Church (U.S.A.) has approximately 2.5 million members, 11,200 congregations and 21,000 ordained ministers. Presbyterians trace their history to the 16th century and the Protestant Reformation. Our heritage, and much of what we believe, began with the French lawyer John Calvin (1509-1564), whose writings crystallized much of the Reformed thinking that came before him.

~ The Presbyterian Church, U.S.A.

Christians have expressed their faith in Jesus Christ in various ways through specific movements and traditions which embrace and express the Authoritative Tradition and the Great Tradition in unique ways. For instance,

Traditions (continued)

Catholic movements have arisen around people like Benedict, Francis, or Dominic, and among Protestants people like Martin Luther, John Calvin, Ulrich Zwingli, and John Wesley. Women have founded vital movements of Christian faith (e.g., Aimee Semple McPherson of the Foursquare Church), as well as minorities (e.g., Richard Allen of the African Methodist Episcopal Church or Charles H. Mason of the Church of God in Christ, who also helped to spawn the Assemblies of God), all which attempted to express the Authoritative Tradition and the Great Tradition in a specific way consistent with their time and expression.

The emergence of vital, dynamic movements of the faith at different times and among different peoples reveal the fresh working of the Holy Spirit throughout history. Thus, inside Catholicism, new communities have arisen such as the Benedictines, Franciscans, and Dominicans; and outside Catholicism, new denominations have emerged (Lutherans, Presbyterians, Methodists, Church of God in Christ, etc.). Each of these specific traditions have "founders," key leaders whose energy and vision helped to establish a unique expression of Christian faith and practice. Of course, to be legitimate, these movements must adhere to and faithfully express both the Authoritative Tradition and the Great Tradition. Members of these specific traditions embrace their own unique practices and patterns of spirituality, but these unique features are not necessarily binding on the Church at large. They represent the unique expressions of that community's understanding of and faithfulness to the Authoritative and Great Traditions.

Specific traditions seek to express and live out this faithfulness to the Authoritative and Great Traditions through their worship, teaching, and service. They seek to make the Gospel clear within new cultures or sub-cultures, speaking and modeling the hope of Christ into new situations shaped by their own set of questions posed in light of their own unique circumstances. These movements, therefore, seek to contextualize the Authoritative tradition in a way that faithfully and effectively leads new groups of people to faith in Jesus Christ, and incorporates those who believe into the community of faith that obeys his teachings and gives witness of him to others.

Appendix B

Defining the "Great Tradition"

The Great Tradition (sometimes called the "classical Christian tradition") is defined by Robert E. Webber as follows:

> *[It is] the broad outline of Christian belief and practice developed from the Scriptures between the time of Christ and the middle of the fifth century*
>
> ~ Webber. **The Ma estic Tapestry**.
> Nashville: Thomas Nelson Publishers, 1986. p. 10.

This tradition is widely affirmed by Protestant theologians both ancient and modern.

> *Thus those ancient Councils of Nicea, Constantinople, the first of Ephesus, Chalcedon, and the like, which were held for refuting errors, we willingly embrace, and reverence as sacred, in so far as relates to doctrines of faith, for they contain nothing but the pure and genuine interpretation of Scripture, which the holy Fathers with spiritual prudence adopted to crush the enemies of religion who had then arisen.*
>
> ~ John Calvin. **Institutes**. IV, ix. 8.

> *. . . most of what is enduringly valuable in contemporary biblical exegesis was discovered by the fifth century.*
>
> ~ Thomas C. Oden. **The Word of ife** .
> San Francisco: HarperSanFrancisco, 1989. p. xi

> *The first four Councils are by far the most important, as they settled the orthodox faith on the Trinity and the Incarnation.*
>
> ~ Philip Schaff. **The Creeds of Christendom**. Vol. 1.
> Grand Rapids: Baker Book House, 1996. p. 44.

Our reference to the Ecumenical Councils and Creeds is, therefore, focused on those Councils which retain a widespread agreement in the Church among Catholics, Orthodox, and Protestants. While Catholic and Orthodox share common agreement on the first seven councils, Protestants tend to affirm and use primarily the first four. Therefore, those councils which continue to be shared by the whole Church are completed with the Council of Chalcedon in 451.

Traditions (continued)

It is worth noting that each of these four Ecumenical Councils took place in a pre-European cultural context and that none of them were held in Europe. They were councils of the whole Church and they reflected a time in which Christianity was primarily an eastern religion in it's geographic core. By modern reckoning, their participants were African, Asian, and European. The councils reflected a church that ". . . has roots in cultures far distant from Europe and preceded the development of modern European identity, and [of which] some of its greatest minds have been African" (Oden, *The Living God*, San Francisco: HarperSanFrancisco, 1987, p. 9).

Perhaps the most important achievement of the Councils was the creation of what is now commonly called the Nicene Creed. It serves as a summary statement of the Christian faith that can be agreed on by Catholic, Orthodox, and Protestant Christians.

The first four Ecumenical Councils are summarized in the following chart:

Name/Date/Location	Purpose
First Ecumenical Council 325 A.D. Nicea, Asia Minor	Defending against: *Arianism* Question answered: *Was Jesus God?* Action: *Developed the initial form of the Nicene Creed to serve as a summary of the Christian faith*
Second Ecumenical Council 381 A.D. Constantinople, Asia Minor	Defending against: *Macedonianism* Question answered: *Is the Holy Spirit a personal and equal part of the Godhead?* Action: *Completed the Nicene Creed by expanding the article dealing with the Holy Spirit*
Third Ecumenical Council 431 A.D. Ephesus, Asia Minor	Defending against: *Nestorianism* Question answered: *Is Jesus Christ both God and man in one person?* Action: *Defined Christ as the Incarnate Word of God and affirmed his mother Mary as **theotokos** (God-bearer)*
Fourth Ecumenical Council 451 A.D. Chalcedon, Asia Minor	Defending against: *Monophysitism* Question answered: *How can Jesus be both God and man?* Action: *Explained the relationship between Jesus' two natures (human and Divine)*

APPENDIX 14

From Deep Ignorance to Credible Witness

Rev. Dr. Don L. Davis

Witness - Ability to give witness and teach
2. Tim. 2.2
Matt. 28.18-20
1 John 1.1-4
Prov. 20.6
2 Cor. 5.18-21

And the things you have heard me say in the presence of many witnesses entrust to reliable men who will also be qualified to teach others. - 2 Tim. 2.2

8

Lifestyle - Consistent appropriation and habitual practice based on beliefs
Heb. 5.11-6.2
Eph. 4.11-16
2 Pet. 3.18
1 Tim. 4.7-10

And Jesus increased in wisdom and in stature, and in favor with God and man. - Luke 2.52

7

Demonstration - Expressing conviction in corresponding conduct, speech, and behavior
James 2.14-26
2 Cor. 4.13
2 Pet. 1.5-9
1 Thess. 1.3-10

Nevertheless, at your word I will let down the net. - Luke 5.5

6

Conviction - Committing oneself to think, speak, and act in light of information
Heb. 2.3-4
Heb. 11.1, 6
Heb. 3.15-19
Heb. 4.2-6

Do you believe this? - John 11.26

5

Discernment - Understanding the meaning and implications of information
John 16.13
Eph. 1.15-18
Col. 1.9-10
Isa. 6.10; 29.10

Do you understand what you are reading? - Acts 8.30

4

Knowledge - Ability to recall and recite information
2 Tim. 3.16-17
1 Cor. 2.9-16
1 John 2.20-27
John 14.26

For what does the Scripture say? - Rom. 4.3

3

Interest - Responding to ideas or information with both curiosity and openness
Ps. 42.1-2
Acts 9.4-5
John 12.21
1 Sam. 3.4-10

We will hear you again on this matter. - Acts 17.32

2

Awareness - General exposure to ideas and information
Mark 7.6-8
Acts 19.1-7
John 5.39-40
Matt. 7.21-23

At that time, Herod the tetrarch heard about the fame of Jesus. - Matt. 14.1

1

Ignorance - Unfamiliarity with information due to naivete, indifference, or hardness
Eph. 4.17-19
Ps. 2.1-3
Rom. 1.21; 2.19
1 John 2.11

Who is the Lord that I should heed his voice? - Exod. 5.2

0

APPENDIX 15

The Way of Wisdom

Rev. Dr. Don L. Davis

The Way of Wisdom {Proverbs 2.1-9; Prov. 8.1-9; 9.1-6; Prov. 1.7; 8.13

Sowing and Reaping {Gal. 6.7-8

You will **sow**
You will **reap** what you sow
You will reap **more than** what you sow
You will reap in **proportion** to what you sow
You will reap **in kind** as you sow
You will reap in a **different season** than you sow
You determine what you sow
You can **sow differently** than you did last year
You reap more if you **cultivate and fertilize**
Your sowing can **affect what others reap** also

What you **think about**
How you **dress**
How you **speak**
Who you **hang out with**
What you **listen to and look at**
What you **read**
Where you **go**
How you **make decisions**
What your **goals** are
What's important to you

The Goal

Be like Jesus
1 Cor. 11.2
Rom. 8.29
Phil. 3.8-12

Loving God with all our heart
Deut. 6.4-6
Matt. 22.34-40

Loving our neighbors as ourselves
Lev. 19.18
Matt. 7.12

The Way of Life { Proverbs 1.7-8; 4.13; 8.10; 9.9; 10.17; 13.18; 15.32-33; 23.23

The Narrow Way {Matt. 7.13-14

Isa. 26.1-9

Instruction in righteousness (On track)
Pss. 31.3; 48.14; Isa. 42.16; Pss. 125; 4-5; 25.5; 27.11

Correction (the way back)
Proverbs 13.1; 19.20; Heb. 5.8; Matt. 26.39; Pss. 31.3;
119.35; 143.10; Prov. 6.20-23; Jer. 42.1-3

Doctrine (The Way)
2 Timothy 3.16-17; John 8.31-32; 1 John 4.6

Rebuke (the way off)
Proverbs 9.9; 11.14; 12.15; 15.22; 19.20;
20.18; 24.6; 13.10; 15.10

The Way That Leads to Death
Prov. 14.12; 16.25; 1.24-33; 2.10-22; 15.9; 15.19, 24, 29; 13.15;
Job 15.20; Ps. 107.17; Rom. 2.9

APPENDIX 16

Chart of Biblical Studies

Rev. Dr. Don L. Davis

Type of Criticism	The Task in Bible Study	What is Studied	View of the Bible	Proof Level	Strengths	Weaknesses	Level of Criticism
Form Criticism	Trace the oral traditions and earliest stories associated with the texts	Oral traditions of the people of God, along with the early Church	Product of human tradition	Low	Evolving sense of the Bible's origin	Too speculative	Higher
Source Criticism	Discover the written sources used in the creation of the books	Comparing texts in various books to see similarities and contrasts	Product of human ingenuity	Low	Ability to identify key sources	No way to prove its claims	Higher
Linguistic Criticism	Study the ancient languages, words and grammar	Study of the ancient Hebrew, koine Greek, and Aramaic	Product of human culture	Mid	In-depth meaning of ancient language	Too far removed from the language	Lower
Textual Criticism	Compare the variant manuscripts to find the best reading	Focus on different manuscripts and their families of texts	Product of textual research	High	Multitude of reliable manuscripts available	Far too extensive number	Lower
Literary Criticism	Determine the author, style, recipient, and genre	Different types of literature, background study on the books	Product of literary genius	High	Discovering what types of literature mean	We tend to read too much into it	Higher

Chart of Biblical Studies (continued)

Type of Criticism	The Task in Bible Study	What is Studied	View of the Bible	Proof Level	Strengths	Weaknesses	Level of Criticism
Canonical Criticism	Analyze the Church's acceptance, view and use of the text	History of the Bible in ancient Israel and the early Church (councils, conventions)	Product of religious community	High	Taking the community's view of the Bible seriously	Tends to make the Bible merely a group book	Higher
Redaction Criticism	Focus on the theology of the person who wrote it	Intense study of individual books to understand the meaning of the author's theme and views	Product of creative personality	Mid	Deep analysis of an author's entire collection of writings	Does not correlate the Bible with other books	Higher
Historical Criticism	Investigate the historical setting, culture, and background	Research of the ancient cultures, their customs, and their history	Product of historical forces	Mid	Firmer grasp of historical issues of the text	Too far removed from the history	Higher
Translation Studies	Provide a clear, readable translation based on the best manuscripts	Understanding of the receiving culture's language along with the meanings of the text for the best translation	Product of dynamic interpretation	Mid	Pursuing a version of the Bible in one's own tongue and thought world	Reflects our own opinions about the text's meaning	Lower

APPENDIX 17

Theories of Inspiration

Rev. Terry G. Cornett

Theory of Inspiration	Explanation	Possible Objection(s)
Mechanical or Dictation	The human author is a passive instrument in God's hands. The author simply writes down each word as God speaks it. This direct dictation is what protects the text from human error.	The books of Scripture show diverse writing styles, vocabularies, and manners of expression which vary with each human author. This theory doesn't seem to explain why God would use human authors rather than giving us a direct written word from himself.
Intuition or Natural	Gifted people with exceptional spiritual insight were chosen by God to write the Bible	The Bible indicates that Scripture came from God, through human authors (2 Pet. 1.20-21).
Illumination	The Holy Spirit heightened the normal capacities of human authors so that they had special insight into spiritual truth.	The Scriptures indicate that the human authors expressed the very words of God ("Thus saith the Lord" passages; Rom. 3.2.)
Degrees of Inspiration	Certain parts of the Bible are more inspired than others. Sometimes this position is used to argue that portions dealing with key doctrines or ethical truths are inspired while portions dealing with history, economics, culture, etc. are less inspired or not inspired.	The biblical authors never indicate that some of Scripture is more inspired or treat only one kind of biblical material as inspired in their use of it. Jesus speaks about the entire scriptural revelation up to his day as an unchanging word from God (Matt. 5.17-18; John 3.34-35).
Verbal-Plenary	Both divine and human elements are present in the production of Scripture. The entire text of Scripture, including the words, are a product of the mind of God expressed in human terms and conditions, through human authors that he foreknew (Jer. 1.5) and chose for the task.	It seems unlikely that the human elements which are finite and culture-bound could be described as the unchanging words of God.

APPENDIX 18

An Example of the Practice of Textual Criticism
Adapted from R. C. Briggs, **Interpreting the New Testament Today.**

Mark 1.1 The beginning of the Gospel of Jesus Christ *(the Son of God)*

According to the critical apparatus, the following manuscripts (or group of manuscripts) read

Ιησοῦ Χριστοῦ υἱού θεοῦ

A (*Codex Alexandrinus*). Fifth century. Byzantine text (in the Gospels).

B (*Codex Vaticanus*). Fourth century. Alexandrian text (in the Gospels and Acts).

D (*Codex Bezae*). Fifth or sixth century. Western text.

W (*Washington Codex*). Fifth century. Western text (in Mark 1.1-5.30).

Ω (*koine*). Group of late uncial and minuscule manuscripts dating from the seventh century. Western text.

λ (*Family 1, Lake Group*). Twelfth century and later. Akin to fourth- and fifth-century Caesarean text.

φ (*Family 13, Ferrar Group*). Twelfth century and later. Akin to Caesarean text.

it (*Itala or Old Latin*). Eleventh century and later. Text is early Western (prior to date of Vulgate).

vg (*Vulgate*). Authorized Latin translation, completed by Jerome in A. D. 405 (Gospels A. D. 385). Western text.

sy[P] (*Peshitta*). Authorized fifth-century Syriac translation. Akin to the Byzantine text (in the Gospels).

sa (*Sahidic*). Fourth-century Coptic (Egyptian) translation. Alexandrian text, with Western influence.

bo (*Bohairic*). Coptic translation, later than Sahidic. Western text. The critical apparatus also lists two significant manuscripts which preserve the shorter reading.

S also designated ~ (*Codex Sinaiticus*). Fourth century. Like B, a primary representative of the Alexandrian text.

Θ (*Codex Koridethi*). Ninth century. Text akin to third- and fourth-century Alexandrian text.

APPENDIX 19

The Compass of Narrative Elements

Charting a Course toward a Story's Meaning

Rev. Dr. Don L. Davis

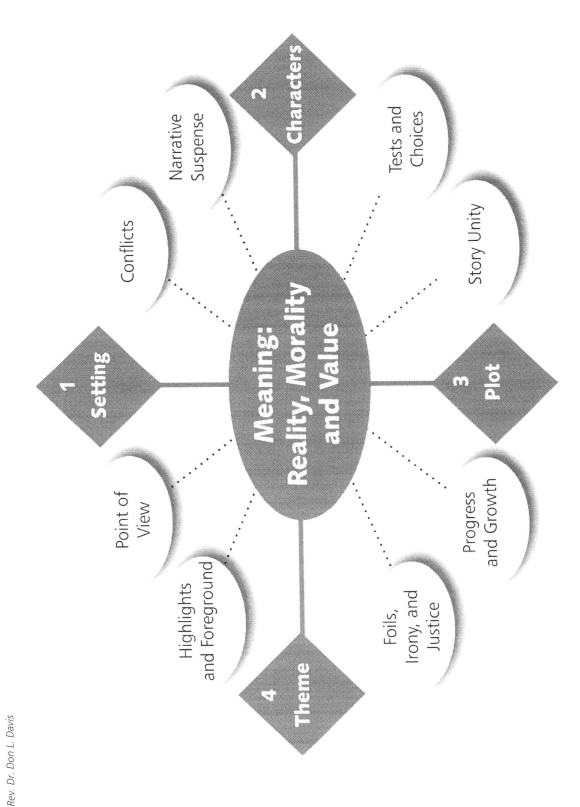

APPENDIX 20

A Comparison of Translation Philosophies
Common English Versions of the Bible
Rev. Dr. Don L. Davis

Most Literally Word-for-Word ◄ · · · · · · ·   · · · · · · · ► *Least Literally Word-for-Word*

Formal Equivalence	**Dynamic Equivalence**	**Paraphrase**
New American Standard Bible (NASB)		
New King James Version (NKJV)		
New Revised Standard Version (NRSV)		
English Standard Version (ESV)		
International Version(NIV)		
New Jerusalem Bible (NJB)		
Revised English Bible (REB)		
Today's English Version (TEV)		
Contemporary English Version (CEV)		
New Living Translation (NLT)		
	JB Phillips Version (Phillips)	
	The Living Bible (LB)	
	The Message	
		Cotton Patch Gospels

APPENDIX 21

Developing Ears that Hear

Responding to the Spirit and the Word

Rev. Dr. Don L. Davis

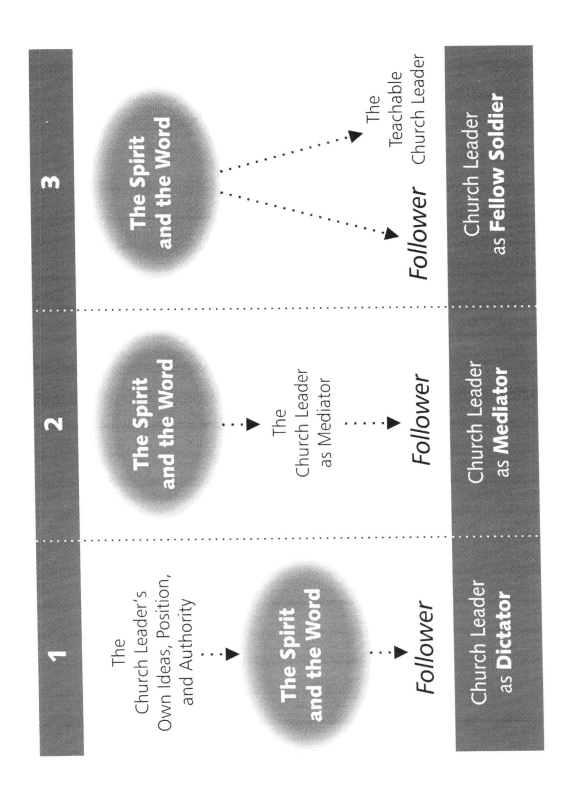

1

The
Church Leader's
Own Ideas, Position,
and Authority

The Spirit and the Word

Follower

Church Leader
as **Dictator**

2

The Spirit and the Word

The
Church Leader
as Mediator

Follower

Church Leader
as **Mediator**

3

The Spirit and the Word

The
Teachable
Church Leader

Follower Church Leader

Church Leader
as **Fellow Soldier**

APPENDIX 22

Translation Methodology

Rev. Terry G. Cornett

	Grade Level	Formal Equivalence	Dynamic Equivalence	Paraphrase
Hard to Read	12th 11th 10th 9th	King James Version (KJV) New American Standard Bible (NASB)		
Average Adult Level	8th 7th 6th	New International Version (NIV) New Revised Standard Version (NRSV) New King James Version (NKJV)	New Living Translation (NLT)	The Living Bible (TLB) The Message
Children's Bibles	5th 4th 3rd	New International Reader's Version (NIrV)	Contemporary English Version (CEV) International Children's Bible (ICB)	

APPENDIX 23

Figures of Speech

Bob Smith. Basics of Bible Interpretation. Waco: Word Publishers, 1978. pp. 113-120.

One of the most enlightening aspects of language is the study of figurative expressions. Milton Terry introduces us to this subject with keen insight:

The natural operations of the human mind prompt men to trace analogies and make comparisons. Pleasing emotions are excited and the imagination is gratified by the use of metaphors and similes. Were we to suppose a language sufficiently copious in words to express all possible conceptions, the human mind would still require us to compare and contrast our concepts, and such a procedure would soon necessitate a variety of figures of speech. So much of our knowledge is acquired through the senses, that all our abstract ideas and our spiritual language have a material base. "It is not too much to say," observes Max Muller, "that the whole dictionary of ancient religion is made up of metaphors. With us these metaphors are all forgotten. We speak of *spirit* without thinking of *breath*, of *heaven* without thinking of *sky*, of *pardon* without thinking of a *release*, of *revelation* without thinking of a *veil*. But in ancient language every one of these words, nay, every word that does not refer to sensuous objects, is still in a chrysalis stage, half material and half spiritual, and rising and falling in its character according to the capacities of its speakers and hearers."[1]

What potent possibilities, then, lie in concepts conveyed by figurative language! So, moving to specifics, let's explore the various figures of speech. I'll list some of them, along with illustrations of their use on the following pages.

[1] *Milton S. Terry.* **Biblical Hermeneutics.** *Grand Rapids: Zondervan Publishing House, n.d. p. 244.*

Figures of Speech

SIMILE (*similis* = like)	A formal comparison using "*as . . . so*" or "like" to express resemblance. "*Even so*, husbands should love their own wives *as* their own bodies . . ." (Eph. 5.28).
METAPHOR (*Meta+phero* = a carrying over)	An implied comparison, a word applied to something it is not, to suggest a resemblance. "*Benjamin is a ravenous wolf . . .*" (Gen. 49.27).

Figures of Speech (continued)

IRONY (*Eiron* = a dissembling speaker)	The speaker or writer says the very opposite of what he intends to convey. "*. . . you are the people and wisdom will die with you*" (Job 12.1).
METONYMY (*Meta+onoma* = a change of name)	One word is used in place of another to portray some actual relationship between the things signified. "*Kill the passover . . .*" (Exod. 12.21 KJV) where the paschal lamb is meant.
HYPERBOLE (*Huper+bole*) = a throwing beyond	Intentional exaggeration for the purpose of emphasis, or magnifying beyond reality. "*If your right eye causes you to sin, pluck it out and throw it away . . .*" (Matt. 5.29).
PERSONIFICATION (to make like a person)	Inanimate objects are spoken of as persons, as if they had life. "The sea looked and fled . . ." (Ps. 114.3).
APOSTROPHE (*apo+strepho* = to turn from)	Turning from the immediate hearers to address an absent or imaginary person or thing. "*Ah, sword of the Lord! How long till you are quiet?*" (Jer. 47.6).
SYNECDOCHE (*sun+ekdechomai* = to receive from and associate with)	Where the whole is put for a part, or a part for the whole, an individual for a class and vice-versa. "*And we were in all 276 souls . . .*" in Acts 27.37, where *soul* is used for the whole person.

Simile

First, let's compare simile and metaphor. Ephesians 5:22-27 is a simile, making a formal comparison between Christ and the church on the one hand, and husbands and wives on the other. The words "as . . . so" or "even so" make this very clear. And this figure heightens our interest and dignifies the marriage relationship, especially if we see it in outline form, like this:

Figures of Speech (continued)

AS with CHRIST AND THE CHURCH	SO with HUSBANDS AND WIVES
CHRIST LOVED THE CHURCH and gave himself up for her (Eph. 5.25)	*HUSBANDS, LOVE your WIVES as CHRIST LOVED the CHURCH* (Eph. 5.25)
"THAT he might sanctify her" (Eph. 5.26) i.e. that we might be put to the intended use for which he created us: a) as an expression of his own *LIFE* and *CHARACTER* b) to fulfill our calling, enjoy our God-given ministries c) and much more (you add the rest)	THAT the husband might sanctify his wife. i.e. that she might SHARE HIS LIFE, be his helper, etc. a) expressing her own personality and life in Christ b) employing her gifts in a spiritual ministry. c) be the *ruler* of the *home*, in all that means to her husband and children
"THAT he might present the church to himself in splendor" (Eph. 5.27) i.e. that he might enjoy the benefits stemming from his unselfish love - in enjoying his Bride. And lead us on to the fulfillment of our manhood and womanhood by his love.	THAT the husband might seek his wife's fulfillment, and enjoy her, i.e. that he may enjoy the beauty and glory of her fulfilled womanhood, as he undertakes the responsibility of his headship leading her with the leadership of love to ultimate fulfillment
"THAT she might be holy and without blemish" (Eph. 5.27). i.e. that his work in us may go on to completion, that we may be wholly his.	THAT the husband be faithful, hanging in there, i.e. that his commitment may be steadfast and permanent, in spite of problems.
"Having cleansed her by the washing of water with the word" (Eph. 5.26) Based on *COMMUNICATION* which his loving heart initiates - to keep us close, mutually enjoying our love relationship.	Husbands are to keep communication channels open, remembering that *LOVE finds a way to COMMUNICATE, and it's his initiative* if he is going to love as CHRIST LOVED.

Figures of Speech (continued)

Metaphor

By contrast, a metaphor is not so straightforward. It communicates an impression more by implication. In the expressions, "You *are the salt of the earth . . .*" (Matt. 5:13) and *"You are the light of the world"* (Matt. 5:14), our Lord Jesus is multiplying metaphors to communicate graphic truth about the determinative role Christians are to play in affecting the world. In those early days, salt was the major means of arresting corruption in meat or fish, so the figure is not lost on those who listened to Jesus. Light, in any age, enables us to function with any degree of confidence. It dispels darkness. When we can't see, we're in trouble! The words "salt" and "light" are used as implied comparison. These metaphors speak with penetrating force, even though they are implicit in nature.

Irony

The use of irony as a figure of speech, though it has a bite to it, often has its humorous side. Our Lord was using both effects when he said, ". . . how can you say to your brother, 'Brother, let me take out the speck that is in your eye,' when you yourself do not see the log that is in your own eye?" (Luke 6:42).

In 1 Corinthians 4:8 the apostle Paul uses irony with great force, "Already you are filled! Already you have become rich! Without us you have become kings! And would that you did reign, so that we might share the rule with you." As we read on, Paul proceeds to contrast the state of the apostles as being the last—not the first, as spectacles to the world, as fools. Then he uses irony again, "We are fools for Christ's sake, but you are wise in Christ. We are weak, but you are strong. You are held in honor, but we in disrepute" (1 Cor. 4:10). Can you imagine how the Corinthian Christians must have felt the shame of their misplaced value systems, how this pointed word of sarcasm must have punctured their swollen pride in men? Would that we should review *our* value systems, today, and discover the only ground of boasting—the Lord Jesus and his life in us.

Metonymy

Then there's metonymy (a change of name). Speaking to the Pharisees concerning Herod, Christ says "Go and tell that *fox . . ." (Luke* 13:32) and with one word he characterized that politically crafty king. And, "The way of the fool is right in his own eyes . . ." (Prov. 12:15) where *eyes* represents the way he sees things, or his mental perspective. And, ". . . *the tongue* of the wise brings healing" (Prov. 12:18) in which *tongue* stands for what the wise one says, his words of wisdom.

In the New Testament, "Then went out to him Jerusalem and all Judea and all the region about the Jordan . . ." (Matt. 3:5) in which it is obvious that *people*, not places, are meant in the mention of these various regions. Then, we look at "You cannot drink the cup of the Lord and the cup of demons. You cannot partake of the table of the Lord and the table of demons" (1 Cor. 10:21). Here *cup* and *table* are used for what they contain and what they offer. Again, in Romans 3:30 *the circumcision is* used to represent the Jewish people, while *uncircumcision* refers to the Gentiles.

I'm sure from these examples you can see how commonly metonymy is used in the Bible. We use the same figure today when we call a person "a tiger" or "a kitten."

Hyperbole

Painting a picture larger than life by intentional exaggeration beyond reality is a common feature of our own speech, so hyperbole (a *throwing beyond*) should be thoroughly familiar to us.

In the anguish of his torment Job indulges in this kind of language. More graphically than any other form of speech it expresses the awfulness of his feeling of affliction.

> And now my soul is poured out within me; days of
> affliction have taken hold of me.
>
> The night racks my bones, and the pain that gnaws
> me takes no rest.
>
> With violence it seizes my garment; it binds me
> about like the collar of my tunic.
>
> God has cast me into the mire, and I have become
> like dust and ashes.
>
> I cry to thee and thou dost not answer me; I stand,
> and thou dost not heed me.

Figures of Speech (continued)

> Thou hast turned cruel to me; with the might of thy
> hand thou dost persecute me.
>
> Thou liftest me up on the wind, thou makest me ride
> on it, and thou tossest me about in the roar of
> the storm.
>
> Yea, I know that thou wilt bring me to death, and to
> the house appointed for all living
>
> ~ Job 30.16-23

Certainly we get the keen sense of his utter despair from this highly expressive, but extravagant, language.

The apostle John in the New Testament uses hyperbolic language in this statement: "But there are also many other things which Jesus did; were every one of them to be written, I suppose that the world itself could not contain the books that would be written" (John 21:25). If we considered Christ's eternal existence, perhaps this statement could betaken literally, but if we limit it to the deeds of the Lord Jesus in his humanity (which I believe is what John has in mind) then it is clearly a use of hyperbole.

Personification

Referring to inanimate objects as if they possessed life and personality is especially evident in the language of imagination and feeling. In Numbers 16:32,". . . the earth opened its mouth and swallowed them up . . ." speaks of Korah and his men. Here the earth is personified as having a mouth to devour these men.

The Lord Jesus uses personification in, "O Jerusalem, Jerusalem, killing the prophets and stoning those who are sent to you! How often would I have gathered your children together as a hen gathers her brood under her wings, and you would not!" (Matt. 23:37). The city of Jerusalem is here personified. Our Lord's concern was for its people, yet he addresses the city as if it were they.

Again, our Lord personifies *tomorrow* in these words: "Therefore do not be anxious about tomorrow, for tomorrow will be anxious for itself" (Matt. 6:34). Here *tomorrow is* invested with characteristics of human personality, as being beset with anxious cares.

Apostrophe

This is a strange but graphic figure which sounds as if the speaker were talking to himself in a sort of externalized soliloquy. For instance, David says to his dead son, "O my son Absalom, my son, my son Absalom! Would I had died instead of you, O Absalom, my son, my son!" (2 Sam. 18:33). What a moving expression of David's grief this is; no other mode of expression could be quite so expressive in this instance.

Then there is the use of this figure in which the kings of earth address a fallen city, "Alas! alas! thou great city, thou mighty city, Babylon! In one hour has thy judgment come!" (Rev. 18:10).

This figure of speech seems best adapted to the expression of deep emotion. As such, it readily grabs our attention and draws out our interest.

Synechdoche

Here's one most of us never heard of, but which we frequently use in everyday speech. We say, "This is his hour" when we don't really mean an hour just sixty minutes long. We mean this is his time of glory, or suffering, or whatever we associate with his current experience. We have substituted a part for the whole. In Scripture it occurs in such passages as this: in Judges 12:7 we are told Jephthah was buried "in the cities of Gilead" (Hebrew) though actually only one of those cities is meant; in Luke 2:1 "all the world" is used to mean the world of the Roman Empire; in Deuteronomy 32:41 "if I whet the lightning of my sword" the word *lightning is* used for the flashing edge of the gleaming blade.

Perhaps now we have seen enough of the prevalence and expressive value of figures of speech to help us appreciate the color and realism they lend to the language of the Bible. Also, interpretively, our review should take some of the mystery out of our encounters with these forms, in studying the Bible.

APPENDIX 24
Bible Study Tools Worksheet

Read through the following Scripture passage and then answer the questions that follow using a Strong's Concordance, Vine's Expository Dictionary of Old and New Testament Words, and the New Bible Dictionary.

Romans 4 (ESV)

What then shall we say was gained by Abraham, our forefather according to the flesh? [2] For if Abraham was **justified** by works, he has something to boast about, but not before God. [3] For what does the Scripture say? "Abraham believed God, and it was counted to him as righteousness." [4] Now to the one who works, his wages are not counted as a gift but as his due. [5] And to the one who does not work but trusts him who justifies the ungodly, his faith is counted as righteousness, [6] just as David also speaks of the blessing of the one to whom God counts righteousness apart from works: [7] "Blessed are those whose lawless deeds are forgiven, and whose sins are covered; [8] blessed is the man against whom the Lord will not count his sin." [9] Is this blessing then only for the circumcised, or also for the uncircumcised? We say that faith was counted to Abraham as righteousness. [10] How then was it counted to him? Was it before or after he had been circumcised? It was not after, but before he was circumcised. [11] He received the sign of circumcision as a seal of the righteousness that he had by faith while he was still uncircumcised. The purpose was to make him the father of all who believe without being circumcised, so that righteousness would be counted to them as well, [12] and to make him the father of the circumcised who are not merely circumcised but who also **walk** in the footsteps of the faith that our father Abraham had before he was circumcised. [13] For the promise to Abraham and his offspring that he would be heir of the world did not come through the law but through the righteousness of faith.

1. Use your concordance to identify the word that is translated "justified" in verse 2 and then write down the word and its Strong's number in the space below:

   Greek word _____ Strong's number _____

2. Look up this word in your *Vine's Expository Dictionary* and read the entry for this word. What does this information add to your understanding of the word and the passage?

_____

_____

_____

3. Use your concordance to identify the word that is translated "walk" in verse 12 and then write down the word and its Strong's number in the space below.

Greek word _____ Strong's number _____

4. Look up this word in *Vine's Expository Dictionary* and read the entry.

Why do you think the Apostle Paul chose this word rather than one of the other Greek words for walking? What does knowing the definition of this word for "walk" add to your understanding of this passage?

_____

_____

_____

_____

5. Using the *New Bible Dictionary*, look up and read the article on "Abraham." In what way does this deepen your understanding of the Scripture passage?

_____

_____

_____

_____

APPENDIX 25

Christ's View of the Bible

Paul P. Enns. The Moody Handbook of Theology (electronic ed.). Chicago: Moody Press, 1997.

In determining the nature of biblical inspiration, nothing could be more significant than determining the view Christ held regarding the Scriptures. Certainly no one ought to hold a lower view of Scripture than He held; His view of the Scriptures ought to be the determinant and the norm for other persons' views. That is the foundational argument of R. Laird Harris. In defending the inspiration of the Scriptures he does not use 2 Timothy 3.16 or 2 Peter 1.21 as the primary argument (although he recognizes their validity); he instead argues from the standpoint of Christ's view of the Scriptures.

(1) Inspiration of the whole. In His use of the Old Testament Christ gave credence to the inspiration of the entire Old Testament. In Matthew 5.17–18 Christ affirmed that not the smallest letter or stroke would pass from the law until it would be fulfilled. In v. 17 He referred to the law or the prophets, a common phrase designating the entire Old Testament. In this rather strong statement, Jesus affirmed the inviolability of the entire Old Testament and thereby affirmed the inspiration of the entire Old Testament.

In Luke 24.44 Jesus reminded the disciples that all the things written about Him in the law of Moses, the prophets, and the Psalms must be fulfilled. The disciples had failed to understand the teachings concerning the death and resurrection of Christ in the Old Testament, but because of the inspiration of the Old Testament, those prophesied events had to take place. By His threefold designation of the Old Testament, Christ was affirming the inspiration and authority of the entire Old Testament.

When Jesus debated with the unbelieving Jews concerning His right to be called the Son of God He referred them to Psalm 82.6 and reminded them "the Scripture cannot be broken" (John 10.35). "It means that Scripture cannot be emptied of its force by being shown to be erroneous." It is noteworthy that Jesus referred to a rather insignificant passage from the Old Testament and indicated that the Scripture could not be set aside or annulled.

(2) Inspiration of the parts. Christ quoted from the Old Testament profusely and frequently. His arguments hinged on the integrity of the Old Testament passage He was quoting. By this method of argumentation, Christ was affirming the

inspiration of the individual texts or books of the Old Testament. A few examples will suffice. In Jesus' encounter with Satan at the time of His temptation, He refuted the arguments of Satan by a reference to Deuteronomy. In Matthew 4.4, 7, 10 Jesus quoted from Deuteronomy 8.3; 6.13, 16, indicating Satan was wrong and emphasizing that these words written in Deuteronomy had to be fulfilled. In Matthew 21.42 Jesus quoted from Psalm 118.22, which teaches that the Messiah would be rejected. In Matthew 12.18–21 Jesus quoted from Isaiah 42.1–4, showing that His peaceable, gentle disposition and His inclusion of the Gentiles had all been foretold in the prophetic writings. These are only selected examples, revealing that Christ quoted from various parts of the Old Testament, affirming their inspiration and authority.

(3) Inspiration of the words. In defending the doctrine of the resurrection to the Sadducees, Jesus quoted from Exodus 3.6 (significant because the Sadducees held only to the Pentateuch), "I am the God of Abraham." In this response Jesus' entire argument hinged on the words "I am." Jesus was apparently supplying the verb which the Hebrew text only implies. Thus He supported the Septuagint (Greek) version which includes the verb. That version was so highly regarded by many of the Lord's contemporaries that it was practically equated with the original Scriptures.

In affirming the resurrection Jesus reminded the Sadducees that Exodus 3.6 said "I am." He elaborated: "God is not the God of the dead but of the living." If the words of the Old Testament were not inspired, His argument was useless; but if the very words of the Old Testament were actually inspired, then His argument carried enormous weight. In fact, Jesus' argument hinges on the present tense of the statement. Because it was written in Exodus 3.6, "I am...." , the doctrine of the resurrection could be affirmed; God is the God of the living patriarchs.

A similar example is found in Matthew 22.44 where Jesus, in debating the Pharisees, explained that their concept of Messiah was wrong. The Pharisees thought of Messiah as a political redeemer but Jesus shows them in His quotation from Psalm 110.1 that David, Israel's greatest king, saw Messiah as greater than himself, calling Him Lord. The entire argument of Christ rests on the phrase "my Lord." In quoting Psalm 110.1, Jesus rested His argument on the inspiration of the precise words "my Lord." If Psalm 110.1 did not read exactly "my Lord" then Christ's argument was in vain. An additional example is

Christ's View of the Bible (continued)

Christ's use of Psalm 82.6 in John 10.34 where His entire argument rests on the word "gods."

(4) Inspiration of the letters. In a number of His statements Christ reveals that He believed the letters of Scripture were inspired. In Matthew 5.18 Jesus declared, "not the smallest letter or stroke shall pass away from the Law, until all is accomplished." The term "smallest letter" refers to the Hebrew letter yodh, which looks like an apostrophe ('). The "stroke" refers to the minute distinction between two Hebrew letters. An equivalent would be the distinction between an O and a Q. Only the little "tail" distinguishes the Q from the O. Jesus emphasized that all the details of the Old Testament writings would be fulfilled down to the very letter.

(5) Inspiration of the New Testament. In the Upper Room discourse Christ made a significant statement that seems to point to the ultimate, accurate recording of the New Testament writings. In John 14.26 Jesus indicated that the Holy Spirit would provide accurate recall for the apostles as they penned the words of Scripture, thus guaranteeing their accuracy (cf. John 16.12–15). This may explain how an old man such as John, when penning the life of Christ, could accurately describe the details of the events that occurred years earlier. The Holy Spirit gave John and the other writers accurate recall of the events. Hence, Jesus affirmed not only the inspiration of the Old Testament but also the New Testament.

An obvious conclusion is that Jesus Christ held a very high view of Scripture, affirming its inspiration in the entire Old Testament–the various books of the Old Testament, the precise words, the actual letters–and He pointed to the inspiration of the New Testament. Surely those who hold to only conceptual inspiration or other variants need to reconsider the attitude of Jesus to the Scriptures. Ought His view of the Bible not to be the standard? Is it legitimate to hold a lower view of Scripture than He held?

APPENDIX 26

Story, Theology, and Church

William J. Bausch. **Storytelling: Imagination and Faith.** *Mystic, CT: 23rd Publications, 1984. pp. 195-199.*

At this point in our book, drawing to a close as it is, it might be well to put aside for the moment the direct story and illustration (to be resumed, however, in the final two chapters) and briefly list ten propositions of a theological nature. This exercise will, I hope, not be heavy or obtuse. It will serve as a means of extracting, for the sake of clarity and reflection, the theological implications of what has been stated here and there in the past chapters. So this is a very brief chapter-an interlude really-and is intended as a kind of theological summary, an overall view of how stories relate to theology and the structures of the church.

First Proposition: Stories introduce us to sacramental presences.

Stories are designed to force us to consider possibilities. To that extent they are grounded in hope. Even the most outlandish fairy tales, for example, raise possibilities and tease our hopes. The biblical stories do the same, only more overtly. Their whole point is to coax us to look beyond our limits and experiences of limitation and to suggest, through the wonderful, Wonder itself. Stories hint that our taken-for-granted daily realities may, in fact, be fraught with surprise. There are "rumors of angels" and grace abounding in our world. If a frog might be a prince, a lost sailor an angel, a pilgrim the Christ, then all of creation may be a sacramental presence pointing to "Something More." Stories declare that this just might be the case.

Second Proposition: Stories are always more important than facts.

Facts, in relation to story, are inert. It is the genius of story to arrange the facts and proclaim the good news about them. For example, the pivotal "fact" of the resurrection is fundamentally less important in its description and verification as a statement of Jesus of Nazareth rising from the dead than as a central proposition of hope. What counts are the implications the resurrection story has for us in our living and in sustaining our outlook on life and death. Otherwise you have reportage, not gospel.

Story, Theology, and Church (continued)

Third Proposition: Stories remain normative.

We have seen in the first chapter of this book that all of theology is but a reflection on the original story. To test a theology, we must always go back to the pristine material (and its subsequent unfolding). To this extent the biblical stories will always remain normative. There is a serious caution, however. Some may go back to the original story and make an idol of it; that is, they will take it as a rigid and finished document, detach it from its history, contemporary and subsequent, and force it to remain compressed and restricted. This is the fault of literalists or fundamentalists.

Fourth Proposition: Traditions evolve through stories.

Traditions evolve through stories: that's the nature of important and critical stories. People "caught" by the story, its hero or heroine and its message, want not only to share an experience but to share an experience faithful to the original story. Hence tradition arises that has two functions: preserving and protecting. Preserving is "handing on," which is what the word tradition means literally. Protecting may need more explanation.

Because stories are really extended metaphors, they are open-ended. They are freely adaptable and can easily be recast and retold. Details, names, and locales are easily accommodated to different audiences and places. We detect this even in the short span of the writing of the four gospels. Still, a boundary is implicitly set beyond which flexibility may not go and still be true to the founding story. To take a secular example: Santa Claus may be metamorphosed throughout the centuries easily enough. He can be tall or short, smooth faced or bearded, clothed in purple or green, rotund or as slim as Ichabod Crane. But Santa can never be a child abuser. After all, he derives from St. Nicholas, who derives from the Christ Child, who derives from the Father of all gifts. The core tradition would not permit a connection between Santa and harm when his whole point is benevolence and kindness. Along the way somewhere, tradition would protect the image from intrinsic contradiction. The biblical stories about Jesus evoke the same process of protection. This is where church tradition fits in. And since the stories of Jesus are varied, varied traditions will not only arise but will be quite legitimate.

Fifth Proposition: Stories precede and produce the church.

This we noted early on. The story exists first, then people are caught by it, savor it, reflect on it, retell it, preserve it, and pass it on (tradition). When many people are caught by, believe in, and celebrate the same story, you have a church.

Sixth Proposition: Stories imply censure.

This proposition is a logical outcome of the preceding two. If you have a tradition dedicated to preserving and passing on the core story, and if you have a church to live by and celebrate the core story, then those of the group who at any time might radically contradict the essential story must be dealt with. This is quite commonplace in all walks of life. Here is where we get-in any religion, government, or university-the censure, the reprimand, the excommunication. Wide latitude may be allowed, but not beyond contradicting what the story stands for. A civil liberties group could not, for example, tolerate an overt bigot. Of course, as history has shown, people tend to be far more restrictive of what they perceive to be the "true" tradition than may be accurate. One person's orthodoxy may be another's heresy, depending on who wields the power. But that is beside the point here. The point is that when story gives rise to tradition, and tradition to a church, then censure is implied sooner or later. (Quite soon, in fact, as we learn from Paul's epistles.) In our Catholic tradition this is the origin of penalties and excommunications.

Seventh Proposition: Stories produce theology.

Reflection on and conclusions from the Jesus stories began early in the church. We see this in the church's earliest writings, the epistles of Paul. When you reflect on the story, make associations, and draw conclusions, you have a theology. We can see this easily, for example, in the faith trajectory concerning the nature of Jesus. In a very special way the story tells us that he is God's man. If he is God's man, then maybe he is his spokesman. If he is his spokesman, then maybe he is his very word. If he is his word, then maybe he has a special relationship with the Father. If he has a special relationship with the Father, maybe he is his son -and in a unique way. If God's son, then maybe he is his equal. If equal, maybe he is God in the flesh. Theology is a putting of pieces together and discovering richer conclusions than might first be grasped.

Story, Theology, and Church (continued)

Or we might put it this way. Theology arises because there is always more to the story than even the tellers either realize or intend. We have a classic example in John's gospel (11:49-52): "But one of them, Caiaphas, who was high priest that year, said to them, 'You know nothing at all; you do not understand that it is expedient that one man should die for the people and that the whole nation should not perish.' " John then goes on to give his reflection and expansion concerning these words (theology): "He did not say this of his own accord, but being high priest that year, he prophesied that Jesus should die for the nation, and not for the nation only, but to gather into one the children of God who are scattered abroad." Time and hindsight often reveal deeper and richer motifs to stories. Theology grabs onto this and draws it out. Theology is rooted in and flows from the story.

Eighth Proposition: Stories produce many theologies.

The Jesus stories themselves are varied and obviously reflect different traditions. Even a casual reading of the four gospels demonstrates this. Since this is so, we expect that such varied story traditions will give rise to varied theologies. No one system is made absolute-nor should it be. The normative stories themselves, after all, are not only open-ended but conditioned by the assumptions and frame of references of their times. There have been and will continue to be many systems of theology in the church. Although there has been a drive in modern times to reduce all systems to one, in the history of the church there has been a wide tolerance of diversity.

Ninth Proposition: Stories produce ritual and sacrament.

We must remember that the experience of Jesus came before reflections about him. This is a way of saying that life came before thought, and that story came before theology. The experience of Jesus was indeed, as we have seen, enshrined in stories, but it must also be noted that it was simultaneously enshrined in ritual and in celebration. Signs, actions, gesture, and symbol also became part of the overall story. Ritual itself is a story line in action. So right away there arose rituals reenacting the death, burial, and resurrection of Jesus. Paul calls this baptism. Then there was a ritual meal breaking bread and sharing a cup, signs of the very givingness of Jesus. In short, there were also lived and shared stories we have come to describe as celebrating the mysteries of God or have come to call simply the sacraments. Story (word), celebration (festivity), and ritual (sacrament) all go together.

Of course, it can happen and has happened that a ritual can lose its story connection through routine, boredom, and repetition. When this happens, people often continue the ritual out of rote, but no longer remember the story it was attached to or expressed. To revitalize or recast the ritual we must go back and remember the story. Church renewals are basically an exercise in this.

Tenth Proposition: Stories are history.

Since stories are open-ended, they cannot be or must not be literalized. Stories have a life of their own and each age extracts from and adds to the story in a kind of symbiotic relationship. The result is a profound enrichment. History is the bridge from which we view the story in all its forms and in all its aspects of truth. Ideally, history saves the story from the twin dangers of idolatry and irrelevance.

APPENDIX 27

Use of Reference Tools for Interpreting the Bible

Rev. Dr. Don L. Davis

	Cross-Reference Aids and Topical Concordances	Theological Workbooks, Dictionaries, and Studies	Bible Dictionaries, Bible Atlases, and Customs References
Purpose	To associate different texts together on a given subject, theme, or issue	To provide an understanding of the meanings of a word or phrase in light of its theological significance	To provide background on the history, culture, social customs, and/or life of the biblical periods
Stage Where Most Beneficial	Finding Biblical Principles	Understanding the Original Situation and Finding Biblical Principles	Understanding the Original Situation
Procedures	1. Find the reference you want to check. 2. Look up the other texts associated with passage in the reference. 3. Associate the verse with a particular theme. 4. Check the theme against those citations given.	1. Attribute the verse or passage you are studying with a particular theme. 2. Find the word or concept you would like to research. 3. Read on the background of the word in the reference or dictionary 4. Associate your text with the theme, gleaning what is helpful and discarding what is not relevant for the purpose of your study	1. Select an item, theme, issue, or custom you need help in understanding. 2. Check the item in the reference text provided. 3. Make note on the background of the issue, and factor the new information in your overall account of the passage.
Benefits	Find texts on same subject throughout the Bible Outlines provided to help digest all Scriptures on a different subject	Thorough scholarship on the various theological usages and meanings of a particular Bible word, wording, or phrase	Wealth of information given on the various sociology, anthropology, historical accounts, customs, society, geography and data on the original situation
Key Caution	Dig deeply into the text BEFORE you begin to look at other similar materials	Do not be confused by the VARIETY of usages and meanings of a theological idea	Stay focused on the meaning of the text and not merely its CONTEXT
Reliability	Good	Very Good	Excellent

Use of Reference Tools for Interpreting the Bible (continued)

	Bible Handbooks, Study Bible, and Commentaries	Topical Bibles, Textbooks, and Thematic Studies	Lexical Aids, Inter-linear Translations, and Word Studies
Purpose	To give a scholarly opinion as to the background, context, and meaning of the text	To give a sophisticated outline of passages on a given theme	To provide insight into the meaning, usage, and grammar of the biblical words and language
Stage Where Most Beneficial	Understanding the Original Situation and Finding Biblical Principles	Finding Biblical Principles	Understanding the Original Situation and Finding Biblical Principles
Procedures	1. After you have completed your own preliminary study, select a commentary or two you will check your findings against. 2. Check your findings against 2-3 other authors to see if yours harmonizes with the meanings they provide.	1. After you have done your study, and made a preliminary judgment as to what you believe the passage teaches, assign your passage a biblical or theological theme. 2. Using that theme, look in the topical reference tools to check other texts on the same subject, and incorporate their meanings into your study. 3. Do not be afraid to modify your findings if the new data illumines your study.	1. Select the words or phrases in the passage which serve as key words to define in order to understand the overall meaning of the passage. 2. Using a concordance, lexicon, or other linguistic tool, look at the various meanings of the word in the context of the book, the author, the author's contemporaries, the Bible, and finally the period. 3. Allow the richness of the biblical meanings to nuance your study's claims on what the passage meant to its original hearers and what it means today.
Benefits	Excellent scholarly opinions on both the background and meaning of the various texts of Scripture	Rich, thorough presentations on various topics, themes, and theological concepts being dealt with in a passage	Abundant expert knowledge given on every phase of the design, use, and meaning of the biblical languages in their own historical and religious setting
Key Caution	Do your own study and reflection before you RELY on the opinion of your favorite interpreter	Do not make a topical listing of texts the SUBSTITUTE for deep digging into individual texts and passages for truth	Do not pretend that a knowledge of the original meanings of the key words DISQUALIFIES a sound knowledge of the text in your own language
Reliability	Good	Good	Excellent

APPENDIX 28
A Bibliography for Biblical Hermeneutics

Archer, Gleason L. *Encyclopedia of Bible Difficulties*. Grand Rapids: Zondervan, 1982.

Black, David Alan. *Linguistics for Students of New Testament Greek: A Survey of Basic Concepts and Applications*. Grand Rapids: Baker, 1988.

------. *Using New Testament Greek in Ministry: A Practical Guide for Students and Pastors*. Grand Rapids: Baker Books, 1993.

Blomberg, Craig L. *Interpreting the Parables*. Leicester: Apollos, 1990.

Bowman, Robert M., Jr. *Understanding Jehovah's Witnesses: Why They Read the Bible the Way They Do*. Grand Rapids: Baker, 1991.

Bray, Gerald. *Biblical Interpretation Past and Present*. Downers Grove/Leicester: IVP, 2000.

Bullinger, E. W. *Figures of Speech Used in the Bible*. Grand Rapids: Baker Book House, 1968.

Caird, G. B. *Language and Biblical Imagery*. Gerald Duckworth & Co. Ltd, 1981.

Carson, D. A. *Exegetical Fallacies*. 2nd ed. Grand Rapids/Carlisle: Baker Books/Paternoster Press, 1996.

Carson, D. A. and John D. Woodbridge, eds. *Hermeneutics, Authority and Canon*. Leicester: IVP, 1986.

------. *Scripture and Truth*. Leicester: IVP, 1983.

Castelli, Elizabeth A. et al, eds. *The Postmodern Bible*. Yale University Press, 1997.

Coggins, R. J. and J. L. Houlden, eds. *A Dictionary of Biblical Interpretation*. London: SCM Press Ltd., 1990.

Cotterall, Peter, and Max Turner. *Linguistics and Biblical Interpretation*. Downers Grove: InterVarsity Press, 1989.

A Bibliography for Biblical Hermeneutics (continued)

Erickson, Millard J. *Evangelical Interpretation: Perspectives on Hermeneutical Issues.* Grand Rapids: Baker Books, 1993.

Evans, Craig A. *Noncanonical Writings and New Testament Interpretation.* Peabody, MA: Hendrickson Publishers, 1992.

Fee, Gordon D. *New Testament Exegesis: A Handbook for Students and Pastors.* Philadelphia: Westminster Press, 1983.

Fee, Gordon D. and Douglas Stewart. *How to Read the Bible for All its Worth: A Guide to Understanding the Bible.* 2nd ed. Grand Rapids: Zondervan, 1993.

Goldingay, John. *Approaches to Old Testament Interpretation.* Updated ed. Leicester: Apollos, 1990.

Greidanus, Sidney. *The Modern Preacher and the Ancient Text: Interpreting and Preaching Biblical Literature.* Grand Rapids: Eerdmans, 1988.

Hendrickson, Walter. *A Layman's Guide to Interpreting the Bible.* Grand Rapids: Zondervan, 1978.

Johnson, Elliott E. *Expository Hermeneutics: An Introduction.* Grand Rapids: Zondervan, 1990.

Kaiser, Walter C., Jr. *Toward an Exegetical Theology: Biblical Exegesis for Preaching and Teaching.* Grand Rapids: Baker, 1981.

Kaiser, Walter C., Jr. Peter H. Davids, F. F. Bruce, and Manfred T. Brauch. *Hard Sayings of the Bible.* Downers Grove: InterVarsity Press, 1996.

Kaiser, Walter C., Jr. and Moises Silva. *An Introduction to Biblical Hermeneutics: The Search for Meaning.* Grand Rapids: Zondervan, 1994.

Klein, William W., Craig L. Blomberg, and Robert L. Hubbard. *Introduction to Biblical Interpretation.* Dallas: Word Publishing, 1993.

Kurht, Wilfred. *Interpreting the Bible: A Handbook of Biblical Interpretation.* Welwyn: Evangelical Press, 1983.

Long, V. Philips. *The Art of Biblical Interpretation. Foundations of Contemporary Interpretation.* Vol. 5. Leicester: InterVarsity Press, 1994.

Longman, Tremper, III. *How to Read the Psalms.* Downers Grove: InterVaristy Press, 1988.

A Bibliography for Biblical Hermeneutics (continued)

------. *Literary Approaches to Biblical Interpretation. Foundations of Contemporary Interpretation.* Vol. 3. Leicester: InterVarsity Press, 1987.

------. *Reading the Bible with Heart and Mind.* Navpress Publishing Group, 1996.

Longenecker, Richard N. *Biblical Exegesis in the Apostolic Period.* Carlisle: Paternoster Press, 1995.

Lundin, Roger. *Disciplining Hermeneutics: Interpretation in Christian Perspective.* Grand Rapids: Eerdmans, 1997.

McKnight, Scot, ed. *Introduction to New Testament Interpretation.* Grand Rapids: Baker Books, 1989.

Marshall, I. H., ed. *New Testament Interpretation: Essays on Principles and Methods.* Rev. 1979. Carlisle: Paternoster Press, 1992.

Neill, Stephen. *The Interpretation of the New Testament 1861-1961.* Oxford: Oxford University Press, 1964.

Osborne, Grant R. *The Hermeneutical Spiral: A Comprehensive Introduction to Biblical Interpretation.* Downers Grove: InterVarsity Press, 1991.

Poythress, Vern Sheridan. *Symphonic Theology: The Validity of Multiple Perspectives in Theology.* Grand Rapids: Zondervan, 1987.

Pratt, Richard L., Jr. *He Gave Us Stories: The Bible Student's Guide to Interpreting Old Testament Narratives.* Phillipsburg, NJ: Presbyterian and Reformed, 1993.

Scalise, Charles J. *From Scripture to Theology: A Canonical Journey into Hermeneutics.* Downers Grove: IVP, 1996.

Silva, Moises. *Biblical Words and Their Meaning: An Introduction to Lexical Semantics.* Revised and expanded ed. Grand Rapids: Zondervan, 1994.

------. *God, Language and Scripture. Foundations of Contemporary Interpretation.* Vol. 4. Grand Rapids: Zondervan, 1990.

------. *Has the Church Misread the Bible? The History of Interpretation in the Light of Current Issues. Foundations of Contemporary Interpretation.* Vol 1. Grand Rapids: Zondervan, 1987.

Sire, James W. *Scripture Twisting: 20 Ways the Cults Misread the Bible*. Leicester: InterVarsity Press, 1980.

Stein, Robert H. *A Basic Guide to Interpreting the Bible: Playing by the Rules*. Grand Rapids: Baker, 1994.

Stenger, Werner. *Introduction to New Testament Exegesis*. Grand Rapids: Eerdmans, 1987.

Stuart, Douglas. *Old Testament Exegesis: A Primer for Students and Pastors*. 2nd ed. Revised and expanded. Philadelphia: The Westminster Press, 1984.

Tate, Randolph W. *Biblical Interpretation: An Integrated Approach*. Peabody, MA: Hendrickson Publishers, 1997.

Thistleton, Anthony C. *New Horizons in Hermeneutics: The Theory and Practice of Transforming Biblical Reading*. Grand Rapids: Zondervan, 1992.

------. *Promise of Hermeneutics*. Carlisle: Paternoster Press, 1999

------. *The Two Horizons: New Testament Hermeneutics and Philosophical Description with Special Reference to Heideggar, Bultmann, Gadamer, and Wittgenstein*. Carlisle: Paternoster Press, 1980.

APPENDIX 29

How to Interpret a Narrative (Story)

Don L. Davis

All stories have a particular shape and possess a number of elements that make it possible to experience the truth of the story, whether historical or imaginative, in a way that is powerful, challenging, and entertaining.

The Elements of Narrative Study

I.   Note with Special Care the SETTING of the Story.

    A.   Place: where geographically is the story taking place?

    B.   Physical surroundings: what are the details physically?

    C.   Temporal (time) setting: what are the time elements of the story?

    D.   Cultural-historical surroundings: what details of culture or history are present?

II. Identify the CHARACTERS of the Story.

    A.   Who are the prime characters in the story? The "hero" and "villain"?

    B.   Note the precise order and details of the actions, conversation, and events of the characters.

C. How are the characters shown to us?

   1. Direct descriptions

   2. Indirect characterization

      a. Appearance

      b. Words and conversation

      c. Thoughts and attitudes

      d. Influence and effects

      e. Actions and character

D. How are the characters tested, and what choices do they make?

E. How do the characters grow or decline (rise or fall) in the story?

III. Watch for the Author's POINT-OF-VIEW and VOICE.

A. Note the author's comments about the characters and events.

   1. Attitude (positive, negative, or neutral)

   2. Judgment (negative or affirmative)

   3. Conclusion (summarizing, absent, closure?)

How to Interpret a Narrative (continued)

B. Consider what voice the story is being written in:

1. The Omniscient narrator (the Holy Spirit)

2. The First-person testimonial

3. The Third-person narrator

IV. Detect the PLOT DEVELOPMENT within the Story.

A. Note the exact order and details of the events and actions.

B. Note also how the story begins, develops, and ends.

C. Ask and answer questions about the actual plot.

1. Why did the events happen as they did?

2. Why did the characters respond as they did?

3. Could they have done things in a different manner?

D. Use John Legget's elements of story.

1. Doormat — the intro of the story

2. Complications — Conflicts, problems, issues, threats

3. Climax — Peak and turning point of the action

4. Denouement — How the story resolves itself

5. End — Finis!

V. Note the THEME of the Story

A. What key principles and truths can be drawn out of this story?

B. What is the "commentary on living" portrayed in this story?

1. What is the story's view of "reality" (what is the world like, and what is our role in it?)

2. What is the story's view of "morality (i.e., what constitutes good and bad in the story?)

3. What is the story's view of "value and meaning" (i.e., what is of ultimate concern and importance in the story?)

C. How do the truths of the story intersect with the challenges, opportunities, threats, and issues of our lives?

APPENDIX 30
Checklist of Narrative Elements

Adapted from Leland Ryken. How to Read the Bible as Literature.

I.   What Is the *Setting* of the Story?

  A. Physical surroundings

  B. Historical environment

  C. Cultural situation

  D. Interpersonal relationships and situation

II. Who Are the *Characters* in the Story?

  A. Who are the main/supporting players in the story?

  B. Who is the "protagonist?" Who is the "antagonist?"

  C. How does the author describe the character's development?

  D. What is the final outcome of the character's life and choices?

III. What Plot *Conflicts* Exist within the Story?

  A. What are the central conflicts with God?

  B. What are the central conflicts with others?

  C. What are the central conflicts within the characters themselves?

  D. What are the central conflicts between the character and their situation?

IV. What Are the Aspects of *Narrative Suspense* Revealed in the Story?

  A. What influences make us sympathize with the characters?

  B. What produces disgust and aversion between us and the characters?

  C. How are we made to approve of what the characters did?

  D. What events or happenings cause us to disapprove of the characters?

V. What Insight Do the Characters Give Us as a *"Commentary on Living"*?

   A. Reality: What is the view of reality portrayed in the story and the character?

   B. Morality: What constitutes good and bad in the context of this story?

   C. Value: What is of ultimate concern and value in the story?

VI. How Does the Story *Unify* Itself in its Various Parts?

   A. How does the organization of the story contribute to its unity?

   B. What is the sequence of events in this story? (Beginning, Middle, and End)

   C. In what way does the story's end resolve the questions raised at the beginning?

VII. How Are the Characters *Tested*, and What *Choices* Do They Make?

   A. What is the dilemma/problem/conflict the protagonist is seeking to overcome?

   B. What character quality is tested in the protagonist ?

   C. What alternative life choices are open to the characters in the story?

   D. Which decisions do the characters make, and what is the result of their decisions?

VIII. How Do the Characters *Progress and Grow* (or Decline and Fall) in the Story?

   A. Where do the characters begin in the story?

   B. How do the experiences of the character affect their development?

   C. Where do the individual characters eventually wind up as a result of their experiences, and the choices they made within them?

Checklist of Narrative Elements (continued)

IX. What *Foils, Dramatic Irony, and Poetic Justice* Are Used in the Story?

   A. Foils: what characters are set against each other as foes in the story?

   B. Dramatic irony: When is the reader informed of situations and realities that the characters themselves are unaware of?

X. What Items Are *Repeated, Highlighted, and Foregrounded* in the Story?

   A. Repetition: what phrases, items, themes, issues, or actions are repeated?

   B. Highlighting: what things in the characters and events are emphasized above other things?

   C. Foregrounding: what things are made to stand out "center stage" in the flow of the story?

XI. What Is the *Point of View* of the Author of the Story?

   A. What comments does the author give us about the characters and events in the story?

   B. What feelings do you believe the story is intending to generate?

   C. How are the materials and details arranged to communicate the author's viewpoint clearly?

APPENDIX 31

Keys to Bible Interpretation

Some Keys to Interpreting the Scriptures Accurately

Terry G. Cornett and Don L. Davis. Revised ed.

Key Principles

To gain an accurate understanding of a book or passage from the Bible, the interpreter must:

Presuppositions

1. Believe that the Scriptures are inspired, infallible and the authoritative rule for life and doctrine.

2. Realize that it is not possible to fully understand and apply the Scriptures without:

    *   having been "born from above" by faith in Christ

    *   being filled with God's Holy Spirit

    *   being diligent to pursue its meaning through regular study

    *   being willing to obey its message, once revealed

3. Allow the process of interpretation to engage the "whole person." The study of Scripture should captivate your emotions and your will as well as your mind. "We aim to be objective but not disinterested readers."

4. Understand that all Scripture is in some way a testimony to Christ. Christ is the Bible's subject; all of its doctrine, teaching and ethics point to him.

5. Take into account both the divine and the human side of Scripture.

Keys to Bible Interpretation (continued)

6. Seek to "extract" or take out the meaning that is in the text (exegesis), not read into the text his or her own beliefs or ideas (eisegesis).

7. Seek to explain:

   • the "unclear" passages by the clearer statements

   • the symbolic portions by the stated teachings of Scripture

   • the Old Testament by the New Testament

8. Take into account the whole context of the book and the passage where any particular text is found.

9. Identify the human author and the intended audience. Start by attempting to discover what the author was trying to say to the original audience. "A passage cannot mean what it never meant."

              Understanding the Original Situation

10. Use information about the manuscripts, languages, grammar, literary forms, history, and culture to help discover the author's intended meaning.

11. Take seriously the genre and types of language used by the author, then interpret the Scriptures literally, meaning that we take the plain sense of the language as it is normally used in that genre.

12. Look for the ideas, values, and truths that a story, command, or prophecy is trying to communicate. Seek to state those principles in a way that is true and useful for all people, at all times, and in all situations.

              Finding General Principles

13. Use Scripture to interpret Scripture. In order to understand any individual part of Scripture, compare that portion to the message of the whole Bible. Once this

understanding has been reached, one must also reinterpret his/her understanding of the whole of Scripture (theology and doctrine) in light of the new information gained from the passage (The Hermeneutical Circle).

14. Understand that reason, tradition, and experience are significant factors in the process of interpreting Scripture. Principles must be clear, logical and defensible; they must be compatible with the way Christians have interpreted the Scriptures throughout history; and they must help to make sense out of human experience.

Applying General Principles Today

15. Carefully move from what Scripture "meant" to its original audience to what it "means" for the current reader.

16. Apply the general truths to specific situations faced by people today.

    • Remember that the Holy Spirit is the primary guide in the application of truth. Ask him for guidance about the meaning for today and then prayerfully meditate on the meaning of the passage.

    • Seek the Spirit's guidance by seeing how he has led other Christians (both inside and outside your own denominational tradition) to interpret the meaning and application of the passage for today.

17. Put the principles and the applications in language that makes sense to modern readers.

18. Keep the proper "end goals" in view. The intent of all Bible study is to mature the reader in the life and love of Jesus Christ, to the glory of God. Not knowledge alone, but life transformation is the goal of Bible interpretation.

Keys to Bible Interpretation (continued)

Key Perspective

Discovering the Word and Works of God in the Lives of the People of Scripture

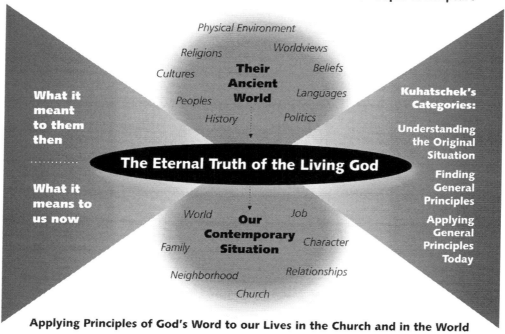

Applying Principles of God's Word to our Lives in the Church and in the World

Note: In this diagram, Kuhatschek's categories refer to the three steps of Biblical interpretation outlined by Jack Kuhatschek in Applying the Bible Downer's Grove: IVP, 1990.

Key Steps to Interpretation

The focus of this step is on understanding the *world of the Bible, the author, and God's message to a particular group of people at a particular time and place.*

Step One: Understanding the Original Situation

A. Ask God to open your eyes to truth through the ministry of the Holy Spirit as you read his Word.

Tell God that you want to be changed as well as informed by your reading of the Scriptures. Ask him to reveal specific actions and attitudes in your own life which need to be changed or disciplined. Ask God to use the Word to reveal Jesus and to make you more like his Son. Thank God for the gifts of his Spirit, his Son, and the Scriptures. Many believers began their study of God's Word by simply praying the words of Psalms 119.18.

Heavenly Father, open my eyes to see wonderful things in your word. Amen.

B. Identify the author of the book, the approximate date it was written, why it was written, and to whom it was written.

Key Tools: Bible Dictionary, Bible Handbook, or Bible Commentary

C. Read the context around the passage.

Key Tool: A standard translation (not a paraphrase) of the Bible

- Look to see where natural "breaks" are in and around the passage and make sure that you are looking at the entire passage during the process of interpretation.

- Read the material around the passage. It is a good rule of thumb to read *at least* one chapter before and one chapter following the passage you are studying.

- The shorter the passage selected for interpretation, the greater the danger becomes in ignoring context. The old proverb is correct: "A text without a *context* is a *pre*text."

D. Observe the passage carefully.

- Identify who is speaking and who is being spoken to.

- Observe the main ideas and the details.

  - Make a simple outline of the passage.

  - Identify the main ideas.

  - Look for repeated words or images.

  - Find "cause-and-effect" relationships.

  - Look for comparisons, contrasts, and connections.

Keys to Bible Interpretation (continued)

E.   Read the passage in another translation of Scripture.

Key Tool: A translation or paraphrase of the Scriptures that uses a different translation philosophy than the version of Scripture you regularly use

*   Write down any questions that this new translation raises in your mind and stay alert for answers as you do further study.

F.   Read any parallel accounts or passages from other parts of Scripture.

Key Tool: A concordance and/or a Bible which includes cross-references

*   Note what details are added to the passage you are studying from the other accounts in Scripture.

*   Why did the author choose to omit some details and emphasize others? What significance does this have for understanding the author's intent.

G.   Study the words and the grammatical structures.

Key Tools: Hebrew and Greek Lexicons and Expository Dictionaries help deepen our understanding of word meanings and usage. Exegetical Commentaries help explain grammatical constructions and how they affect the meaning of the text.

*   Make a note of words that are being used in a unique way by the writer and of special grammatical forms like imperatives, verbs that show continuous action, etc.

H.   Identify the genre (type of literature) and consider any special rules that apply to it.

Key Tool: Bible Dictionary and Bible Commentaries

*   Each type of literature has to be taken seriously for what it is. We must not interpret poetry in the same way we interpret prophecy, or narratives in the way we interpret commands.

I. Look for literary structures that might influence the way the text is understood.

Key Tool: Exegetical Commentaries

- Literary structures include figures of speech, metaphors, typologies, symbols, poetic structures, chiasmic structures, etc.

J. Identify the historical events and the cultural issues which might effect the people or influence the ideas described in the passage.

Key Tools: Bible Dictionaries and Bible Commentaries

- Constantly ask, "What was happening in history and society that would affect the way the audience heard the message in this text?"

K. Summarize what you believe the author was trying to say and why it was important for the original audience.

- Your goal in this step is to write the key truths of the passage in such a way that the original author and the original listeners would agree with them if they heard them.

Step Two: Finding General Principles

The focus of this step is identifying *the central message, commands, and principles in a portion of Scripture* which teach God's purposes for all people.

A. List in sentence form what you believe are the general principles in the passage which apply to all people, at all times, in all cultures.

B. Check these statements against other parts of Scripture for clarity and accuracy.

Key Tools: Concordance, Topical Bible

Ask yourself:

- Are the principles I listed supported by other passages in the Bible?

Keys to Bible Interpretation (continued)

- Which of these principles might be difficult or impossible to explain when compared with other passages of Scripture?

- Must any of these principles be ruled out in light of other passages of Scripture?

- What new information about God and his will does this passage add to my overall knowledge of Scripture and doctrine?

C. Adjust or modify your statements of God's principles in light of the discoveries you made above.

- Rewrite your key principles to reflect the insight gained from other portions of Scripture.

D. Read commentaries to discover some of the key principles and doctrines that others in the Church have drawn from this passage.

- Compare and contrast the information from the commentaries with your own reading. Be willing to abandon, change, or defend your views as necessary as you come across new information.

E. Again adjust or modify your statements of God's principles in light of the discoveries you made above.

The focus of this step is on moving *from what Scripture "meant" to what it "means."* What does obedience to God's commands and purposes look like today in our culture, with our families and friends, and with the problems and opportunities that we face in our lives?

Step Three: Applying General Principles Today

A. Ask God to speak to you and reveal the meaning of this passage for your life.

- Meditate on the passage and the things you have learned from your study so far while asking the Holy Spirit to point out the specific applications of the truths discovered for yourself and those around you.

B. How is this passage "Good News" to me and others?

- How does it reveal more about Jesus and his coming Kingdom?

- How does it relate to God's overall plan of salvation?

C. How should knowing the truth from this passage:

Affect my relationship with God?

- Try to determine how the principles and examples from these Scriptures might help you to love and obey God more perfectly.

Affect my relationships with others?

- This includes my church family, my physical family, my co-workers, my friends, my neighbors, my enemies, strangers, and the poor or oppressed.

Challenge beliefs, attitudes, and actions that my culture views as normal?

- How must my thinking and acting be different from those in the world around me?

D. Attempt to answer the questions "What am I to believe?" and "What am I to do?" now that I have studied this passage.

- Do I need to repent from old ways of thinking and acting?

- How can I act on this truth so that I become a wise person?

E. How can I share what I have learned with others in a way that draws attention to Christ and builds them up?

Documenting Your Work
A Guide to Help You Give Credit Where Credit Is Due
The Urban Ministry Institute

Plagiarism is using another person's ideas as if they belonged to you without giving them proper credit. In academic work it is just as wrong to steal a person's ideas as it is to steal a person's property. These ideas may come from the author of a book, an article you have read, or from a fellow student. The way to avoid plagiarism is to carefully use "notes" (textnotes, footnotes, endnotes, etc.) and a "Works Cited" section to help people who read your work know when an idea is one you thought of, and when you are borrowing an idea from another person.

Avoiding Plagiarism

A citation reference is required in a paper whenever you use ideas or information that came from another person's work.

Using Citation References

All citation references involve two parts:

- Notes in the body of your paper placed next to each quotation which came from an outside source.

- A "Works Cited" page at the end of your paper or project which gives information about the sources you have used

There are three basic kinds of notes: parenthetical notes, footnotes, and endnotes. At The Urban Ministry Institute, we recommend that students use parenthetical notes. These notes give the author's last name(s), the date the book was published, and the page number(s) on which you found the information. Example:

Using Notes in Your Paper

> In trying to understand the meaning of Genesis 14.1-24, it is important to recognize that in biblical stories "the place where dialogue is first introduced will be an important moment in revealing the character of the speaker . . ." (Kaiser and Silva 1994, 73). This is certainly true of the character of Melchizedek who speaks words of blessing. This identification of Melchizedek as a positive spiritual influence is reinforced by the fact that he is the King of Salem, since Salem means "safe, at peace" (Wiseman 1996, 1045).

Creating a Works Cited Page

A "Works Cited" page should be placed at the end of your paper. This page:

- lists every source you quoted in your paper

- is in alphabetical order by author's last name

- includes the date of publication and information about the publisher

The following formatting rules should be followed:

1. **Title**

   The title "Works Cited" should be used and centered on the first line of the page following the top margin.

2. **Content**

   Each reference should list:

   - the author's full name (last name first)

   - the date of publication

   - the title and any special information (Revised edition, 2nd edition, reprint) taken from the cover or title page should be noted

   - the city where the publisher is headquartered followed by a colon and the name of the publisher

3. **Basic form**

   - Each piece of information should be separated by a period.

   - The second line of a reference (and all following lines) should be indented.

   - Book titles should be underlined (or italicized).

   - Article titles should be placed in quotes.

   Example:

   Fee, Gordon D. 1991. *Gospel and Spirit: Issues in New Testament Hermeneutics.* Peabody, MA: Hendrickson Publishers.

Documenting Your Work (continued)

4. Special Forms

A book with multiple authors:

> Kaiser, Walter C., and Moisés Silva. 1994. *An Introduction to Biblical Hermeneutics: The Search for Meaning.* Grand Rapids: Zondervan Publishing House.

An edited book:

> Greenway, Roger S., ed. 1992. *Discipling the City: A Comprehensive Approach to Urban Mission.* 2nd ed. Grand Rapids: Baker Book House.

A book that is part of a series:

> Morris, Leon. 1971. *The Gospel According to John.* Grand Rapids: Wm. B. Eerdmans Publishing Co. The New International Commentary on the New Testament. Gen. ed. F. F. Bruce.

An article in a reference book:

> Wiseman, D. J. "Salem." 1982. In *New Bible Dictionary.* Leicester, England - Downers Grove, IL: InterVarsity Press. Eds. I. H. Marshall and others.

(An example of a "Works Cited" page is located on the next page.)

Standard guides to documenting academic work in the areas of philosophy, religion, theology, and ethics include:

Atchert, Walter S., and Joseph Gibaldi. 1985. *The MLA Style Manual.* New York: Modern Language Association.

The Chicago Manual of Style. 1993. 14th ed. Chicago: The University of Chicago Press.

Turabian, Kate L. 1987. *A Manual for Writers of Term Papers, Theses, and Dissertations.* 5th edition. Bonnie Bertwistle Honigsblum, ed. Chicago: The University of Chicago Press.

For Further Research